Melancology

Black Metal Theory and Ecology

Melancology

Black Metal Theory and Ecology

Scott Wilson

Winchester, UK
Washington, USA

First published by Zero Books, 2014
Zero Books is an imprint of John Hunt Publishing Ltd., Laurel House, Station Approach,
Alresford, Hants, SO24 9JH, UK
office1@jhpbooks.net
www.johnhuntpublishing.com
www.zero-books.net

For distributor details and how to order please visit the 'Ordering' section on our website.

ISBN: 978 1 78099 189 4

A CIP catalogue record for this book is available from the British Library.

Design: Stuart Davies

Printed and bound by CPI Group (UK) Ltd, Croydon, CR0 4YY

CONTENTS

Catena

The words are barely discernible, thin, fragile shapes formed out of the hoarse yet bellicose raging of a desiccated, cadaverous throat, leprous, shredded; its death-rattled breath conveyed by the thundering vibrations of drums breathlessly pummelled without pause. There is no rock 'n' roll backbeat here, just a furious cacophony. Voice smashed and sliced open by explosions of percussion challenging the darkness, buzzing guitar chords rising and falling up the scale, lurching, striving like a swarm of ravenous insects dipping and swerving in the frozen, airless void, defying gravity, seeking the taste of death ...
Scott Wilson Introduction to Melancology

Melancholy is experienced as both a heightened contemplation of heavenly mysteries and a depressive submergence into thing-like muteness. Frozen in a philosophical trance indistinguishable from catatonia, melancholy sage and melancholy idiot join in aping the posture of a corpse. This distortion of temporality is also a distortion of tempo: melancholy models a time that is at once 'ancient' and 'to come', and, accordingly melancholy keeps a time that is at once fast and slow.
Drew Daniel, 'Corpsepaint as Necro-Minstrelsy, or Towards the Re-Occultation of Black Blood'

The black metal musician ... is not subdued by solar tyranny, but opens him/herself to the abyss through defilement and necrophilic mess. In this space life feasts on death, and the black metal persona is laid opened.
Aspasia Stephanou, 'Black Sun'

Melancology and the blackening of the green treads into the blackness of the forest to the point where there is no forest; 'the eternal forest ... where all things seem to have deceased' (Absurd, 'Deep Dark Forest', 1996).
Niall Scott, 'Blackening the Green'.

Once when Merwan was banging his head on the floor at home, his mother heard a thudding sound coming from his room… . [he] had blood all over his face. Crying she asked, 'Merog, have you gone mad? Are you totally mad?' Wiping the blood off with a towel, he said, 'I am not mad! I have become something else!' Bang your head into a black hole, make space for the worm to crawl. Black metal is the spice, boring into my skull. Ego … sum vermis et non homo *(Psalm 22.6), For I am a worm and not a human.*
Nicola Masciandaro, 'WormSign'

The music itself is a kind of dry sterile thunder, performing its own collapse into the earth, into its black space. It waits for rain, for the stench of life: the cycle is renewed, but only through breaking the dead grip of self-reflection. This is larval music, in a process of becoming without clear ends.
Steven Shakespeare, 'Shuddering: Black Metal on the Edge of the Earth'

It is as the lightening which gives 'a dense and black intensity to the night it denies:' Not here! *It cries.* Not that! *The lightening flashes, and is gone, and the pitch-black night sky rejoices; primordial order, status quo. In the methodology of black metal then, in imagining a black metal art history, it has been integral to define the sonic and visual language of black metal by its absence, by its formlessness, its crevices, and its voids.*
Amelia Ishmael, 'Black Metal in the White Tower: Metal's Formless Presence in Contemporary Art'.

The main characteristic and novelty of black metal is indeed not to bring the world's mysteries to light but to increase them 'much as the moon with its white beams does not diminish but increases the shimmering mystery of night'.
Liviu Mantescu, 'In the Abyss of Lies'

While for some bands the chthonian earthing of man's existence abounds, for still others seek to oppose this gravity and fly with the skies, rather than the earth, at their feet. ... 'To the mountains!'
Dominik Irtenkauf, 'To The Mountains: The implications of Black Metal's Geophilosophy'

On this occasion, I do not venture a claim of the 'fundamental politics' beneath the intent to talk about melancology nor to jibe at the fact that similar ecological-aesthetic inheritances run very close to a fascist political-aesthetic inheritance. All the same, it must be held in the air. It does not mean necessarily that melancology is fascistic. It does mean that fascist aesthetics are melancological.
Evan Calder Williams, 'The Hot, Wet Breath of Extinction'

Black metal presents a music that negates some aspect of musical form – a song against all melody, a rhythm against all tempo, and a harmony against all tonality. What results is not an absence of music per se, but rather a form of anti-music expressed through music. At its limit, black metal brings us back to an even more basic distinction – that between music and sound – the former continually threatening (or promising) to dissolve into the latter.
Eugene Thacker, 'Sound of the Abyss'

My wager is that the inhumanness of black metal's blackening is in fact more ecologically useful than reliance on either the image of humans reunited with nature or with an original home earth, a tranquil Edenic earth as originary ark, or any other paganesque purification of the planet that Wolves in the Throne Room have sonically engineered, narrated, and continue to support.
Ben Woodard, 'Irreversible Sludge: Troubled Energetics, Eco-purification, and Self-Inhumanization'

In black metal's buzzing, its musca amusica, *sound takes flight, the noise of Ba'al Zebûb's divinely inexistent ascension, into the heart of*

the impossible. The sound resonates along a vector of amusical existence towards an altogether other, nonanthropomorphic environment. Collective and multiple, 'through compound eyes / I envision eternity' (Lugubrum, 'Attractive to Flies').
Scott Wilson, 'Musca Amusica'

The impulse [of Black Metal Theory] from the beginning has been for something that goes beyond, without necessarily precluding, diagnostic or analytical discourse about black metal. No one merely listens to *music, without participating* in *it. It is an object that infects and possesses the subject. So philosophy stands for the practice of thought, for thought as participation, as more than just studying or thinking about something. On this point black metal theory opposes the perverted secret identity between fan and philosopher in contemporary culture, namely, the situation according to which the fan is an unconscious or sleeping philosopher and the philosopher a mere fan.*
Dominik Irtenkauf & Nicola Masciandaro

Introduction to Melancology

Scott Wilson

Melancology

Black metal irrupts from 'a place empty of life / Only dead trees ...' (Mayhem, 'Funeral Fog', 1992) where 'Our skies are forever black / Here is no signs of life at all' (Deathspell Omega, 'From Unknown Lands of Desolation', 2005). In its evocation of a landscape that is already divested of nature, black metal could be described as a negative form of environmental writing bearing on a world that has become blackened, or perhaps bearing on an entirely other, black world heterogeneous to the green one that is the object of ecological concern. The least Apollonian of genres, black metal is both terrestrial and cosmic – indeed subterranean and infernal – inhabiting a dead forest that is at once both mythic and material, in which 'darkness shows the way' (Mayhem, 'De Mysteriis Dom Sathanas', 1992). For black metal, darkness shows the way along an atheological horizon that marks the limit of absolute evil where there are no *goods* or resources to distribute and therefore no means of power and domination, a mastery of nothing.

Black metal is a musical genre – one would hesitate to call it popular – that owes its origins to heavy metal and certain stylistic traits introduced by bands like Black Sabbath, Motörhead, Venom, Hellhammer, Celtic Frost and Bathory finding perhaps its ultimate definition in the Scandinavian 'second generation' bands Mayhem, Burzum, Darkthrone, Emperor, Beherit among others. The characteristic generic traits of black metal will become evident throughout the following chapters, but readers should be advised that this is not a book that takes black metal as an object of study. *Melancology* is not an example of 'metal studies'. For the latter, readers should look elsewhere.[1] Rather, it is a work that seeks inspiration from black metal, and writes alongside and in conjunction with it. The chapters in this book address black metal as a strange form of environmental writing that 'blackens' or addresses a 'blackened' cosmos, responding to the conjuration of a new word and concept that conjoins 'black' and 'ecology': *melancology*, a word in which can be heard the melancholy affect appropriate to the conjunction. Black metal resounds from what is called in black metal the 'abyss', and it is precisely only in relation to its abyssal sonic forces, this book suggests, that the question of intervention in the environment can be posed in the articulation of a melancological ethos that does not take the green world as its primary reference. But before we progress any further with this articulation, it is necessary to distinguish melancology from the 'dark ecology' suggested by Timothy Morton.

Dark ecology

In his book *Ecology Without Nature* (2007) Timothy Morton calls for a theory of ecological writing and criticism that is similarly divested of nature since he argues that it is nothing but a locus of fantasy; nature is the reference of an 'ecomimetic' art that 'offers the illusion of a false immediacy that is belied by the immersed yet laid-back aesthetic distance it demands'.[2] For Morton, ecomimesis is the aesthetic support of an empty signifier in which diverse contents (from heterosexuality to the market) may be legitimated through the normativity assumed by the natural. In contrast, Morton recommends a 'dark ecology' that recognises that nature, if it is anything at all, is not a locus of pleasure but of discomfort that he nevertheless evokes through the means of a different aesthetic. Morton's ecological thought involves

> The thinking of interconnectedness [that] has a dark side embodied not in a hippie aesthetic of life over death, or a sadistic-sentimental Bambification of sentient beings, but in a

> 'goth' assertion of the contingent and necessarily queer idea that we want to stay with a dying world: *dark ecology*.[3]

This 'goth' ecology is also a 'dualist' 'melancholic ethics' that both accepts and insists on human separation from 'nature' even as it recognizes human complicity in the destruction or deleterious transformation of the world and its creatures. On the basis of this double position Morton's ethics are essentially Kantian: we can be kind to animals and treat the world as an end not a means because we must do so. The melancholic attitude of this ethic is in turn supported by an aesthetic form that is invigorated by its preservation of 'the dark, depressive quality of life in the shadow of ecological catastrophe'.[4]

While it is certainly not Goth, black metal is a musical genre with adherents all around the world that is characterized by melancholy, misanthropy and anti-modernity. As Aaron Weaver, drummer in the American band Wolves in the Throne Room, comments, 'it's possible to define the essence that unites artists within black metal. It is a revolt against the modern world; it is rooted in bitterness and hatred; it is mythic and spiritual ...'[5] Wolves in the Throne Room are the band most associated with the ecological impulse in black metal, at least from a non right-wing perspective.[6] WITTR's own perspective is more anarchist than left wing, and is tied to nostalgia for a pre-modern existence: 'A deep sense of yearning to a forgotten past is what gives our music its melancholy spirit ... We are empty, meaningless corpses. Look at the lost, ancient world, where things were whole and full of depth. And now look at us. The world is doomed, and we are lost'.[7]

While it is possible that the ecological impulse in some black metal, particularly Wolves in the Throne Room, might approximate to something like Morton's melancholic ethic, I suspect that he would regard the source of the band's melancholy to be essentially part of a hippie aesthetic that remains at the level of the same fantasy that he believes plagues environmentalism generally. Nevertheless, I assume that he would concur with them in their rejection of the Satanism and pagan fetishism that they suggest characterizes much of the black metal scene.[8] Perhaps this is one of the reasons why, along with fellow USBM band Liturgy, Wolves in the Throne Room are one of the bands that black metal 'kvltists' love to hate. Because Satanism and all the paradoxes that it involves are, of course, absolutely essential to black metal.

The importance of Satan

The impasse that Morton recognises in the ecological split between immanence and transcendence – which produces his melancholy dualist ethic – is essentially an effect of the split between atheism and religion. Either Man, as the image of God and his representative on Earth, is charged with tending for His creatures (Morton's 'distance') or humanity is just one creature among others with no special privileges ('immediacy'). But as simply one creature among others humans could hardly be expected to do anything other than treat the environment and its resources as a means for survival; this is what all the other life forms do. The Kantian imperative that Morton adopts for ecology, that human beings can treat the environment as an end rather than a means, is an attempt to retain a trace of God's transcendence in an essentially secular, atheist world of immanence. All it does, however, is to internalize God as a principle of self-punishment in order to produce a creature that is a slave to its own bad conscience, condemned to an abyssal feeling of guilt, hollowing out the vicious circle of superego in which every attempt to treat nature simply as an end rather than a means just discloses the ultimate human instrumentality of that end thereby producing more guilt, more self-abnegation, renunciation and so on.

Most forms of secular politics and ethics retain 'God' in this way, that is to say a God who, in a circular manner, was Himself never much more than an effect of the human desire for meaning and purpose. As the officially atheist regimes of the twentieth century showed (USSR, Maoist China), the rejection of God did not result in a sense that 'all is permitted' but on the contrary demanded a redoubling of prohibition in an austere world slavishly dedicated to production and utility. For Quentin Meillassoux, atheism is complicit with religion in accepting and thereby 'ratifying the religious partition between immanence and transcendence: for *atheism consists in being satisfied with the unsatisfying territory that religion cedes to it*. Atheism is a strategy of the besieged'.[9] In the rejection of religious transcendence the atheist also 'devalues' the world of imagination and its desire to transcend the 'misery of the condition of immanence'.[10] But that does not therefore imply a return to God, or to the God who sits at both the origin and the promised end of the misery as its ultimate justification. As such God is simply a figure representing the desire for consistency that atheists seek in scientific reason. This is a God that even God, if He existed, would fail to believe in, in fact could only rage against since it reduces His sovereignty to a servile construct of the limits of human rationality. This essential loathing of God, then, in which God Himself if he actually existed could only partake paradoxically opens up a more radical, even divine space for atheism in the form of a void filled with 'His horrible absence' rather than his imbecilic, stupefied presence.[11]

A radical, paradoxically divine atheism that loathes God and thereby embraces Satanism opens itself to such a world of transcendent imagination that Meillassoux argues secular atheism precludes. Indeed, Nick Land maintains that this kind of satanic blasphemy is precisely what atheism must sustain if it is not to subsist in miserable banality. For Land, the fact that 'God has wrought such loathsomeness without even having existed only exacerbates the hatred pitched against him. An atheism that does not hunger for God's blood is an inanity'.[12] Proving himself a direct contemporary of Norwegian black metal and a black metal theorist *avant la lettre*, Land goes on, 'anyone who does not exult at the thought of driving nails through the limbs of the Nazarene is something less than an atheist; merely a disappointed slave'.[13]

Satan's role, as it has been handed down from Romanticism, is to sustain a trace of the divine in the wake of the death of God. As such, the Prince of Darkness, in the playful gravity of his perpetual insurgency, is of course a negative support of modernity's Enlightenment project, both as its defining obscurantist opposite and its very impulse as a mode of transgressive negativity. Satan, as the untenable metaphor for nonknowledge, marks the boundaries of being and nothingness, joy and the abyss, centre and margin, life and death, man and beast; as the demonic figure of paradox, possession and the impossible, Satan threatens the undoing of these distinctions, holding them both together and apart, the locus of desire and imagination in a Godforsaken universe.

In their pre-(as opposed to anti-)enlightenment nostalgia, Wolves in the Throne Room are anomalous in the field of black metal because the desolate and infernal landscapes that feature in the genre have no reference either to nature in the sense understood by Morton or to the objects of ecological concern.[14] While it may appear, superficially, that Morton's melancholic dark ecology informs the melancology that is elaborated in this book, there is in fact no relation. The melancholy that one should hear in the conjunction of black and ecology in melancology does not at all concern regret about 'distance' or mourning for the loss of 'immediacy'. Rather it involves a Satanic blackening of ecology that transforms the very notion of ecology and the terrain of immanence that it takes, impossibly, as its reference.

Death and the horror of scientific realism

In another statement in which he distinguishes the specific project of Wolves in the Throne Room from black metal generally, Aaron Weaver notes that 'current conditions in the world make misanthropy and suicide valid endpoints for many. A lot of black metal envisions the universe as a cold, mechanical, meaningless trap. I find this interpretation very compelling, but it is not what our band is about'.[15] Black metal seems to inhabit an entirely spiritual, infernal realm populated by Satan, his rebel angels, and legions of the dead, damned or forgotten. And yet, as Weaver says, this is also directly related to 'current conditions' and the understanding of the universe as 'a cold, mechanical, meaningless trap'. An understandable response to this bleak, materialist conception of the universe might well be to reject it in either an affirmation of a deeper, metaphysical realm or in nostalgia for an ancient, more enchanted past, also 'whole and full of depth'. And indeed this is the response of much pagan and folk metal. But it is not the response of black metal, or at least the black metal that concerns us in our development of the concept of melancology. Here, black metal's response to the austerity of the material universe is to evoke an even more desolate place, or, as we shall see, to evoke through mytho-poetic means the full horror of the real and eternal desolation of the material universe itself.

What is essential to remember with regard to the black metal thematic is that the nightmarish, quasi-theological hell evoked in the lyrics of so many songs and the 'cold, mechanical, meaningless trap' is exactly the same place. Moreover, the former does not imply a denial of the science, but on the contrary a full engagement with it in different terms. The black metal universe is atheological in the sense that it is paradoxically both Godless and evil, with the emphasis falling on the latter. For scientific materialism, however, the universe is merely Godless, if complex and ultimately systematizable. For the neuroscientist Paul

Churchland, it is still thermodynamics, understood within complex systems, that renders every aspect of the universe intelligible to human thought, including thought itself:

> It is [thermodynamics] that renders physically intelligible such things as the process of synthetic evolution in general, and the Sun-urged growth of a rose in particular. And what is human knowledge but a cortically embodied flower, fanned likewise into existence by the ambient flux of energy and information?[16]

The universe is a great flux or churn of forces of expenditure, or entropy, temporarily fixed or captured by informational systems that transform energies into different orders of action and expenditure. The theorist who connects the energetic model of the material universe with its atheological double is, of course, Georges Bataille whose system of general economy relates cosmic forces to human societies, inner experience and evil.[17] In common with the black metal band Impaled Nazarene, Bataille views the crucifixion of Christ to be 'the most sublime of all symbols' because it links an 'extremely equivocal expression of evil' (for Christians, 'the greatest sin ever committed') with 'an exuberance of forces. It brings about a maximum of tragic intensity. It relates to measureless expenditures of energy and is a violation of the integrity of individuals'.[18] For Bataille this constitutes a 'moral summit' that is quite distinct from any good, in which human communication is attained in the presence of an evil with which it is complicit. Evil is this force of measureless expenditure that overwhelms the integrity of individuals and their thought, the very force that black metal, at its finest, invokes in its drive towards sonic ecstasy. In this regard, recourse to a mytho-poetic language is necessary to supplement a sonic force which is, of course, entirely a matter of physical form and energy.

The specific problem that seems to exercise black metal the

most, the problem of evil that science fails to confront is that of death, the violation of the integrity of individuals. Science fails to confront this problem because death has essentially no scientific meaning, and as such of course fails to recognise evil in any sense (indeed there is no place for sense or meaning of any kind in science at all): it is simply entropy or the transformation of energy into different forms of matter. But there is an irony here because the social understanding of death as an evil has encouraged techno-science to find ways of circumventing it, ways precisely enhanced by the scientific indifference to the integrity of individuals with the result that both the determination and function of death has been transformed. The advent of transplantation, prostheses, life support technology and artificial intelligence has disclosed that the precise definition and determination of death is scientifically impossible, and thus must become an object of biopolitical decision; the sovereignty of life is abolished relative to the sovereign decision of biopower.[19] These are the 'current conditions [that] make misanthropy and suicide' not only 'valid endpoints' but genuine political acts. The suicide of Mayhem's vocalist, Dead, for example, takes on symbolic significance in this context. With the scientific dissolution of death comes the biopolitical co-option of life, a co-option that for some renders us all equivalent to 'meaningless corpses'. The self-named 'Dead's' fascination with death can be seen in this light as an attempt to reclaim his own life in the instance of death.[20]

The mourning and melancholy of black metal is essentially this mourning for death – not the death of someone, or something or some lost past, but for death itself. It is felt in the love and fascination that black metal has for death. The elegiac black funeral doom metal of Nortt for example conveys a loving identification with the dead. In an interview with Brandon Stousey, Nortt remarks, 'Death within my lyrics is erotic, I desire death'.[21] At the same time, black metal is continually haunted by the spectre of the undead, eternal bleakness of the universe. Black metal's melancholy is the ecstatic agony of this revelation of eternity, melancholy not because things are going to die, but because death has no dominion and the planet revolves scorched and frozen alternately in an unremittingly bleak and pointless cosmos. Even the reassuring notion of a beginning and end to the universe in the idea of the big bang and the gradual unbinding of matter has apparently been supplanted by the unravelling of the physical understanding of the universe and the formal necessity of multiple universes and new dimensions of dark matter and energy to support the maths.

Understandably given the history of Mayhem, the suicide of Dead and the murder of Euronymous, its founder and guiding spirit, death is a major theme in the band, constantly revisited. For example relatively recent tracks from *Chimera* (2004) exemplify the distinction and contrast between an individual death and the undead drive of scientific reason for ever more reduced forms of simplicity, coherence and efficiency that circulate the voided God of meaning and purpose: 'The sum of all you ever knew equals zero. You are not dead, you never existed. You are not dead, you never existed ... You are not dead, you never existed' (Mayhem, 'Chimera', 2004). This is contrasted with the glorification of that emptiness that arises through the influx of the 'lifeforce' that can only be unleashed in the affirmation of death in all its singularity: 'Into your glory of emptiness, I send my lifeforce, my death be death with me, be death with me, death with me, death with me' (Mayhem, 'My Death', 2004). The two are linked because it is of course precisely the singularity and sovereignty of death (a death that is at once both intimate and absolutely exterior to oneself) that marks the limit of scientific knowledge, rendering it zero, since all the latter can do is observe the transformation of matter. It is through this narrow aperture of science's unthought that black metal lyrics pour in speculations concerning a domain beyond strictly scientific concerns that is both intimate and absolutely exterior, speculations inspired by the horror and fascination of death in which the world is extinguished time after time. 'Funeral Fog', the song that opened this section, is such a figure for this unknown, intimate yet non-natural exteriority. It is a fog that does not descend from the sky but rises from the depths of the tomb, into a world in which 'all natural life has for a long time ago gone', a fog of darkness that is 'thin and so beautiful / but also so dark and mysterious' taking life and nurturing it in death (Mayhem, 'Funeral Fog', 1992).

The other song that opened this Introduction, Deathspell Omega's 'From Unknown Lands of Desolation' (2002), explicitly makes the correspondence between the world of black metal's Satanic mytho-poetic atheology and the universe of science where the former is populated by strange, oppositional and insurrectionary forces that irrupt from the same cosmic chaos as matter. But theirs is it seems a darker, more imperceptible matter: 'no eyes can see us, no one believes in us, we are not made of flesh and blood'. Their destination is the despoliation of the world, where they already reside like a black hole consuming the souls of those who 'don't understand the meaning of death'. 'The apotheosis of Satan approaches / He who is inside of us', the song ends, the 'us' having been throughout an ambiguous, shifting marker of identity and invocation. The words are barely discernable, thin, fragile shapes formed out of the hoarse yet bellicose raging of a desiccated, cadaverous throat, leprous, shredded; its death-rattled breath conveyed by the thundering vibrations of drums breathlessly pummelled without pause. There is no rock 'n' roll backbeat here, just a furious cacophony. Voice smashed and sliced open by explosions of percussion challenging the darkness, buzzing guitar chords rising and falling up the scale, lurching, striving like a swarm of ravenous insects dipping and swerving in the frozen, airless void, defying gravity, seeking the taste of death ...

Our skies are forever black
Here is no signs of life at all
For burning spirits we are
Consuming your small universe
Slowly but surely
No one believes in us
We came from realms of Hell
No eyes can see us
We're not made of flesh and blood
In times past we reigned everywhere
One day life emerged from the chaos
We still dominate but this error must end
The void shall swallow the decease / disease
Slowly but surely
Changing from one dimension to another..
of being possession
Out of the nihilistic kingdom
to spread destruction
An unseen invasion to conquer
the spoiled land ... till total extinction
The human claim to rule their world
They don't even understand the meaning
of death
A black hole is eating each soul
The ultimate desolation will suppress
life and prevail again
Then there won't be mistakes anymore
The apotheosis of Satan approaches
He who is inside of us
(Deathspell Omega, 'From Unknown Lands Of Desolation', 2002)

The death of God and the music of the environment

'Whatso of bliss is among men, ne'er does it appear unmingled with woes.' (Pindar, Pythians Ode XII)[22]

Since Pythagoras and the music of the spheres, a long tradition has regarded music not just as a sound that can create an ambient environment, but as the very form of the cosmos itself. This tradition is the reference of ideas of 'acoustic ecology' that attempt to monitor the changing soundscape and the 'noise pollution' caused by the activities of technological and economic development around the world. The founder of the idea of acoustic ecology in the 1970s is the composer and theorist F. Murray Schafer. In a chapter called 'The Music of the Environment', Schafer refers to two apparently contrary Greek myths concerning the origin of music. The most familiar myth, from Homer, accounts for the invention of the lyre by Hermes when he discovers that a turtle shell can produce sound. With this discovery that given materials of the universe have pleasing sonic properties, comes ultimately the whole post-Pythagorian notion (also corroborated by the *anahata* of Indian mystics according to Schafer) that 'the universe is held together by the harmonies of some precise acoustic design, serene and mathematical'.[23] The contrary myth, from Pindar's Twelfth Pythian Ode, concerns Pallas Athena who, upon hearing of Perseus's slaying of Medusa, attempts to 'connect' with 'the sorrowful lamentations' of her sisters, and 'framed the full-sounded harmony of the reeds that she might imitate with instruments the deep groans proceeding from Euryale's fell cheeks'.[24] Thus, Athena passes on the invention of the flute to mortals for the entertainment of the people even though music never quite escapes the melancholy tenor of its origins, 'Whatso of bliss is among men, ne'er does it appear unmingled with woes'.[25] All music, according to this myth, is infused with death and mourning.

For Schafer it is this latter myth that provides the model for music as a form of human expression that reaches its peak in Western romanticism and the 'subjective and irrational' discordance of individualism. By contrast, Schafer's ecological goal is to reaffirm music as a model for 'the harmonizing influence of sounds in the world about us' that have been lost in the cacophony of the modern world.[26] Congruent with the Pythagorian view of the musical cosmos, of course, is the scientific belief in its ultimate mathematical consistency that also precludes any subjective dimension, mortal or immortal.

Perhaps in the spirit of universalism, both monotheistic and mathematical, it is possible to unify the two myths. There is only one God, and His Eternal Omnipotence, absolutely appalled at the image that His creation offers to Him, and filled with loathing for it, annihilates Himself in a profound groan of agony and despair. Imagine the agonies of Christ on the Cross multiplied to infinite proportions, the maximum of tragic intensity giving rise to measureless expenditures of energy in the form of sonic vibrations. This is the sound of the universe, the melancholic sound that *constitutes* the universe, the cosmic noise from which all form and structure derives as oscillations coalesce into dark matter, atomic matter and light,[27] producing the stars from which life ultimately derives, a universe in which, with supreme irony, human forms of life will perceive divine harmony and mathematical consistency, the very image of creation that God sought to avoid, but through avoiding, in his tragic stupidity brings about.

No wonder Lucifer rebelled, becoming Satan, the great adversary, patron of black metal which if it cannot break the chain of eternal repetition, affirms the divine cacophony and pandemonium that results from the death of God, therein returning harmony to dissonance all the better to affirm the primordial impulse, the sovereign gesture, in which God negates himself in the slavish image of man, the divine hatred of the divine returning each time in an ecstasy filled with woe of a different force and quality.

Melancology: concept and ethos

A new word implies a new concept and according to Gilles Deleuze and Félix Guattari concepts have to fulfil three criteria, they require a plane of immanence, a delimited number of characteristics and embodiment in a conceptual persona. For melancology, the plane of immanence is death and extinction: that which negates thought (and indeed science) since it both ties and limits thought to its always excessive (im)perishable conditions of existence. As Eugene Thacker notes, 'extinction can never adequately be thought, since its very possibility presupposes the absolute negation of thought'.[28] But further, Thacker suggests that notwithstanding its inadequacy, the idea of extinction does indeed sustain a notion of species 'life', as the 'null set of biology', that is distinct from the life that is led by any individual organism. As such, 'extinction is *the non-being of life that is not death*'.[29] This describes very well the plane of immanence of melancology upon which the melancholic mourning for death of a life without being resounds in the doom of howling winds. The vanishing point of a horizon of incommensurability between philosophy and science, ontology and biology, 'life as non-being' can only be situated beyond the domain of the human, either above or below its scale among 'spiritual creatures' or 'the strata of demonic multitudes or that of subhuman plague and pestilence', forms of 'a misanthropic quality of Life [that] sustains itself with a certain inaccessibility'.[30] Its legions swooping among the obscure and noisy strata of non-human forms, in black metal's sonic pandemonium can be heard the radical heterogeneity of life-as-non-being, its violent clamour the formless form of being's negation and transformation.

This undead, heterogeneous life-without-being finds in melancology its *conceptual personae* in the black metal 'kvltists' whose ethos runs across the spectrum of melancholy from bile and rage to sorrow, depression and the delectation of evil all the better to affirm the desolation that is contemplated in the clamour of black metal's ecstatic woe. For Freud, 'the complex of melancholia behaves like an open wound, drawing to itself cathectic energies ... from all directions, and emptying the ego until it is totally impoverished'.[31] Sick, wan, as pale as death, the melancholic, corpse-painted figure of the black metal kvltist presents an undead *memento mori* to the plane of immanent and imminent extinction. In the melancholic refusal of nourishment, of the consumption of goods, the oral drive of the melancholic is displaced by the invocatory drive of song, or rather black metal's rasping death-rattle battle-cry, the call and invocation of the cosmic abyss (plunged apart by God's conversion to atheism and suicide) that is inseparable from the radical impoverishment and dissolution of ego. The melancholic invocation is an effect of binding with the locus of sound itself, the acosmic sonic drive evoked by black metal's sovereign dissonance.

Sovereign yet essentially anonymous because devoid of being melancological self-consciousness is paradoxically projected outside of oneself (on a path of ex-sistence) into the heterogeneous domain of non-being. This domain of excess (the excessive negation of being) and of absolute evil is therefore exactly the same as the absolute good of black metal itself: the expenditure of a sonic drive that propels a blackened self-consciousness, a melancological consciousness without being that is necessarily prior to any positive 'ecological' intervention in the 'environment' that could only repeat the process of its human exploitation and subjugation.

This is why we need to reject ecology in favour of a different term that denotes above all an ethos rather than an '*oikos*', the (restricted) economic basis of ecology. This ethos, or style, is of course related to an ethics, but it is not the same as ethics. It is perhaps appropriate here to emphasise what the ethos of melancology is not: it is not a form of morality; it is not a set of rules relating to social behaviour, civic duty, code of conduct, biopolitical governance, nor does it relate to any form of socio-political order dedicated to organizing and improving human survival or the survival of any other form of (inter-)planetary life. Neither does it, nor should it, set out to legislate for or produce new rules for the revolutionary transformation of society or the world. It is not a call to order; it is not a *savoir vivre*.

On the contrary, this ethos is supremely indifferent even, at least in the first stage, vehemently hostile to all the above. Since, for black metal, the environment is a place of absolute evil, there are no *goods* to distribute (or re-distribute) and therefore no means of power and domination, no 'good', that is, except for the sovereign good of the music itself. Stage two, therefore, involves the question: what is that musical good, that sole and only good in which or in relation to which we might confront in non-knowledge the exteriority of one's (non)relation to oneself and all that which is exterior to the chain of being? The tautological non-answer then is black metal (about which, as every kvltist says, nothing can be said) since in black metal we glimpse something that is otherwise and beyond being, indeed the very possibility of beyond. Black metal delineates the locus of desire upon which we do not give up, and from which everything can be questioned – including ecology, the environment and so on.

In order to regard extinction as a speculative opportunity for thought, including ecological thought, black metal provides the locus of the atheological a-musicality of the cosmos denoting the intimacy of and with exteriorization and with cosmic processes of binding and unbinding, consciousness, unconsciousness and even nonconsciousness. Life's undead sonic drive towards and beyond being, black metal provides a locus from which one might question human intervention in and adaptation of 'its' environment through the articulation of melancology with ethics that projects the latter beyond the threshold of the human. That is to say in deciding with which forms to dwell and expire, in deciding how to discover death rather than seek its perpetual inhuman deferral, and in rediscovering death, deciding with what processes of expenditure and decay, with what heterogeneous forms, what surpluses, what waste, what dust and detritus to unravel and decay in mutual processes of unbinding that traverse the planet.

Notes

1. For an online lecture on the musical influences and development of black metal see Gylvo 'Fenriz' Nagoll, 'Black Metal 101: A Vague Teaching' accessible on *Black Metal Theory* http://blackmetaltheory.blogspot.com. For an academic account of black metal in the context of other 'extreme' forms of the genre such as death metal and grindcore see Keith Kahn Harris, *Extreme Metal: Music and Culture on the Edge*. London: Berg, 2006. For a somewhat sensationalist, journalistic account of the notoriety that has come to be associated with the genre because of various criminal acts perpetrated by members of the Norwegian inner circle (most notably church burning and murder) see Didrik Søderlind and Michael Moynihan, *Lords of Chaos: The Bloody Rise of the Satanic Metal Underground*. Feral House, 2003.
2. Timothy Morton, *Ecology Without Nature*. Harvard University Press, 182.
3. Ibid., 185.
4. Ibid., 187.
5. Aaron Weaver quoted in Nathan T. Birk, 'Hungry for Heaven: Spirituality, Transcendence and black metal' *Zero Tolerance* 042 Aug/Sept 2011, pp. 014-019; 017-019.
6. There are indeed a significant number of right-wing and even self-styled National Socialist black metal bands almost all of whom advertise their ecological concerns in their imagery and on their websites. The most famous of these is Varg Vikernes whose music is branded under the name of

Burzum. In a recent interview with *Terrorizer* Vikernes was happy to justify his racism in biological terms: 'All sane and healthy biological creatures are racist'. In the same interview he also complains about 'the rape of Mother earth' blaming wasteful consumption and the actions of bankers (a recent concern). Nevertheless he has in common with the super rich contempt for 99% of the population. His deep ecological solution is thus: 'We should line 99 per cent of the world's population against a wall and execute them. That's the best we could do for the environment, but I guess I might come out looking quite unsympathetic if I say that in public'. Robyn Dorien, 'Burzum' *Terrorizer* 217 December 2011, pp. 20-24. It is interesting that Vikernes cannot help but wryly acknowledge the self-defeating nature of his views. The almost comic hyperbole of the statement (almost comic because Vikernes is indeed a committed if ineffectual fascist) conceals a serious and more general point about the relation between ecology and the political economy to which it inevitably becomes bound. Ecology and economy are virtually the same word and when the former becomes the basis of the latter there is always the serious danger of a drift towards fascism because it is always a question of deciding who or what lives and dies usually on an aesthetic/utilitarian (or ends/means) basis.

7. Ibid
8. Weaver insists that their nostalgia is not romantic, but a semi-strategic position from which to critique the present. 'A deep sense of yearning to a forgotten past is what gives our music its melancholy spirit. But to be trapped and engulfed by the ghosts of the past is a different thing. We have no interest in dressing up as Vikings and cobbling together a religion from a lost culture. We don't romanticise the past; we criticise the present ... There is no reason why a return to a world of smaller-scale, earth-based, bioregional

cultures *needs* to have a right-wing ideology attached to it. The vast majority of people who are actually developing new rural cultures are anarchists and peaceful hippies. Neo-Nazis like to have armchair fantasies about forging a pure agrarian utopia, but in fact they tend to be useless failures who accomplish nothing. My hatred for the blowhards on the far right knows no bounds'. Ibid., 019.

9. Quentin Meillassoux, 'Divine Inexistence' in Graham Harman, *Quentin Meillassoux: Philosophy in the Making*, 2011. Edinburgh: Edinburgh University Press, p. 226.
10. Ibid.
11. 'God is only aware of His own nothingness, and that's why He is an atheist, profoundly: he would immediately cease being God (instead of His horrible absence there would be only an imbecile, stupefied presence, if He saw himself in that way)'. Georges Bataille, *Inner Experience*, trans. Leslie-Anne Bolt. SUNY Press, 1990: 103. See also Allan Stoekl, *Bataille's Peak: Energy, Religion and Postsustainability*. Minneapolis: Universtity of Minnesota Press: 88-9.
12. Nick Land, *Thirst for Annihilation*. London: Routledge, 1992.
13. Ibid.
14. This is acknowledged by Bradley Smith of WITTR when he says, 'Our music, then, is not "true" Black Metal for we have moved beyond this fantasy of a nihilistic apocalypse ... Our relationship with the natural world is a healing force in our lives'. Cited in Steven Shakespeare, 'Blackened Notes' in *Hideous Gnosis* edited by Nicola Masciandaro, CreateSpace, 2010, pp. 5-22, 7.
15. Weaver, *Terrorizer*, 19.
16. PM Churchland, *Scientific Realism and the Plasticity of Mind*. Camb UP, 1979, 151.
17. See especially Georges Bataille, *The Accursed Share*. New York: Zone Books, 1988 and Georges Bataille, *Literature and Evil*. London: Marion Boyars, 1971.

18. Georges Bataille, *On Nietzsche*. New York: Paragon House, 1992, p. 17.
19. See Giorgio Agamben *Homo Sacer*. Stanford University Press, 160-65.
20. The adoption and association of corpsepaint by Norwegian black metal bands is of course of relevance here and dates from this point. For a discussion of corpsepaint see Drew Daniel below, pp. 16-29.
21. www.pitchforkmedia.com/article/feature/50777-column-show-no-mercy
22. Pindar, 'Pythians Ode XII: To Midas of Agragas', Gilbert West, *The Odes of Pindar in English.*
23. F. Murray Schafer, 'The Music of the Environment' in Christoph Cox and Daniel Warner (eds) *Audio Culture.* London: Continuum, 29-39, 30.
24. Pindar, 'Pythians Ode XII'.
25. Ibid.
26. Schafer, 31.
27. For astrophysicist Mark Whittle, this is indeed more or less how the universe began, describing the 'big bang' as a kind of 'primal scream', 'a moment of silence followed by a rapidly descending scream which builds to a deep roar and ends in a deafening hiss'. See 'Primal Scream: Sounds from the Big Bang'. http://astsun.astro.virginia.edu/~dmw8f/index.php
28. Eugene Thacker, *In the Dust of this Planet*. Winchester: Zero Books, 123.
29. Ibid., 126.
30. Ibid., 131.
31. Sigmund Freud, Mourning and Melancholia. *The Standard Edition of the Complete Psychological Works of Sigmund Freud, Volume XIV (1914-1916): On the History of the Psycho-Analytic Movement, Papers on Metapsychology and Other Works*, 237-258, 256.

Corpsepaint as Necro-Minstrelsy, or Towards the Re-Occultation of Black Blood

Drew Daniel

A Melancholy Prolegomena

What forces are at work when blood runs black? From Beherit's 'Oath of Black Blood' to Mütilation's 'Black Imperial Blood' to Behexen's 'My Stigmas Bleeding Black' to Xasthur, for whom 'shadows of human suffering have found a home, watered with blackened blood', black metal hotwires the historical poetics of early modern humoral theory, summoning the sanguine urge of celebration, and the choleric rage of the berserker, only to pollute these Hippocratic streams of blood and bile with the cold and dry essence of black bile.[1] As the sallow face of Dürer's angel becomes the absolute pallor of a corpsepainted 'frozen moon', the signature affect of ancient Greek medicine and Renaissance high culture undergoes a paroxysm of parody, profanation, and ruin in which black metal whitewashes early modern melancholy, and speeds it up. Yet the infusion of melancholy's 'wretched wisdom' (Krallice) into black metal modulates the black metal war machine just as strongly, detuning downwards towards despair. In this essay I wish to consider the complex, polychronic encounter between black metal as an already self-belated formation and black bile as a material substance perpetually archaic and passé with respect to itself. But before the amps and distortion pedals of black metal theory are engaged at full volume, some preliminary tunings, mic-checks, and clarifications of the essentially vague and murky nature of black bile's intellectual history are required.

As a humoral fluid in circulation alongside and mixed within other liquid substances, melancholy is always already fundamentally impure. But the circulation of black bile within black metal, aptly described by Nicola Masciandaro as the 'thrown conceptual space' of Melancholy Black Metal,[2] models with particular virulence a kind of temporal distortion already implicit in the early modern archive of melancholy representation, an impurity which is theoretical insofar as it is a categorical encounter with temporality: the past of an archaic origin and the endpoint of an extinct finitude yet to come are both brought into a present moment. As is well known, melancholy is experienced as *both* a heightened contemplation of heavenly mysteries and a depressive submergence into thing-like muteness. Frozen in a philosophical trance indistinguishable from catatonia, melancholy sage and melancholy idiot join in aping the posture of a corpse. This distortion of temporality is also a distortion of tempo: melancholy models a time that is at once 'ancient' and 'to come', and, accordingly melancholy keeps a time that is at once fast and slow.

This conundrum derives from a basic push-pull between philosophy and medicine articulated by the two core authority figures within the intellectual archive of black bile: Aristotle and Galen.[3] In pseudo-Aristotelian panegyrics, the presence of an excess of black bile manifests a manic state of enervated inspiration: melancholy is a kind of genius. In Galenic pathological writings, the presence of an excess of black bile manifests a stupefied state of vegetal shutdown: melancholy is a kind of sickness. The result for the medieval and early modern inheritors is that melancholy names neither a substance nor a subject but an essentially incoherent problem space stretched between the two incongruous definitions of the same object. Preceding their clinical separation into the forked or horned pairing of bipolar disorder, the speed of mania and the slowness of despair remain mixed and mutually enmeshed in the symptomatic spectrum of ancient Greek humoral thinking and its subsequent citation in Christian Europe, and this fundamental discordance is carried over into black metal's re-use of humoral poetics. Thus, an impurity of historical location and an impurity of mixed feelings are made simultaneous: what we are feeling and when we are feeling it are called into question, swirled into a state Watain evoke as 'Lawless Darkness'. How does melancholy time operate within black metal? Reading black bile's circulation within black metal on behalf of a metallic blackening of the archive of early modern melancholy, I seek to translate the darkness of this thrown conceptual space of Black Metal Melancholy in terms of the historical/political temporal dynamic that Alain Badiou in *Logics of Worlds* has christened 'occultation'.[4]

If the warlike clustering of black metal collectivities has recently been theorized in terms of the multiplicity of wolf-packs, acephalous hordes and kvlts (formations which themselves recall the swarming, cross-species manifolds implicit in Renaissance representations of atrabilious temperament as a plane of indivisibly black immanence), the rise to prominence of so-called 'depressive / suicidal' black metal would seem to compromise the viability of those models. For the entrenched and domestic Werther-ism of so-called 'depressive / suicidal black metal' risks collapse into the perfect commodity-form of private, solitary, defeatist quietism, leaving black metal ripe for critical re-territorialization as nothing more than ambient shoegaze dressed up with gothic posturing (something for lone wolves rather than for packs). In his polemic of 1931, 'Left Wing Melancholy', Walter Benjamin long ago flagged the quietistic implications of this emotion, lambasting the ultimately harmless and conciliatory aura of 'tortured stupidity' that it proffers as an inadequate response to capitalism.[5] As an aesthetic mode staked upon intoxicating reveries of suicide, masochism, failure and retreat, the necro-politics of melancholy seem perfectly suited to index the vanishing point of the pagan and ancestral collectivities mourned within black metal, re-presenting them as lost objects of love impossibly canceled by the politics of the present.

For this very reason, black metal's embrace of melancholy

constitutes a contemporary expression of the process which Alain Badiou, in *Logics of the Worlds* (2009), terms 'occultation' and defines as 'the descent of the present into the night of its non-exposition'.[6] Neither the faithful subject standing in a stance of fidelity to the politics of the event (a Communist) nor the reactive subject who simply subverts/denies the event (a neoliberal reformist), the 'obscure subject' constitutes a third option: a temporal stance of revolt, but a revolt against living within the present as such, a flight not simply backwards but *out of time*. The black metal kvltist chooses to drown the present in a fog of black bile, offering what Badiou terms 'the paradox of an occultation of the present which is itself in the present'.[7] The passé nature of melancholy, at once exhausted as an aesthetic and discredited as science, constitutes a means of subtraction from its grip. It is here that the critical disjunction between modern 'depression' and early modern 'melancholy – to most, a purely pedantic distinction without a difference – offers us some critical leverage. I am indebted here to Dominic Fox's account of depressive black metal as 'a reaction to belatedness' in his book *Cold World: The Aesthetics of Dejection and the Politics of Militant Dysphoria*.[8] Fox takes the belatedness to function at the level of the black metal scene itself, which it does; but I think it can be stretched further back to the self-belatedness of melancholy as an already inherently 'polychronic' substance.[9] Therefore, I want to offer an account of *black blood* as neither a matter of race nor face but instead as a radically impure phenomenon of what I term *melancholy assemblage*, temporally and materially distributing black blood across subjects and across time, rather than essentially compressing and preserving any racial or subjective essence inwards within particular bodies in the hopes that this might darkly illuminate the political scene of 'occultation' staged within black metal.

Trying to make good upon the imperative to 'blacken' theory, in the space thus opened out I will offer not an argument but an invocation. My essay's title is a spell whose sequential order I shall immediately revile and overthrow through a suitably satanic inversion: not the Lord's Prayer backwards or, as Marlowe's Doctor Faustus puts it, 'Jehovah's name / Forward and backward anagrammatized', but the sequential progression of rational argument turned deliberately arsey-versey.[10] This inversion is itself a working outwards through five onionskin layers of inclusion, which could be formalized thusly:

> *(TOWARDS THE (RE-(OCCULTATION OF (BLACK (BLOOD)))))*

Accordingly, this text begins in blood and ends in the gestural leap towards its very beginning: inverting its own titular order, we move from blood to black blood, from black blood to its occultation, from the occultation of black blood to its re-occultation, and finally, the full spell will be articulated as the movement towards the re-occultation of black blood. The first shall be last and the last shall be first.

BLOOD

'Blood' names the sanguine humour that sustains life, whose revelation and ecstatic exposure reminds us of the liquid basis of our being. Crawling back into the original darkness, John Donne points out in his final sermon 'Death's Duell' (1630) that: '... in the womb we are fitted for works of darkness, all the while deprived of light; and there in the womb we are taught cruelty, *by being fed with blood* ...'[11] Blood was our first food, and we learn in darkness to drink, forgetting our primal encounter only with training and shaming. But behind the civilized restraint is a chthonic thirst; at some level we still know, with *Dracula*'s crazed Renfield, that 'The blood is the life!'[12] To spill blood is to remind us of this fact, and also to bring us closer to the end of life. Metal constitutes a music that sings in and of our blood, pulsing with the longing to surge and flow and spill and drink. As Mika from Impaled Nazarene put it with characteristic bluntness: 'I feel like I'm reborn after I have been covered in blood'.[13] From Slayer's climactic declaration in 'Raining Blood' that 'Now I shall reign in blood' to Exodus's evocation in 'Bonded by Blood' of 'Metal and blood come together as one' to Hellhammer's evocation of 'Blood Insanity' to Gorgoroth's 'Blood Stains the Circle' to Leviathan's 'Vesture Dipped in the Blood of Morning', we can say that the definitive humoral substance that unifies metal aesthetics is blood, and that it does so under the sign of unification: blood as seal for the blood oath or pact which solders together multiple persons into a social assemblage.[14]

BLACK BLOOD

Contrarily, 'Black Blood' evokes the pollution of this life force, the contamination of the blood that sustains life by a counter-force of negativity: melancholy, *melaina khole*, or black bile, the humor associated in Hippocratic medicine and its Galenic, medieval and early modern inheritors with autumn, cold, solitude, night-time, old age, and a wildly variant affective spectrum: sorrow and anxiety above all, but also rage, lycanthropy, psychotic hallucinations, religious devotion, sexual jealousy, artistic inspiration, catatonia and mania.[15] If we can regard the humoral aesthetics of heavy metal generally as alternately sanguine and choleric, black metal's turn to melancholy jumps from Mötley Crüe's 'red hot' to Mayhem's 'true' black. To move from Exodus's 'Bonded by Blood' to Beherit's 'The Oath of Black Blood,' is to reject the jocular and homosocial bonds of friendship in favor of the sorrowful, creaturely solidarity of melancholy suffering.[16]

It must be said that such a formulation, (melancholy solidarity) sounds 'wrong', discordant: the association of melancholy with solitude and isolation, with the figure of the lone wanderer reflecting upon a depopulated natural landscape or posed/poised within some scenic spot of retreat, rises in the mind as an immediate, overfamiliar and ready to hand cliché, seemingly definitive of melancholy as a congenital withdrawal from the social. This cliché is itself born out by countless musical anthems to, about, or upon solitude (Black Sabbath 'Solitude', Candlemass, 'Solitude' Drudkh's *Songs of Grief and Solitude*).[17] In the face of such an overpopulated field of melancholic solitude, why invoke melancholy solidarity?

The quick and dirty and unsatisfying answer is 'Because melancholy battens upon paradox.' As a cold and dry humor, black bile constitutes an essentially contradictory substance: a dry liquid that cools when it is burned. Accordingly, we might also say that melancholy generates assemblages of social relation even and especially when they are figured through the seeming cancellation of the social itself. The slower and (perhaps) more satisfying answer to the question 'why invoke melancholy solidarity?' would run as follows: because melancholy's ontology of planetary/biological correspondence blurs and violates the very distinction of figure/ground upon which such framing relies. 'The Oath of Black Blood' binds together the melancholic with the world that surrounds them, creating an extended scene of pathetic correspondence and mutually blackened resonance between mind and world: a melancholy – or, better, melancological, assemblage. We can see this at work in even the most schematic, crude representations of melancholy. A case in point is offered by the depictions of the four humoral temperaments in the Augsburg Calendar, in which 'Melancholy' is modeled as a tenuous relational network – at once proposed and canceled – between two limp figures.

The man sits at a table with his head in his hands, face entirely obscured. His partner rests beside him with her hands at her sides, her spinning wheel left untouched, looking away from him, neither acknowledging the viewer nor her companion. This offers the viewer a gathering together of persons and things

Fig. 1. 'Melancolicus', Augsburg Calendar.[18]

under the sign of Saturnine despair, a degree zero of sociality which is not about dialogue or even spectatorship but mere abeyance: being melancholic together, these forms and postures and objects are aligned into an affective dump site in which bodies become as still and enigmatic as the discarded tools that surround them: a melancholy assemblage.

Melancholy assemblages perform a simultaneously damping and reinforcing function in relation to the forward drive of metal aesthetics: what was hot becomes icy and cold, what was a vigorous expression of life force becomes deathbound, moribund, or in black metal parlance, 'necro'. There are so many examples of this affective claiming of melancholy by metal bands in general and black metal in particular that a list of exemplary bands, song titles, album titles, and, yes, file-sharing websites would far exceed the space provided, but here are just a few examples from the ocean of black bile: Sargeist, 'Black Treasures of Melancholy', Mütilation's 'Tears of A Melancholic Vampire', Striborg's 'Autumnal Melancholy' and 'The Grandeur of

Melancholy', Agalloch's 'The Melancholy Spirit', Ulver's *A Quick Fix of Melancholy*, Cold World's *Melancholie 2*. One could go on. Bracketing this personal hit parade, the Encyclopaedia Metallum indicates at least five bands simply called Melancholy from Greece, Mexico, Lebanon, Poland and Russia, not to mention Czech Republic's Melancholy Pessimism.[19] Dan Nelson's abcedarian art world gag / tome *All Known Metal Bands* (2008) provides a suitably exhausting list of related outfits which overlaps with the Encyclopeaedia that runs, in part, as follows:

> Melancholia, Melancholic Art, Melancholic Demise, Melancholic Seasons, Melancholic Silence, Melancholic Winds, Melancholy, Melancholy, Melancholy, Melancholy Cry, Melancholy Pessimism, Melancholyc Sunrise, Melancolasi, Melancolia, [...] Melencolia, Melencolia Estatica, Melencoliam, Melencoliasi ...[20]

What was true at the level of the medieval and early modern melancholic image remains also present within the social surround of the dark flowering of depressive and suicidal black metal. Far from isolating and disconnecting the solitary sufferer, nothing brings people together like the collective evocation of melancholy solitude.

THE OCCULTATION OF BLACK BLOOD:

'The Occultation of Black Blood' names the repression or concealment of the possibility of black blood within the body. Early modern physiology expected a dark complexion to be found in the face of melancholics because the physical surplus of black bile within a living system could be seen in and through the skin itself. If we look at *Melencolia I* (1514), we see that Dürer's angel has a noticeably dark face: she is not, as it were, 'white' but is quite literally a dark angel. This is because the blood within the body of a melancholy person was imagined to run black. As

Marsilio Ficino puts it in the chapter of *De Vita Libri Tres* (1489) titled 'How Many Things Cause Learned People Either to Be Melancholy or to Become So', this is a result of a drying of the brain caused by agitation:

> when the more subtle and clear parts of the blood frequently get used up, the rest of the blood is necessarily rendered dense, dry and black. [...] All these things characteristically make the spirit melancholy and the soul sad and fearful – since, indeed, interior darkness much more than exterior overcomes the soul with sadness and terrifies it.[21]

The result of this can be read into the face, as Burton notes in *The Anatomy of Melancholy* (1621): 'This diversity of Melancholy matter, produceth diversity of effects. It if be within the body, and not putrefied, it causeth black Jaundice.'[22] Within Renaissance medicine, black blood within the body lends a legibly black cast or color to the skin surface of the affected person.

The first 'occultation' of black blood therefore occurred with the dawning of 'pallor' as the epidermal signifier of emotional melancholy. As melancholy lost its humoral meaning and became an elite aesthetic mode of 'sadness', what was bleached away, literally, was its association with dark-skinned faces. Through the recession of Galenic schemes and the aesthetic triumph of Romanticism, 'pallor' becomes an index of a bloodless-ness, a draining away of life force, which purifies melancholy of its attachment to a thingly, materially embodied substantial form of black bile. This achieves its zenith in the romantic cult of languid pallor and the crypto-sexualization of the symptoms of tuberculosis.[23] Tom Moore, visiting Lord Byron in Patras in 1828, hears the poet declare 'I look pale. I should like to die of consumption'; taking the bait and asking why, he is told 'because the ladies would all say "Look at that poor Byron, how interesting he looks in dying".'[24] Thus, the first 'occultation of black blood' is a historical phenomenon which tacitly racializes an already ambient (and Aristotelian) poetics of 'genial' melancholic greatness, sensitivity, intellectual achievement, refinement or excellence by connecting a trait to a skintone, and, implicitly, a diseased state, albeit one no longer supported by humoral fluid but instead produced by fluid in the lungs. What persists is the idea that the excellent, distinctive, artistic and thoughtful person has a legible skintone that symptomatically, and morbidly, expresses this quirk of temperament. There is then, a pronounced irony at work in an 'occultation', a darkening, that works through the imposition of whiteness, but this sleight of hand in which the sallow, jaundiced, dark-faced early modern melancholic gearshifts into the pallid and tubercular Romantic offers us a 'Just So Story' of intellectual history as a racial fantasy: How the Melancholics Became White.

THE RE-OCCULTATION OF BLACK BLOOD:

This passage into physiological abeyance is only further reinforced by a second historical occultation through which melancholy yields to the lucrative pharmaceutical and diagnostic supremacy of 'depression.' The dawn of depression banishes the old world of humoral physiology, ushering in a modern psychology of affect management that monitors workflow and sleep patterns and sex lives for slumps and drops in productivity and prescribes accordingly. In *The New Black*, psychoanalyst Darian Leader describes this massive cultural shift in a paragraph worth quoting in its entirety:

> Historians of psychiatry and psychoanalysis have mostly agreed that depression was created as a clinical category by a variety of factors in the second half of the twentieth century: there was a pressure to package psychological problems like other health problems, and so a new emphasis on surface

> behavior rather than on unconscious mechanisms came to the fore; the market for minor tranquilizers collapsed in the 1970s after their addictive properties were publicized and so a new diagnostic category – and remedy for it – had to be popularized to account for and cater to the malaise of urban populations; and new laws about drug-testing favored a discrete, simplistic account of what illness was. As result, drugs companies manufactured both the idea of the illness and the cure at the same time. Most of the published research had been funded by them, and depression came to stand less for a complex of symptoms with various unconscious causes than simply that which anti-depressants acted on. If the drugs affected mood, appetite and sleep patterns, then depression consisted of a problem with mood, appetite and sleep patterns. Depression, in other words, was created as much as it was discovered.[25]

In a Foucaultian parable of social construction that should be familiar to veterans of theory in the 1990s, we see here the sequential replacement of one medically constructed identity by another. To rewind to the beginning of this process, the 'melancholic' as an individual was produced as a consequence of a theoretical commitment to a temperamental tetrad embedded in a web of synergistically confirming Ancient Greek attitudes and ontologies: the Pythagorean worship of the numeral four begat the Empedoclean combinatorial model of the elemental composition of the universe out of earth, air, fire and water, and this led in turn to a Galenic medical practice fashioned after this Pythagorean/Empedoclean image, populated by four broad types of human beings: sanguine, phlegmatic, choleric and melancholic. Fast forwarding several centuries, this stubbornly tenacious model yielded to experimental science and the dawn of biopolitics, the socially constitutive process of identity by which kinds of selves are named into existence by systems and regimes of knowledge which replaced the melancholic of the fifteenth century with the splenetic of the eighteenth century, the neurotic of the nineteenth century, and, finally, the depressive of the twentieth and twenty-first century. Doubly 'occulted', black blood is banished from our bodies as humoralism enters the purgatory of discredited pseudo-science. This has consequences for the immediate recognizability of the subject in question: pallor triumphs over sallowness as the default complexion of melancholy feeling.

TOWARDS THE RE-OCCULTATION OF BLACK BLOOD:

In the wake of these two Occultations, which are, from the perspective of mainstream culture, definitive and final, the further twist of 'Re-Occultation' that concerns me here is the contemporary flowering of so-called 'Depressive / Suicidal' Black Metal. How can we work through this inner darkening? 'Towards' marks the asymptotic approach, the poetics of a gesture that reaches out for something, a solicitation, a tease, the shortfall between two points that do not quite intersect. In reaching 'towards', we mark the failure of something to overlap successfully with itself. Considered historically, this 'towards' marks the failure of early modern melancholy to overlap with modern depression; considered phenomenologically, it marks the asymptotic disjunction between the completeness of the specular image and the incompleteness of the 'I,' that Lacan famously evoked as a 'discordance' within the dialectic of the self.[26] Considered politically, the asymptotic 'towards' marks our position in time, but also our relation to the political event, a relation which, as Badiou describes it, can be one of fidelity, reaction, or occultation. Describing the obscure subject as willfully submerged in a 'night' of obscurity which suppresses the revolutionary possibility of evental political truths in his *Logics of Worlds,* Alain Badiou writes that 'this night must be produced under entirely new conditions which are displayed in the world by the rebel body and its emblem.'[27] Speaking the words of the nightspirit, the rebel body of the black metal kvltist has chosen as its emblem a powerful sigil of melancholic 'occultation': corpsepaint

To speak of corpsepaint at all is to risk providing aid and comfort to the enemy. The mainstream media, predictably ravenous in its cool-hunting search for hotzones radioactive with even the most notional cachet of authenticity, has predictably fastened onto the comedic potential of corpsepaint as a means to both co-opt and condescend to black metal as an extremist subculture. Exhibit A of this process is the thinly veiled transposition of Immortal's Abbath into the avatar Lars Umlaut in the *Guitar Hero* video game franchise. Current retail for this series is over 2 billion dollars, and with more than 25 million units sold, it is safe to say that *Guitar Hero* constitutes the most widely disseminated representation of a black metal musician on this planet. It is hardly surprising that the visual look of corpsepaint has become a legible meme, but the price of its very success as a consistent and strong image is that it is also, by that token, ripe for parody, appropriation, and various modes of repressive tolerance. The same is the case for more ad hoc and apparently underground encounters with the image of the corpsepainted black metal kvltist. The recipe for such encounters is simple: take a press photo of Immortal, replace battle-axes with kittens, and you've got yourself a hilarious new image to use as an online avatar which shows that you're aware of 'that stuff but that you don't take it too seriously.' Such clichéd substitutions (kittens for battleaxes) tell us nothing about black metal and everything about a rapacious and alienated culture that insists upon leveling down all that it touches. Infinitely worse than contempt, censorship or repression, neutralizing fondness of this sort constitutes an inevitable response, but hopefully one that will spur black metal ever earthwards towards a more torturous and inaccessible stance of obscurity and hateful recalcitrance.

Corpsepaint also constitutes a point of contact between black metal as a subculture and a broader taxonomy of mainstream performance history, celebrity culture, and animal morphology. As UK artist Bunny Bissoux points out in her 'Creatures of Corpse Paint' graphic illustration, the family tree of this practice includes, as any metal fan acknowledges, Arthur Brown, Alice Cooper, Kiss, King Diamond, Sarcofago and The Misfits, but it also includes Ronald McDonald, Brandon Lee, Insane Clown Posse, Marilyn Manson and, from the animal kingdom, badgers, pandas and raccoons.[28] The undeniably humorous but effectively trivializing nature of such assemblages indexes a classic capitalist technique: the insistence upon plurality and multiplicity is used to level down the intensity of any particular affirmation with the sheer fact of generalized clutter. Such acts of inclusion reassure the consumers that there is, luckily, 'nothing special' about Hellhammer, Abruptum, Satyricon, Immortal, Behemoth, Vondur or Gorgoroth; they are just more trash to be heaped alongside some wrestler named Sting.

But what unites Guitar Hero, Bunny Bissoux, and various online borrowers and parodists is a shared recognition: there is something powerful, totemic and incomplete about the graphic and somatic sigil of the corpsepainted face. It communicates powerfully by virtue of a certain disconnection from the practical temporality of everyday life – it is anti-quotidian in its essence. Corpsepaint seems to focus the will of those who wear it; as Bard Faust of Emperor put it in an interview immediately preceding his incarceration for the murder of a gay man, corpsepaint brings darkness forward and prefigures 'dark events,' and for this reason cannot become an accessory to a daily lifestyle:

> When we, under a gig or during a photo session, are using corpsepaint, we are usually in a state of mind that makes us feel like we are getting nearer darkness (and maybe even one

> with darkness). Corpsepaint shouldn't be used everyday. It should only be used when you feel like some dark event would happen [...] At such events, I look at myself as one of creatures of the night ... a child of darkness.[29]

There are at least two temporal dynamics that the corpsepainted face makes available to thought: one is the tension between the *punctum* of the 'dark event' and the 'everyday' which it cancels and ruptures. The regularity of an ordered, productive, adult existence in the light summons its hateful opponent in Bard Faust's dark child. The other temporal dynamic concerns the longer arc of intellectual-historical time which corpsepaint folds, tesseract-like, into a new polychronic alignment. Transforming the face into a battlefield of relational struggle between a black surface and a white surface, corpsepaint enacts the historical disjunction between the absolute black of early modern melancholy blood and the absolute pallor of post-Romantic depressive whiteness. Through corpsepaint, black metal achieves the re-occultation of black blood as an immanent experience of asymmetric struggles between life and death, dark and light, then and now.

Corpsepaint thus marks the juncture of a number of troubling insufficiencies: the insufficiency of any face to secure a solid and persuasively stable, singular subjectivity is foregrounded in the construction of personalized, 'signature' modes of make-up. The insufficiency of racist ideologies of whiteness, already belied by the merely ontic pinks and browns of actual skintone, is staunched through the purely artificial whiteness of make-up. This transformation of the face of the entertainer into a cartoonishly legible form thus recalls the minstrelsy tradition of white European and American entertainers 'blacking up' so that they can look like African-Americans, a dialectical process that foregrounds the artificiality of race as a construction while still effectively reinforcing that construction's normative force.

Which ought to give one pause. While it might seem a merely risible stretch, if not trivializing, to transpose the nationwide, socially situated history of harm implicit in American minstrelsy performer's stagings of black subjectivity into the more localized subcultural register of black metal musicians' imposture of dead subjectivity in this manner, such a risk seems to me worth taking. To state the obvious, though the jury is out on the question of whether such encounters are long overdue or pre-emptively rigged, black metal theory awaits its rendezvous with both queer theory and critical race theory. Given the presence of nationalist and racist rhetoric, images, lyrics and opinions within some but by no means all of its practitioners, black metal's partial overlap with neo-Nazi politics and crypto-supremacist or openly white supremacist positions at once calls out for theorization precisely as a counterpart to, and component of, any ethical judgment and at the same time raises basic questions about the fundamental disjunction of aesthetics and ethics. Mention of such facts and indications of such problems typically cues the presentation of well meaning apologias, numerous counterexamples of non-racist black metal, and awkward changes of the subject from fans and, by extension, fans-who-theorize (myself occasionally included).[30] The relative absence from view of queer theory and critical race theory at the scene of black metal's theorization may tell us something about the demographics of its participants, or it may indicate an intellectually hygienic impulse towards the ontological over the ontic, or the instrumental use of the latter to paper over embarrassment at the former. But it might also be a register of fatigue with certain stances of reading, and betray a collective sense that the theoretical conversation itself has simply migrated elsewhere; if the productions of symposia are any indication, participants are simply more interested in religious history, cosmology, and ecological thought than in shoving one more subculture through the cultural studies meatgrinder in order to produce a politically well-intentioned exposé of racism which is already so grotesque as to hardly merit the intrigue of symptomatic unpacking. Obsessed as it is with thinking negation, negativity, hostility and failure, recent queer theory might yet constitute a particularly generative lens through which to think about the fetishistic circulation of the Third Reich as a 'lost cause – melancholically embraced because it is lost – within black metal aesthetics.[31]

But for the purposes of this essay, one cannot invoke the paradigmatic ventriloquism of the minstrelsy tradition in relation to black metal performance and kvltist identity without also thinking the corpsepainted subject as at once hyperbolically racialized and strategically subtracted from racial legibility—and to see this feeling of 'empty fullness' as paradigmatically melancholic in the process. While the raced dynamic of imposture in its American nineteenth-century context has already been the subject of outstanding scholarship from Eric Lott, Daphne Brooks and others, their formulations undergo a theoretical re-'blackening' when adjusted to the frozen northern wastelands lyrically evoked by black metal, if not actually inhabited by its increasingly global performers, practitioners, and fans.[32] At the level of scene politics, if the commentary of its pioneers is any indication, the *Ursprung* of corpsepaint may not lie in Norway, Finland, or Sweden but in Brazil: whenever the origins of this make up style are discussed, mention is swiftly made of the foundational influence of Sarcofago's debut album 'I.N.R.I.' (1987) upon the visual presentation of the first wave of Scandinavian black metal artists, who more or less copied the signature look from these citizens of Belo Horizonte: spiked bracelets, bullet belts, white cheeks, black circular eye makeup. Corpsepaint might well have been required in order for South American musicians to look sufficiently 'vampiric' and 'ghoulish', i.e. white—but even if corpsepaint is quite specifically about looking like a dead white person, its ultimate horizon gestures beyond racial legibility towards the species-being based project of turning the human face – any human face – into a skull. Accordingly, the models proposed by minstrelsy scholarship require a paradigmatic adjustment when performers are not masquerading across racial lines but are instead ostensibly pretending to be dead versions of themselves. To corpsepaint the face is to render it at once whiter than white, exposing the insufficiency of biological whiteness, and to become, as Dead from Mayhem put it in an interview, blacker than black and 'darker than death' – that is, not dead, but somehow, *more dead than the dead.*[33]

Corpsepaint is thus *not not* part of the minstrelsy tradition, but the dynamic of cross-identification is pulled in a different direction: the thrilling yet normative project of shoring up 'blackness' and 'whiteness' is bypassed in favor of Necro-minstrelsy, the cross-identification of the living with the dead, permitting the fantasy of their liminal border as a life-in-death. To wear corpsepaint while alive is to put on a kind of travesty of being dead, which is epistemologically reliant upon the audience's recognition of a fundamental artificiality. In a dynamic of impurity familiar from the theorization of drag performance, this very falseness offers a violation of a boundary that reifies the very line that it also subverts through crossing.[34] Which means that corpsepaint is about the necessary- and comforting-failure of the living to be dead, *and* the longing of the living to already be dead. Corpsepaint is a performative melancholic technology through which the notional certainty of a future status of being dead can be borrowed upon and brought into the lived present: an epidermal vacation into the future. Corpsepaint hypertrophically externalizes the internal affective dynamic already implicit in what one could call melancholy self-presentation or, termed less kindly but more accurately, melancholy posturing: the social production of a legible outward display of an inward relation to death. As Robert Burton memorably defined it in *The Anatomy of Melancholy*, melancholy is 'the character of Mortality', the affective signature of the proleptic presence of our own mortality within our life.[35] Not just, or not only, a curiously stylized working through of 'white' racialization as an incomplete project, corpsepaint also stages our asymptotic proximity to death itself. We are discordant with respect to ourselves because of the impossible certainty of our own knowledge that we are going to die. Thus the surface announcement that 'I am dead' proclaimed by corpsepaint is, as paint, also the declaration 'I am (not yet, not quite, not really) dead'. This stalling of the obscure subject within the night of an 'occultation' operates in two directions: it is both the refusal of a particular political present in favour of a discredited past and a virulent frontloading of the certainty of our own future extinction into the lived present. Stranded in the past of Ancient Greek medicine and already laid out upon the morgue table that awaits, daubed with the pallor of modern depression and the darkness of early modern black bile, the body of the black metal kvltist becomes morcellated, strewn across history. We can formulate this as a final melancholic malediction which occults the present moment on behalf of what it cannot fully contain: When blood runs black, time runs back.

Notes

1. Beherit, "The Oath of Black Blood", *The Oath of Black Blood,* Turbo Records, 1991; Mütilation, "Black Imperial Blood", *Vampires of Black Imperial Blood,* Drakkar Productions, 1995; Behexen "My Stigmas Bleeding Black", *My Soul for His Glory,* Hammer of Hate, 2008; Xasthur, "Xastur Within", *To Violate the Oblivious,* Total Holocaust Records, 2004. The notion of black blood has since triggered other iterations in black metal aesthetics; notably, the Italian label Black Blood Productions, which has released recordings by Pyre, Common Grave, Darkened Nocturn Slaughtercult, Aryan Terrorism, and other groups. Outliers are numerous, the most prominent being Los Angeles based metalcore band

As Blood Runs Black; more relevant to my argument is the anachronistic medievalism of the gothic folk trio Tbe Soil Bleeds Black, whose nominal indication of the melancholy element of earth suggests a grounding in the Empedoclean material tetrad upon which humoral medicine is based.

2. Nicola Masciandaro, "Anti-Cosmosis: Black Mahapralaya", *Hideous Gnosis: Black Metal Theory Symposium I*, 2010, 90.
3. For a basic account of the Aristotle/Galen split, see Lawrence Babb, *The Elizabethan Malady: A Study of Melancholia in English Literature from 1580 to 1642*, East Lansing: Michigan State University, 1951.
4. "The production is neither that of the present nor of its deletion, but instead that of the descent of this present into the night of its non-exposition." Alain Badiou, "Formal Theory of the Subject (Meta-Physics)" *Logics of Worlds*, Trans. Alberto Toscano, London: Continuum, 2009, 59.
5. Walter Benjamin "Left Wing Melancholy", *Selected Writings, Vol. 2, Part 2, 1931-1934*, Cambridge: Belknap Press, 1999, 425.
6. "The production is neither that of the present nor of its deletion, but instead that of the descent of this present into the night of its non-exposition." Alain Badiou, "Formal Theory of the Subject (Meta-Physics)" *Logics of Worlds*, Trans. Alberto Toscano, London: Continuum, 2009, 59.
7. Alain Badiou, "Formal Theory of the Subject (Meta-Physics)" *Logics of Worlds*, Trans. Alberto Toscano, London: Continuum, 2009, 60
8. See Dominic Fox, "A Sermon in the Name of Death", *Cold World: the Aesthetics of Dejection and the Politics of Militant Dysphoria*, London: Winchester: Zero Books, 2009, 43- 57.
9. For more on "the polychronic", see Jonathan Gil Harris, *Untimely Matter in the Time of Shakespeare*, Philadelphia: U of Pennsylvania Press, 2008.
10. Christopher Marlowe, *The Tragical History of Doctor Faustus,*

Ed. Roma Gill, New York: W.W. Norton / New Mermaids, 1989, (1.3.10) 17.

11. John Donne. *Death's Duell, or a Consolation Against the Dying Life and Living Death of the Body. Delivered at a Sermon at Whitehall, Before the King's Majesty, in the Beginning of Lent, 1630. By that Late Learned and Reverend Divine, John Donne, Dr. in Divinity, and Dean of St. Paul's, London. Being His Last Sermon, and Called by His Majesty's household, the Doctor's own Funeral Sermon*. 347, italics mine.
12. "He was lying on his belly on the floor licking up, like a dog, the blood which had fallen from my wounded wrist. He was easily secured, and to my surprise went with the attendants quite placidly, simply repeating over and over again, "The blood is the life! The blood is the life!" Bram Stoker, *Dracula,* ch. 11. 1897.
13. Jon Kristiansen, "Slayer 9: Alternative Death Mental Zine", *Metalion: The Slayer Mag Diaries,* Brooklyn: Bazillion Points Books, 2011, 241.
14. Exodus, "Bonded by Blood", *Bonded by Blood,* Torrid Records, 1985.
15. For a historical account of the clinical shift from early modern melancholy to modern medicine, see Dr. Stanley Jackson, M.D. *Melancholia and Depression from Hippocratic Times to Modern Times,* New Haven: Yale University Press, 1986.
16. Beherit, *The Oath of Black Blood,* Turbo Records, 1991.
17. Black Sabbath, "Solitude"; Candlemass "Solitude"; Drudkh, *Songs of Grief and Solitude,* Supernal Music, 2006.
18. Raymond Klibansky, Erwin Panofsky, and Fritz Saxl. *Saturn and Melancholy: Studies in the History of Natural Philosophy, Religion and Art,* New York: Basic Books, 1964, plate 89b.
19. Sargeist, "Black Treasures of Melancholy", *Disciples of the Heinous Path,* Moribund Records, 2005.
20. Dan Nelson, *All Known Metal Bands,* San Francisco:

McSweeney's, 2008.

21. Marsilio Ficino, *Three Books On Life*, Book I, Chapter IV, Trans. Carol. V. Kaske and John R. Clark, Tempe: Renaissance Society of America, 2002, 115.
22. Robert Burton, *The Anatomy of Melancholy*, Part I, Section I, Member 3, Subsection 4. Eds. Faulkner, Kiessling, Bamborgouh. Vol. I., Oxford: Oxford University Press, 1989.
23. See Jean Dubos, *The White Plague: Tuberculosis, Man, and Society*, New Brunswick: Rutgers University Press, 1987, 246.
24. As cited in Susan Sontag, *Illness as Metaphor*, New York: Farrar, Strauss, and Giroux, 1977, 31.
25. Darian Leader, *The New Black: Mourning, Melancholia, and Depression*. Minneapolis, Graywolf Press, 2008,15.
26. Jaques Lacan, *Ecrits*, 76/94, as quoted in Alain Badiou, *Theory of the Subject*, Trans. Brian Bosteels, London: Continuum, 2009, 197.
27. Alain Badiou, "Formal Theory of the Subject (Meta-Physics)" *Logics of Worlds*, Trans. Alberto Toscano, London: Continuum, 2009, 59.
28. http://bunnybissoux.blogspot.com/2009/08/corpsepaint-creatures-limited.html
29. Jon Kristiansen, "Slayer 8: Jesus Is Dead", *Metalion: The Slayer Mag Diaries*, Brooklyn: Bazillion Points Books, 2011, 209.
30. For a direct examination of the NSBM phenomenon and Peste Noire in particular, see Benjamin Noys, "*'Remain True to the Earth!'*: Remarks on the Politics of Black Metal", *Hideous Gnosis*, 105-127.
31. See in particular Judith Halberstam "'The Killer in Me Is the Killer in You': Homosexuality and Fascism", *The Queer Art of Failure*, Durham: Duke University Press, 2011, 147- 173.
32. See Eric Lott "The Blackening of America: Popular Culture and National Culture", *Love and Theft: Blackface Minstrelsy and the American Working Class*, Oxford: Oxford University

Press, 1993, 89-111; Daphne Brooks, "The Deeds Done in My Body: Performance, Black(ened) Women, and Adak Isaacs Menken in the Racial Imaginary", *Bodies in Dissent: Spectacular Performances of Race and Freedom, 1850-1910*, Durham: Duke University Press, 131-207.

33. Jon Kristiansen, "Slayer X: Past Present Forever", *Metalion: The Slayer Mag Diaries*, Brooklyn: Bazillion Points Books, 2011, 275.
34. With reference to the contretemps surrounding the drag performances in *Paris Is Burning*, Judith Butler notes the same issue: "Heterosexuality can augment its hegemony through its denaturalization, as when we see denaturalizing parodies that reidealize heterosexual norms without calling them into question." Judith Butler, "Critically Queer", *Bodies That Matter*, London: Routledge, 1993, 231.
35. Robert Burton, *The Anatomy of Melancholy*, Part I, Sect. I, Member I, Subsection 5. Eds. Faulkner, Kiessling, Bamborgouh. Vol. I., Oxford: Oxford University Press, 1989.

Black Sun

Aspasia Stephanou

The sun has failed
Darkness spread its wings.
Marduk, 'The Sun has Failed' (1994)
Reveal to me the flames of Gnosis by the absence of Light.
Immanifest, 'Among the Dead' (2010)
I had a dream, which was not all a dream.
The bright sun was extinguish'd, and the stars
Did wander darkling in the eternal space,
Rayless, and pathless, and the icy earth
Swung blind and blackening in the moonless air;
Lord Byron, 'Darkness' (1816).

David Michael Levin, following Derrida's reading of Levinas states that 'in our time, we can see the tain of the mirror: the other side, a phallocentric, logocentric 'heliopolitics' driven by 'the violence of light' and threatening to impose the ontological order of presence whenever its mastery can reach'.[1] For Levinas, Derrida writes, perceives 'a Greco-Platonic tradition under the surveillance of the agency of the glance and the metaphor of light'.[2] Derrida finds in Western philosophical thought a helio-centric tendency which prioritizes light (truth, reason) over darkness (error, unreason). Similarly, Luce Irigaray refers to the metaphor of light and photology or the language of metaphysics, the fantasy of heliocentrism which gives precedence to the masculine and posits difference and the maternal origin as absence or invisibility.[3] This is what she calls the light of the Same, of (masculine) form as opposed to the difference of maternal origin as matter, which remains outside of thought.[4] For Bataille, apart from the sun of truth and illumination exists another sun. Against the elevating sun of Icarian heights and consequently against traditional heliocentrism, there is the destructive sun, 'a filthy parody of the torrid and blinding sun'.[5] This sun is the solar anus, the darkest hole or the rotten sun which sparks the subject's desire to stare at it and be annihilated. Bataille's resistance against Plato's sun and the tradition of heliopolitics is manifested in the notion of the scrutinized sun associated with the Mithraic cult of the sun. On the one hand, the sun offers 'spiritual elevation', but on the other hand, 'the scrutinized sun can be identified with mental ejaculation, foam on the lips, and an epileptic crisis. In the same way that the preceding sun (the one not looked at) is perfectly beautiful, the one that is scrutinized can be considered horribly ugly'.[6] Bataille relates the act of staring at the rotten sun to the artist's creative imagination and limit experience. Van Gogh's cutting of his ear and his sun paintings are the result of staring at the sun and losing one's self. Thus the artist's sacrificial mutilation is an 'act of deindividuating freedom, an expression of ecstatic and "sovereign" heterogeneity'.[7] The encounter with the destructive sun becomes here a liminal experience whose violence leads to the dissolution of the subject.

Bataille's 'sun of malediction' remains however,[8] according to Negarestani, trapped in a solar economy and the tyranny of heliocentrism. In 'Solar Inferno and the Earthbound Abyss' he proposes instead a radical ecology outside the empire of the sun, where both the sun and earth are envisioned as dying and where such ecological death 'becomes a form of descent into the cosmic abyss'.[9] 'The sun', he writes, 'should neither be embraced as the dark flame of excess nor glorified as a luminous end, but rediscovered as an infernal element in the chain of complicities which open the Earth into a universe that is more weird than infernal'.[10] His desire is to 'subvert the Sun's thirst for annihilation' and embrace the 'dark corpse of the sun' through a pact between the earth and the sun.[11] 'To make a pact with the Sun, to love the Sun terrestrially' is, for Negarestani, 'more than a mere act of obliteration; it goes further in the direction of mess rather than that of death'.[12] The sun's pact with the earth imbues the sun with 'terrestrial characteristics' and introduces it to 'terrestrial becomings'.[13] Thus the sun's transformation produces 'heretical innovations' and 'inexhaustible becomings of perversion, deviations, and insurgent creativities'.[14] In this way, the Earth and Sun are 'bound or grasped as merely contingent and hence, necessarily perishable entities'.[15] For Negarestani, there is no hegemony of the sun or the image of the earth as a blue marble, but only the effects of the 'perverse immanence' of a decaying earth with the sun.[16]

If Negarestani's decaying sun in its alliance with the perishable earth unleashes perverse and multiple possibilities, then we have to look into the core of blackness and the black sun of alchemists. There is a connection between Negarestani's descent into darkness, alchemical processes and Jung's psychology of the unconscious. Stanton Marlan in *The Black Sun: The Alchemy and Art of Darkness* (2005) approaches the notion of a black sun or Sol Niger and blackness not as a representation of the nigredo or blackness phase in the process of the alchemical opus that disappears when the work is completed, or in terms of Jungian psychology where the black sun of the nigredo phase is associated with suffering and the melancholic soul's struggles with this shadow of darkness.[17] Instead, Marlan's analysis focuses on the image of the black sun and blackness itself a descent into darkness and the unconscious which can be seen as transformative. He sees our time as one that is trapped by 'the tyrannical shadow of the Sun King who bears within himself the seeds of his own destruction'.[18] He envisions darkness and the blackening alchemical process 'as a dying of immature innocence – a nigredo that holds a transformative possibility and an experience that opens the dark eye of the soul'.[19] It is in this blackened geography that the black metal Orpheus opens himself, by his katabasis, literally or metaphorically, into the abyss and the black sun of melancholia. The melancology of the black metal musician, in its double movement conjures up a black ecology and a black logos, a blackening of symbolic structures propelled by desire and not lack.

This katabatic logic of the black metal musician can be connected to Negarestani's reading of the rite of *nekyia* in Odysseus's katabasis to the underworld which results in 'his openness to and by the dead'.[20] Orpheus' *katabasis* or descent into the subterranean realm can be paralleled to the similarly schizotrategy of the black metal musician whose 'becoming chthonic' entails a non-escapist flight into the chthonic earth and a radical openness, seeking to devour and be devoured. While Orpheus' logic and virtue shines in the underworld—it is the act of seeing or turning back to look at Euridice that brings her annihilation as well as annuls necrophilic contact with her body—the black metal musician on the other hand, is not subdued by solar tyranny, but opens him/herself to the abyss through defilement and necrophilic mess.[21] In this space life feasts on death, and the black metal persona is laid opened:

> In the darkest night of the soul,
> It begins the long descent to the kingdom of Hades,
> The doors of hell open, The kingdom of shades,
> My Ego's, Erebo.
> Here begins the slow agony,
> Divine in primordial chaos,
> to purify the seven metals,
> to reach the root of life,
> to be reborn in the womb of the matter
> As a pure regenerated spirit (Arcanum Inferi 'Obscura Nox ad Inferos').

The rite of *nekyia*, in the place where Sol Niger burns blackened landscapes of desolation and death, leaves the soul bare.[22] In order to be reborn, the black metal musician descends into the darkest night, where the sun of life and the darkness of death are mutually contaminated: Black Sun.

It is in this realm of the blackening sun that the poetic persona expresses death and melancholia. In his lyrical poem 'The Disinherited' (1859) Gerard de Nerval writes:

> I am saturnine—bereft—disconsolate,
> The Prince of Aquitaine whose tower has crumbled:
> My lonestar is dead—and my bespangled lute
> Bears the Black sun of Melancholia.[23]

Nerval inscribes in language the black sun of melancholia, and the sonnet becomes, according to Kristeva, an 'antidote to depression', his 'Noah's Ark'.[24] In *The Black Sun: Depression and Melancholia* (1989) Kristeva offers an analysis of Nerval's lyric poem through the development of Freudian notions of mourning and melancholia as well as a Kleinian prioritising of the maternal. For Kristeva, the subject in order to enter the symbolic needs to abject the mother: 'For man and for woman the loss of the mother is a biological and psychic necessity, the first step on the way to becoming autonomous. Matricide is our vital necessity'.[25] In order that the matricidal drive does not 'pulverize me into melancholia', 'the maternal object having been introjected, the depressive or melancholic putting to death is what follows, instead of matricide. In order to protect mother I kill myself while knowing – phantasmatic and protective knowledge – that it comes from her the death-bearing she-Gehenna...'[26] The inversion of the maternal object into an image of death is necessary in order to separate from her and become an autonomous being. For Kristeva, Nerval's language replays the loss of the archaic mother. Language stages the melancholic void, emptiness and loss by giving presence to the Thing, the abject mother. Kristeva finds in Nerval's poetic language traces of the archaic Thing:

> By means of a leap into the orphic world of artifice (of sublimation), the saturnine poet, out of the traumatic experience and object of mourning, remembers only a gloomy or passional tone. He thus comes close, through the very components of language, to the lost Thing. His discourse identifies with it, absorbs it, modifies it, transforms it: he takes Eurydice out of the melancholy hell and gives her back a new existence in his text/song.[27]

For Kristeva, however, the condition of melancholia is debilitating for the subject and the triumph over melancholia and the black sun must be achieved by the re-establishment and illumination of the symbolic order in terms of the poet's creation of a symbolic family in 'The Disinherited' and also of the creation of the sonnet itself, as a cultural artefact. The sonnet becomes a substitute for the lost thing while it transforms 'woeful darkness into a lyrical song that assimilates 'the sighs of the saint and the screams of the fay''.[28] This symbolic anthropophagy keeps, for Kristeva, the darkness at bay. On the other hand, it is exactly through this metaphoric descent into the abyss that language is transformed into an infernal element with creative results. The encounter with the black sun of melancholia and the identification of the poetic persona with Saturn who is associated with melancholy, winter, night, the myth of devouring his children and death are significant in the poem in terms of messing up with the luminous order of language. For the poetic voice confesses that: 'I've twice, yet alive, been across the Acheron,/ Modulating and singing on Orpheus' lyre/The sighs of the saint and the screams of the fay'.[29] It is not the fact that symbolic illumination has prevailed, but that the journey through Acheron, the river of pain in the Underworld, has transformed

Orphic melody into the blackened litany of the saturnine prince of the sonnet. Through symbolic language and contact with the unsymbolized, the underworld of the archaic mother, the she-Gehenna, an amalgam of abyssal illumination and symbolic fragmentation is produced.

If for Kristeva the black sun of melancholia is an expression of some lost unity with the archaic mother, then the black metal space opened by the black metal musician messes up any notion of a nostalgic return to the mother. Unlike her salvationist project, the black metal musician does not mourn for the lost Thing. If ecological decay and the death of the earth do not, according to Negarestani, 'demand an appropriate mourning',[30] then, the sorrow of the black metal musician is not associated with loss or nostalgia for a feminized, anthropomorphic earth, both notions expressing an essentialist position. Moving away from Kristeva and negative representations of melancholy, Deleuze's fold offers an affirmative architecture, where melancholy is not a loss of the object but an opening, new relationships to other relations, a renewal and productive beginning: 'a process of folding, unfolding and refolding' that liberates 'the subject from the melancholy of the unrepresentable'.[31] Images of life metamorphose into images of death, of melancholic contemplation amidst an open graveyard. The black metal musician's melancholy is associated with ecological death, and a mourning that is not lack but desire towards renewal through decay. For Mayhem 'birth is pain/All the stars in the north died/We move towards a new constellation ('Completion in Science of Agony', 2003). Similarly, Imago Mortis 'see a new sun, black and shining' and wait for 'the Phoenix [to] ... arise from the abyss' ('Black Arctic Sun'). 'Under the black sun', Alttari are 'celebrating the time of crushing tyranny/Time of purification and honor' where 'black towers will rise from the ashes of the earth/ After the destructive wave of plague and curses', a 'world without lies of deceitful messengers of light' (Alttari 'Black Angel

Wings').

While the melancholic consciousness of the black metal musician embraces a perishable universe which might open the way to a blackened horizon of possibilities, at the same time the contemplation of such blackened geography results in desperation and nothingness. In the song 'Demonic Crown of Anticreation' (2002) by the Russian black metal band Ithdabquth Qliphoth, the satanic voice conjures up Nachiel, the intelligence of the sun in order to tear his heart out and be transformed into the Blackest Sun. In this 'coming of nonexistence' and the 'end of space and time' 'oceans boil and soil is aflame/Raining storm of molten lead'. This is an 'unholy place' where 'No life shall ever touch/This scorched ground of sorrow'. There is nothing but a 'barren landscape, untamed and bleak' as Bathory describe in 'Nordland' (2002).

Negarestani refers to the openness to the cosmic abyss as the result of 'intimacy with the cold' and Sol niger is, as portrayed in Dante's ice world and Cocytus, the eternally frozen lake of the Underworld, extremely cold.[32] In the blacker than black phase of the nigredo, where matter decays, Sol niger shows its coldness and indifference. Darkthrone's universe is made of 'dark and cold wastelands' ('Sunrise over Locus Mortis'). For Mayhem 'everything here is cold/ everything here is so dark' ('Freezing Moon'). The 'dark cold emptiness' (Pest 'Dark Northern Winters') and extreme cold landscapes haunted by monstrous entities create an Arctic Gothic atmosphere. Terror arises from the arctic void itself, but also from what Edmund Burke has defined as the characteristics of the sublime: 'Vacuity, Darkness, Solitude, and Silence'.[33] The vast and limitless cold spaces, things of great dimensions when imbued with an 'adventitious idea of terror and populated with entities 'considered as objects of terror' can indeed convey a sense of terror and fear:[34] 'In the dead of the Satanic Winter/Lord Sathanas returns' (Pest 'Satanic Winter'), 'gleaming beyond the subterraneous black sun'

(Sanguinary Misanthropia, 'A Glimpse of the Image of Lucifer Gleaming beyond the Subterraneous Black Sun'). The cold earth gives birth to evil demons: when 'the Blackened sun has set' the 'Root of evil grows in the ground; 'Dark and cold as ice/The season of evil demoncy' (Ezurate 'Season of the Witch'). The Burkean sublime shares much with the darkness and terror of black metal's arctic gothic atmospheres and resonates with what Eugene Thacker calls 'the world-without-us'; a world neutral to humans which can be found 'in the very fissures, lapses, or lacunae in the World and the Earth', in 'a nebulous zone that is at once impersonal and horrific'.[35] In Nabaath's 'Eternal Silent Forest of Frost' the 'horizon is black as the blackest night' and 'Frozen trees stay eternally dead/The darkness rules the silent forest/cold demons of frost, of eternal sorrow.' In the 'frozen arctic kingdom' 'eyes of despair are lifted/Towards a sky dressed in black/A monument moulded of agony/Beholding itself bleeding the dark' (The Moaning 'Dying Internal Embers'). Darkness bleeds into the frozen kingdom, spreading despair and an uncontrollable menacing emptiness.

But as the darkness is growing, the cemetery lights up again (Mayhem 'Freezing Moon') to accept those souls that followed the freezing moon. Immortal have created such a frozen universe, the fictional kingdom of Blashyrkh where the mighty Ravendark reigns in eternal frost and winter. In Blashyrkh's 'deepest realms' ('At the Heart of Winter') and 'Unearthly Kingdom' the sun no longer rises (2010) and the realm consumes all light. Funeral Mist's song 'Sun of Hope' presents a world of 'Panic, hysteria, infernally raging chaos' where 'salvation [is possible] through destruction' and the 'Cold black sun of hope' will bring the death of all and purity.

Sol Niger can also be the burning heat of the cremation ground of Kali. In the *Descent to the Goddess: A Way of Initiation for Women* (1981), Sylvia Perera describes this domain as the land of the dead of the Sumerian goddess Ereshkigal where there exists

> an energy we begin to know through the study of black holes and the disintegration of elements, as well as through the process of fermentation, cancer, decay and lower brain activities that regulate peristalsis, menstruation, pregnancy, and other forms of bodily life... Ereshkigal is like Kali, who through time and suffering... 'pitilessly grinds down... all distinctions ... in her undiscriminating fires' ... She symbolizes the abyss that is the source and, the end, the ground of all being.[36]

Kali, who represents the process of dying and is the 'terrible Mother of the cremation ground',[37] is worshipped by the Tantrics who believed that, '[s]itting next to corpses and other images of death, one is able to transcend the 'pair of opposites' (i.e., good-bad, love-hate, etc.)' The terrible images 'arouse instant renunciation in the mind and help the Tantric to get rid of attachment to the body'.[38] Death and transformation through decaying matter is evident in such images of Kali where she copulates with Siva over a dead burning body. Dissection's single 'Maha Kali' investigates this idea of contact with Kali's fire of darkness and decay as a rebirth experience. The satanic voice conjures up 'Maha Kali', the 'dark mother' to dance and awaken him with her pure nakedness. He exclaims that, 'Yours are the fires of deliverance which shall bring me bliss' and that her 'black tongue of fire' will embrace him and awaken him in order to transcend the limits of the flesh and become a body without organs: 'I burn myself for thee/ I cut my own throat in obscene ecstasy/ I make love to abominations, embrace pain and misery/Until my heart becomes the burning ground'. The black metal musician opens himself to the darkness and the abyss, a descent into the black sun of melancholia and Kali's realm in order to set his rage against a world he desires to cremate and set his essence free.

The descent into the abyss, likened to the alchemical stage of the nigredo and putrefaction,[39] is nothing but a place of decay:

'stench, disintegration, repulsion and depression...Things must rot thoroughly like garbage, before they can be reduced to...rubble...It seems as though the feelings of emptiness and isolation will last forever...It is a bottomless pit'.[40] For Abgott, the 'Season of darkness' unveils a 'Rotten land /Infested in decay', a 'season of the end' ('Synapses'). However, in this void and emptiness that recalls Odysseus and Aeneas's journeys to the underworld, the descent is a transformative process, an opening:

> The dynamic vector for being opened might be katabatic, but its medium is surely communication with the dead or the rite of Nekyia. Odysseus' ascension to the outer surface is not a return to the economical openness of his superficial journeys but the continuation of his descent, for every ascent is the sublimation of descent. To ascend and descend are both alike acts of opening.[41]

For Jungian analyst David Rosen 'egocide' or symbolic death is the result of such a descent into the abyss. For him the soul in depression enters a void and through suffering or a 'death-rebirth experience' the psyche is born again. In the alchemical process this is likened to the mortificatio process or putrefaction which leads to nothingness. This process, a 'journey into the dark night of the soul',[42] results in mourning for the lost ego. But this kind of egocide is a transformative experience, a metaphoric entrance into Hades and death and a renewal of the self; an opening to new possibilities and creativity. Without entrance into the nigredo and without the mortificatio there is no transformation.[43] For Satan's Host the world's collapse and 'destruction [equals] re-creation' ('End All, Be All 2012') a new aeon of darkness and epiphany.

Pseudo-Dionysius the Areopagite defines Divine darkness as a luminous darkness, 'the unapproachable light', the place where God is.[44] Divine darkness is similar to descending into the realm of Sol Niger, or Hades and is made manifest only to those who travel through foul and fair, who pass beyond the summit of every holy as- cent, who leave behind them every divine light, every voice, every word from heaven, and who plunge into the darkness where ... there dwells the One who is beyond all things'.[45]

In Jungian terms this is the darkness of the Self, the no-Self which can be seen as the Sol Niger both dark and luminescent, present and absent, a 'Divine darkness beyond affirmation and negation'.[46] In Pseudo-Dionysius' negative theology, Divine darkness is equal to mystical ecstasy, where there is nothing more to say, beyond good or evil, a poetic, fiery, mad illumination of darkness.

But this emptiness that is also fullness, the light in the darkness, leads to a blackening joy, the joy of the underworld; the *jouissance* of the blackening abyss. In the dark of night, in nothingness there is light. This is also linked to Pseudo-Aristotle's notion of melancholia 'that reveals the true nature of Being' and is associated with intellectual genius and creativity.[47] The idealization of melancholy, a convergence of the Neoplatonic idea of Saturn as the highest of all the planets and pseudo-Aristotelian beliefs in the creative temperament of melancholic men,[48] finds expression in the role of the black metal musician whose melancholy becomes a creative energy rendered through litanies of a blackened universe. Darkthrone's song 'Blasphemer' expresses this well: 'Forlorn I was as poets should be/ I am as chosen as the weaver himself'. 'From darkness we create light' ('A Grand Declaration of War'), Mayhem announce, and for Darkthrone 'Sunrise over Locus Mortis' (2008) is but the rise of the dark side. It is in such a Qliphothic, infernal universe where the black sun is the devouring essence of the Qliphoth, the fearful light, that black metal musicians such as Immanifest, enter into in search for gnosis and illumination. In the 'realms of eternal night' (*Immanifest*, 'Revelations in Darkness') Mayhem greet those 'who still have eyes to observe and see/ And who still have courage to break through into the dying light' ('View from Nihil, Part I of II). Darkthrone in 'The Watchtower' (2008) refer to darkness and the rotten earth which opens itself to the black metal musician who is himself open to such possibility: 'Nocturnal flight, no shadows cast/ a distant symbol of our beyond/ life lies in front of us/ Sacred Ground, rotten earth/ashes to dust/flesh decomposed/ Caressing the sacred ground/where the deadened corpses lie/ A sepulchural misty night/ with a whiff of the Macabre/.../ Our minds united; a force is lit, and insight creates/A humanoid watchtower, reaching for their souls to the Sky,/ For a glance onto /The other Side....' In 'Cromlech' Darkthrone plunge into the abyss where 'Dark is the reich of the dead' in order to 'flee over the River Styx/ and join the dead with joy/ An ocean of Blasphemy/ Heathenish realm/and 'Do What Thou Wilt' as decoy/My Prophecy is true... /We'll All Make It Through'. In Dark Funeral's journey to the underworld, the black sorcerer asks from the Lord of darkness the dark flame of the abyss, the keys of mystical knowledge ('The Secrets of the Black Arts'). In the underworld, where Satan's Host call upon Satan, the 'dark aeon of Set' has come and 'the black sun [is] burning' illuminating with wisdom, 'a witching-chaos purified/ divine~kliffothic' ('Throne of Baphomet'). The black metal musician constructs perverse strategies to navigate into darkness and nothingness, embracing death and the realm of the black sun in his complicity with the dark forces of decay and death, in order, as Abgott remind us, to 'shine in a new divine light ... darkness' ('Disharmonic Requiem').

Notes

1. David Michael Levin, 'Introduction.' *Modernity and the Hegemony of Vision*. Ed. David Michael Levin. Berkeley and Los Angeles, California: University of California Press, 1993, 7.

2. Jacques Derrida, *Writing and Difference*. London: Routledge, 2001, 109.
3. Cathryn Vasseleu, *Textures of Light: Vision and Touch in Irigaray, Levinas and Merleau-Ponty*. London: Routledge, 1998, 7.
4. Ibid., 10.
5. Georges Bataille, 'The Solar Anus.' *Visions of Excess: Selected Writings, 1927-1939*. Ed. Allan Stoekl. Minneapolis, MN: University of Minnesota Press, 1985. 5-9, 9.
6. Georges Bataille, 'The Rotten Sun.' *Visions of Excess: Selected Writings, 1927-1939*. Ed. Allan Stoekl. Minneapolis, MN: University of Minnesota Press, 1985. 57-8.
7. Martin Jay, *Downcast Eyes: The Denigration of Vision in Twentieth-Century French Thought.* Berkeley and Los Angeles, California: University of California Press, 1994, 255.
8. Nick Land, *The Thirst for Annihilation: Georges Bataille and Virulent Nihilism*. London: Routledge, 1992, 20.
9. Reza Negarestani, 'Solar Inferno and the Earthbound Abyss.' *Our Sun*. (Pamela RosenKranz). Milan: Venice Branch & Mousse Publishing, 2010. 3-8, 7.
10. Ibid., 3.
11. Negarestani, Reza. *Cyclonopedia: Complicity with Anonymous Materials*. Melbourne: re.press, 2008, 175, 158.
12. Ibid., 175.
13. Ibid.
14. Ibid. 176.
15. Negarestani, 'Solar Inferno', 7.
16. Negarestani, *Cyclonopedia*, 147.
17. Stanton Marlan *The Black Sun: The Alchemy and Art of Darkness.* College Station, Texas: Texas A&M University Press, 2005, 10
18. Ibid., 17.
19. Ibid., 23.

20. Negarestani, *Cyclonopedia*, 207.
21. Ibid., 204-5.
22. This echoes Emil Cioran's musings *On the Heights of Despair*, of death's immanence in life and life's 'beastly Satanism' where 'forms are given birth only to be destroyed'. For him there is no salvation in life or death, and the only solution is the destruction of the world (qtd. in Marlan, 62).
23. Nerval quoted in Julia Kristeva *The Black Sun: Depression and Melancholia*. Trans. Leon S. Roudiez. New York: Columbia University Press, 1989, 141.
24. Kristeva, *Black Sun*, 170, 144.
25. Ibid, 27.
26. Ibid., 28.
27. Ibid., 160.
28. Ibid., 162.
29. Ibid., 140.
30. Negarestani, 'Solar Inferno', 7.
31. Gilles Deleuze. *The Fold: Leibniz and the Baroque*. London: Athlone Press, 1993, 59-60.
32. Negarestani, *Cyclonopedia*, 207; Marlan, 59-60.
33. Edmund Burke, *A Philosophical Enquiry into the Origin of Our Ideas of the Sublime and Beautiful*. 2nd ed. London: R. and J. Dodsley, 1859. *Google Book Search*. Accessed 1 Jan. 2012, 125.
34. Ibid., 97.
35. Eugene Thacker, *In the Dust of this Planet*. Winchester: Zero Books, 2011, 8, 6.
36. Sylvia Brinton Perera, *Descent to the Goddess: A Way of Initiation for Women*. Toronto: Inner City Books, 1981, 24-5..
37. Elizabeth U. Harding, *Kali: The Black Goddess of Dakshineswar*. York Beach, Maine: Nicolas-Hays, 1993, 38.
38. Ibid.
39. Marlan, 66.
40. Bosnak, quoted in Marlan, 66-7.
41. Negarestani, *Cyclonopedia*, 207.

42. Marlan, 73.
43. Ibid., 79.
44. Ibid., 176.
45. Dionysius quoted in Marlan, 176.
46. Marlan, 177.
47. Kristeva, 8.
48. Radden, 14.

Blackening the Green

Niall Scott

Nature throws us into darkness. The blackening of the green is a foretelling, part of a melancological claim of an oncoming darkness, an oblivion. It is a double blinding through the absorption of all light and the reduction of the myopic perspective of the observer to its becoming sightless. It is an invitation extended to us by black metal's Wolves in the Throne Room: to head for the darkest place we know, into the woods beyond the briar thickets to a place even beyond the relative comfort of darkness. The blackening of the green is not a *weltanschaung*; it is indeed opposed to perspective, to observer, to the position of watcher. The blackening of the green is not whitewash; if it was then it would merely be an attempt to mask or obscure. Blackening the green is not opposed to progressive change in the sense of negating it, rather it is something emerging but inactive. Jonathan Selzer's phrase to which this piece is indebted echoes the woodland truths of Negura Bunget and Wolves in the Throne Room, that an awareness of nature is an awareness of vacuity. This awareness turns on itself to become a vacuous awareness. Negru of Romania's Negura Bunget has presented their and black metal's working with nature as ideas that are rooted in a spiritual and metaphysical concept that goes beyond the music and shapes the music.[1] The extension of black metal sound into the green outlines of the forest that give way to shadows and then black returns without coming back, as a silence and a green blackened. The key to this work is that it is not done without blackness.

The green that is to be blackened

The green that is to be blackened refers to lush nature and the ideologies that posit a moral and political community aiming to rescue humanity's relationship with the environment, but more importantly to rescue that environment from humanity's effect on it. Such positions are described metaphorically as existing along a colour spectrum from light to dark green; shallow or deep ecology, indicating theoretical differences.[2] This green is not limited to the environmentalists and green activist perspective, its roots burrow deep into evolutionary thought concerning purpose and the organisational nature of the biotic world. In a sense borrowing evolutionary language, the green movement generally speaking is a movement about adaptation to change in order to slow down or halt the environmental crisis that is argued to threaten humanity and the biosphere's degradation from a human point of view. The green movement broadly speaking commits itself to this colour, representing vitality, life and flourishing and a caring commitment to life on the planet, promoting a drive to a benign relationship with the environment. But as the deep ecology movement considers man to 'be a danger to the whole of nature' and a danger to mankind,[3] it appears to be heading in the direction of blackening. In denying special moral consideration to human beings deep ecology argues for a non-anthropomorpic and anti-anthropocentric position.[4] A route to achieving this insight, some deep ecologists hold, is through a self-realisation that one becomes aware of metaphysical holism and connectedness with nature that does not recognise an ontological divide between a human and non-human world.[5] This identification is predicated on a sense of unity with the biotic community, a belief about an at-one-ness and interrelatedness with the biosphere, promoting a vitality expressed as a consciousness rather than an ethical stance.[6] It is hard to see though how a process of self-realisation leads to an anti-anthropocentrism, whereas a blackening of the green in the removal of the observer can do exactly this. Much of the discourse and argument surrounding nature is abstract, conceptual, even the natural environment to which green ecological positions refer is abstract, rather than particular. The use of nature and environment refers above all to no place in particular with the hope of transcending place and time.[7] Tim Ingold has drawn attention to a point of view that treats the environment as a thing distinct and separate from people: a world divorced from life that is yet complete in itself and human life.[8] The blackening of the green proposed in this melancological meditation points to a more harrowing solution. A solution that does not advocate a change in the way of life, nor a biocentrism or ecocentrism or even an attempt to judge actions from a point of view on or of nature. Instead it seizes the opportunity to herald the obliteration of the point of view. Blackening requires that one is blinded by light, but also that light burns earth to blackness so that it can no longer reflect light, so that light is consumed and vision is impossible. Blackening thus generates a double blindness. Melancology in this blackening expresses a loss of sight and of vision, a destruction of all colour, grey then fading to black, so that even the remaining pathological monochrome that Maurice Merleau-Ponty describes, is banished. Those allied to the green then are drawn to contemplate not the verdant, illuminated, visual fringes of the forest, but are challenged to be drawn deep into darkness and further. Black metal addresses this darkness, but going beyond the African song cited by anthropologist C.M. Turnbull: 'There is darkness all around us; but if darkness is and the darkness is of the forest, then the darkness must be good'.[9] It goes beyond this because darkness still allows a relational position to light and thus is never pure blackening. Melancology and the blackening of the green treads into the blackness of the forest to the point where there is no forest; 'the eternal forest ... where all things seem to have deceased' (Absurd, 'Deep Dark Forest', 1996). The vehicles for blackening, black metal and black metal theory, take on the role of the ferryman, both blind and deaf in leading humanity in to the abyss.

The blackening of the green is a dawning, a realisation of this that has begun with a shadow cast over the eyes of the overconfident observer. The shadow moving over the gaze of the melancholic moment in ecology is a slow movement, but one that foretells of an ultimate all-encompassing darkness. It is an ecology that looks forward to the oblivion of the observer, yet without looking forward. At its heart is a dark impenetrable depth not open to reflection, like that which Merleau-Ponty characterises as an 'instability of levels producing not only the intellectual experience of disorder, but the vital experience of giddiness and nausea, which is the awareness of our contingency, and the horror with which it fills us'.[10] This blackening has then the characteristics of Merleau Ponty's treatment of space. Even deep ecology's hope for a value without a perspective is oxymoronic; the positioning intrinsic worth of a system is arguably still bound by a point of view. The deep ecologist maintaining the possibility of adhering to a non-instrumental value of nature argues against mere utility, but retains the gaze of judgement of value. It is worthy that deep ecology attempts to push a case against anthropocentrism, but at the same time the theory calls for a human self-realisation as a route to the awareness of value inherent in nature. Blackening the green does not, instead it calls for an eternal end: 'Blackened in the end / throws all you see into obscurity / death of mother earth / never a rebirth / evolutions end / never will it mend' (Metallica, 1988). The blinding in this blackening is also encountered in Abgott's 'Blizzard': 'I can see what you see not / vision milky eyes then rot / when you turn they will be gone / then you see what cannot be / shadows move where light should be' (Abgott, 2000). It follows that this leads to an 'out of darkness out of mind' in the prospect of the observerless world that is no longer a world.

The Putrefaction of Ideas

The pathway now being trodden in this grey climate celebrates the dual processes of fermentation and putrefaction as an introduction to blackening; the decomposition of plant matter and the process of the decomposition of flesh are entropic aids to blackening the green: the decomposition of ideas about nature; a *putrefactio philosophorum*. Putrefaction has a stench of inactivity about it – the presence of pathogenic clostridia in the soil has little or no invasive power.[11] Putrefaction is brought about from that which is simply already present, the ingredients for rot are already here producing exotoxin proteins, such as botulism and are pure intoxication. According to the sayings of Arnold de Villanova in the alchemical *Rosarium Philosophorum*, Aristotle the king and philosopher holds: 'I never saw any thing that has life to grow and increase without putrefaction and vain would the work of alchemy be unless it were putrefied'.[12] So ecology and environmentalism must also be putrefied so that following Bacchus 'when natures are corrupted and putrefied they engender'.[13] This alchemical expression of the value of decomposition continues, supporting putrefaction as potential:

> The philosophical putrefaction is nothing else but a corruption and destruction of bodies. For one form being destroyed, nature presently brings into it another form, more better and subtle. Putrefaction is the same thing that fraction of filthiness is. For by putrefaction every thing is digested, and fraction is made between that which is filthy, that which stinks, and that which is pure and clean. For a pure and clean body being putrefied doth immediately grow and increase, as is manifest in a grain of corn, which after it has stood many days under the heat of the earth, then it beginneth to swell, and that which is pure grows out of it and multiplies, but that which is filthy and naught, vanishes away. Therefore putrefaction is also necessary in our work, by reason of the

aforesaid causes.[14]

Tudianus's description of putrefaction is held to be philosophical putrefaction and yet is also the corruption and destruction of bodies. This putrefaction occurs almost simultaneously with conception where putrefaction was treated as a separation of parts – on the one hand that which is filthy, wretched and stinking, on the other hand that which is pure – one thing being destroyed, and the pure remaining. The alchemist's belief that putrefaction led to the spontaneous creation of new matter is now of course treated as rather amusing, but its metaphorical significance remains. Couples conjoined in conception are in their simultaneous putrefaction both made black in alchemy and the colour black too is putrefied. It would be mistaken to see this blackening as something in opposition to verdant growth of the green *oikos*, so not as an evil in opposition to a good, where evil is characterised by chaos, dissonance and dissociation, good by harmony, flourishing and order. It must be remembered that blackening of the soul for the alchemist as well as the biological putrefaction and decomposition is required for transformation. However there needs to be a commitment to a complete blackening with no hope for transformation before blackening as potential can be contemplated. The error is made to try and insert hope into the blackening process prior to its running its destructive course, and seek refuge in such hope. Osiris, god of resurrection is depicted in both black and green, yet in this ambiguity, green is favoured, sending the herds of ecologists and environmentalists chasing in the wrong direction. Thus we see forms of pseudo blackening, a clinging on to the edge of the abyss rather than an authentic committal to its depths. Accounts of decomposition focus on the life emerging from the black, the emergence of maggots, carrion food, mould and fertile nutrients for the next vital surge. By way of rot and decay detritus fills the floor, but also it should be known that the earth is sufficient for blackness to be brought about. The total blackening with no vitality to follow seems to be uncontemplatable, yet this melancological blackening of the green requires precisely this. Depth Psychology too attempts to head for the transformative potential of decomposition. Blackening the green is not limited to the alchemical glass chamber, the blackened crow's head or the psyche, but considers a blackening of the entire unity of being, ideas and object. These writings provide for a black confession with no hope or thought of redemption or absolution.[15]

False and Pseudo-Blackening

There are many types of pseudo-blackening. Pseudo-blackening is like the blackening that provides a chemical coating for ferrous metals, through an oxidation process, to aid in the prevention of corrosion. Commonly applied to bolts, chemical blackening gives protection to the metals that maintain structures, even giving structure to unarranged objects. By extension then metal is protected from corrosion. But where the structures are flawed and the metal in a state of fatigue, this is nothing but a whitewash, a postponing of decay. True blackening is thorough and deep; all pervasive and total rather than superficial. If, where it is used as a coating to aid light rejection, it is still nothing other than a coating with the function of protecting that which is beneath. The biblical revelation of John understands this: the pouring out of the seven bowls of wrath in the *Book of Revelation* block out life entirely. Blackening the green heralds an essence of black purity in which a watcher's position will not last for long: 'A watcher of your pallid and fading grace/for I can see a dawn / swept in darkest haze' (Watain, 'Rabid Death's Curse' 2001/2008).

Black metal brings on a blackening of the green through encouraging a sonic shadow. The sound that introduces the silence is either mistaken or revelatory. If it is revelatory it is a sound that dethrones tranquillity. It is part of the shadow that blackens the green, desecrating life in tandem with light desiccating soil in favour of a lifeless erosion, turning all to dust. There is no halting this, not even a chemical oxidation blackening of metal. In as much as DH Lawrence's (1960) machinery in service of the bitch goddess brings forth black from the earth, the machinery will inevitably rust, so life will rot and become grainy. That which is brought up as blackening in its terminal force cannot be conceived of: 'We see and know also some things that we know not of what nature cometh forth, although we know it sufficeth us, but cannot give any reason for it, because they are dark and profound and perhaps hidden underneath the earth' (Villanova). The remnant shapes from humanity's exploitations are anthropomorphised as scars. There are no scars in nature; that is just a foolish way of thinking, wishful thinking, as if wanting somehow that which is out there is in some way like us; the anthropocentric joke. A criticism may be levelled that the sound of black metal is not one that ushers in the blackening or the silence, but rather that it represents merely a thrashing about in darkness in an aimless waste of energy, much like the environmentalisms that achieve little in the oncoming blackening. This error highlights the enthusiastic sometimes unconscious human attempts to bring about a blackening, but is an aimless, fake blackening like that of urbanisation. Much like the pseudo blackening analogy of chemical coating is the misplaced belief that blackening out the green is the expansion of concrete urban shadows that slab over verdant village greens and cricket creases that birth out an architecture that is ripe for decay. The environmentalists' optimism in nature being able to overcome betonisation permits cracks to open to abyssal holes; a true blackening though would only treat these temporary monolithic buildings like icebergs floating on an erupting loam, ordering 'superficial worms to die' (Abgott , 2003). These are cities that are born to crumble, one Detroit after another casting shadows over grass, crude oiling lubrications for death to slide in and suffocate the living of an entirely human making. The attempts at a blackening of this kind has been encountered before, but guided by human agency and such mistaken projects fail precisely because they are bound, limited by human agency and are eventually corrected by a politics or a higher morality. Thus the futurist goal for generational purge in the sonorous call for displacement of the old, abolition of nostalgia, declaring death to archaeology in Italy was such an attempt at blackening. Marinetti's promotion of the young, the celebration of the forward lush expansion of industrialisation and technology should have eventually lead to rust and decay, either at the hands of an alternative human agency in moral politics, or the more powerful creep of techno-erosion. The result instead has been no decay, rather an expansion of technology and the celebration of speed, productivity and waste. A blackening on the other hand has as its consistent throng being that not of overcoming, growth, animism and vitality but of rot. Nothing but 'dead will rise from rotten earth to you' (Abgott, 'Lanrutcon Nyarlathotep', 2003).

At the heart of the environmentalist's case is the realisation (in biological discourse) of humanity's lack of adaptive fit to its environment. Deep ecology answers this with arguments to locate value intrinsic in nature, to develop a biotic egalitarianism independent of human perspective, and action based on self realisation of unity and equal value of things in nature. Although this is not without criticism the very possibility of biotic egalitarianism gives voice to the concept of life, of vitality in the *oikos*, which a blackening sees fit to remove. Now we see delayed reactionary solutions to this realisation that deep ecology tries to address, typifying it as the great environmental crisis. We behold movements that on the one hand promote degrees of regression, to ecological awareness, to primitivism or on the other hand to the frantic appropriation of technology's capacity of the creation of hospitable environmental conditions permitting the future of humanity. Yet the latter contains within it an air of nostalgia for the hospitable. Identifying crisis and attempting to address it has often been the way; Max Horkheimer's identification of science in crisis where science does well to aid production and the promotion of industry, but fails in its responsibility to deal with the problems of social processes, holding that a deadening and disorganising factor had entered science.[16] Blackening opens the possibility of moving beyond the boring monotony of the crisis, the crisis of science, the crisis of the economy, the crisis of culture, the crisis of the environment. Crisis has an affinity with the leper; instead of allowing the leper to be healed, the leper is perpetually re-infected. Horkheimer's identification of crisis is not in science itself, rather it is in the social conditions which hinder its development. Science's capacity to cope and to respond positively to the demands of the environmentalist movement and bring a halt to the 'social causes of the stunting and destruction of human life' would also need to address ideological disorder within the green movements which cynically can be seen as self-referential theoretical arguments with not enough application.[17] Even the possibility that science with the right ideology can bring about change in response to the green crisis is an optimism of adaptation-immediacy. Carolyn Merchant's *The Death of Nature* (1990) lays the blame for the crisis at the foot of an enlightenment history of masculine dominated science that models nature as a mechanism.[18] Blackening the green goes further than Merchant's ecotheology and is a defamation of science in the sense that not only the mastery over the object is removed, but also the possibility of any perspective on the object. The optimism of human overcoming is built on the mistaken belief that the best adapted, the fittest survives, a thought that hangs in the optimist discourse of change and potential. Yet this has been already discredited in biology as a product of perniciously circular thinking founded on the conflation between description and explanation: 'In the study of evolution, the concept of fitness, which once referred to a property of appropriateness to the environment, became identified with a concept of natural selection, the hypothetical mechanism by which appropriateness to the environment is to be explained'.[19] An optimism is expressed that humanity will adapt to fit and at the same time biology tells us that the processes grounding the environmental mechanism are purposeless.

Blackening Purpose

Blackening embraces the purposelessness thoroughly: there is no purpose, no goal nor end in nature; there is not even negation, there is nothing, only a final *endstille*. The obliteration of the observer leads to the removal of purpose, with no mind present to intend. In the green perspective, adherence to an organisational quality in nature of a kind that is inclusive of humanity yet independent from it requires blackening. The arguments supporting what this organisational quality is like go deep into evolutionary biology. Thus there is arguably a language that links the scientific goal of objectivity in the evolutionary process to the independence of nature from humanity's perspective. Yet here too in the biological sciences we have seen a pseudo blackening – a shift from multiple colours to monochrome grey, to darkness in the form of the move from teleology (function that is purposeful goal directed orientation) to teleonomy (purposeless function) to an autopoetic unity.[20]

Teleonomy is the evolutionary progression of teleology; the latter requiring mind, the former one where mind is apparently absent. Teleonomy concerns the study of goal directed processes without need for teleological explanation one can have function without purpose and adaptation. Yet teleonomy comes across as a biological fudge, a way of paying lip service to purposiveness without purpose, a clinging on to the observer's stance on the natural system. Jaques Monod recognised this as an epistemological contradiction, to be resolved where the (observer's) claim to scientific objectivity binds one to recognise the teleonomic character of organisms, to admit that in their structure and performance they act projectiveley – 'realise and pursue a purpose'.[21] Monod's solution was to secure teleonomy as a secondary property of invariance arguing the underlying purposelesness at the molecular level giving rise to evolutionary change. He sought to divide the spheres of interest of teleonomic systems into those that are vitalist (implying a difference between the living and the inanimate) and animist culminating in mankind as a product of evolution. However not only has it been argued that these terms are misappropriated, suggestions have been made that this thinking is still saturated with purpose and mindful intention and can be more aggressively dispensed with through a blackening. Understanding the organisation and mechanism of living systems arguably do not require the application of teleonomic discourse. Such discourse holds that a developmental project internal to the system or organism is present allowing it to function in relation to its environment. 'Purpose or aims ... are not features of the organisation of any machine (allo- or autopoetic); these notions belong to the domain of our discourse about our actions, that is they belong to the domain of descriptions, and when applied to a machine, or any system independent from us, they reflect our considering the machine or system in some encompassing context'.[22] These articulations concern arguments about theoretical, conceptual and definitional frameworks to try to understand the nature of living things and their contexts and what is involved in an organism's adaptation to an environment as well as the nature of that environment to be fit for sustaining life. Attempts to dispense with teleonomy are replaced with unity and autopoesis; and a slow progression is at work. Autopoeisis rejects Monod's vitality and animism and instead looks at living systems as unitary. Important to this autopoetic understanding of living systems as a unity is the observer in the role of describer of said system where the observer too is a living system. The observer as living system like any other living system has circularity in its organisation and is a self-referring system. The maintenance of the organisation of the human as a self-referring system includes its interactions with its environment, and continued change in response to it are part of a capacity to predict and infer, maintaining a circularity in interactions expressed as a niche. This for humans is not just a function of mere mechanism but a cognitive function, and Maturana holds that the observed cannot be part of the environment that is the exclusive domain of the observer. The contemplation of the blackening of the green is a move on from this autopoetic suggestion; that is, it announces a journey to an obliteration of the observer which is outside the cognitive domain of the very thing that is the living system that thinks it. This is the black domain of the forest, of the abyss. In as much as humans have thought up accounts of their own origins, blackening the green can be the contemplation of humanity's end, removing also the entirety of the biosphere from a cognitive domain. Marturana's position on the observer as a living system is openly optimistic in that he considers 'the possibility of enlargement of the cognitive domain' to be 'unlimited; it is a historical process. Our brain, the brain of the observer, has specialised during evolution as an instrument for the discrimination of relations'.[23] This progression of thought from teleology to autopoesis returns to hope, reanimates the observer. Where biological discourse was heading towards the looming failure of perspective in purposelessness, it has fallen foul of arrogant optimism. The contemplation of humanity's end would fall outside the cognitive domain of the human as a living system, but blackening the green allows for a melancological account of the end of the human as a living system. Then for consistency's sake, a blackening is demanded, rather than a final explanation, a call for a shadow leading to the blinding of the observer.

What remains is nothing.

Blackening the green is the poetry of entropy, the law of insipid inevitability. Once committed to this, 'every colour will appear after blackness, and where thou see thy matter wax to black, then rejoice because it is the beginning of the work'.[24] What is difficult to comprehend is that once the green has been blackened, there is no longer any function in ecology; the melancological realisation that where there was function without purpose, this blackening and the removal of the eyes of the witness lead to the loss of function, cognition and perspective. What remains is nothing.

Accepting the blackening of the green is an accepting of the oncoming silence: from colour to monochrome, grey to black. From teleology to teleonomy to autopoesis to nothingness, from melody to the monotone to the *Endstille*: 'he therefore that maketh the earth black shall come to his purpose and it shall go well with him'.[25] This ought to be the final movement to every melancological black metal offering. Against ecotopia, blackening the green proposes a metanoic turn to the abyss, an abystopia.

Notes

1. Jonathan Selzer, 'Seasons in the Mist', *Metal Hammer* May, issue 204 (2010), 126.
2. A. Dobson & P Lucardie, *The Politics of Green Thought*. London: Routledge, 1993.
3. Ibid.
4. Richard A. Watson, 'A Critique of Anti-anthropocentric Biocentrism', *Environmental Ethics* 5 (3) (1983), 245-256.
5. Warwick Fox, 'Deep ecology a new philosophy of our time?' *The Ecologist* 14 . 5,6 (1984), 194-200, 196.
6. M.M. Gunter, 'Deep Ecology' in *Encyclopedia of Environmental Ethics and Philosophy* ed. Baird Callicot Robert Frodeman. NewYork: Macmillan, 2009, 209.
7. J.G. Carrier, *Confronting Environments : Local Understanding in a Globalised World*, California: Alta Mira press, 2004, 5.
8. Tim Ingold, 1993, 35
9. C. M. Turnbull, (1962) 'The Forest People' in: McLuhan T.C.

The Way of the Earth: Encounters with Nature in Ancient and Contemporary Thought, Simon and Schuster: New York, (1994), 92-93.

10. Maurice Merleau Ponty, *The Phenomenology of Perception.* London : Routledge, 1962, 254.
11. R. Stanier, J.L. Ingraham, M.L. Wheelis and P.R. Painter. *General Microbiology* (5th ed.) Macmillan Education Basingstoke, 1986, 487.
12. Arnold da Villanova, (no date, prob 13th century) *Rosarium Philosophorum* http://www.rexresearch.com/rosarium/rosarium.htm
13. Ibid.
14. Ibid.
15. See Niall Scott, 'Sin-Eaters etc.' in Nicola Masciandaro (ed) *Hideous Gnosis.* Create Space, 2011.
16. Max Horkheimer, 'Notes on Science and the Crisis', *Critical Theory and Society, a Reader* S. Bronner, and M.C. Kellner, London: Routledge, 1989, 54.
17. Ibid., 56.
18. Carolyn Merchant, *The Death of Nature.* New York: Harper Collins, 1990.
19. N. S. Thompson 'The Misappropriation of Teleonomy' in: P. G. Bateson & P H. Klopfer (Eds.). *Perspectives in Ethology.* Vol. 6. New York: Plenum Publishing Corporation, 2000, 260.
20. See H. R. Maturana and J.V. Varela *Autopoesis and Cognition: The Realisation of the Living* Kluwer science, Dordrecht Netherlands, 1980.
21. J. Monod *Chance and Necessity,* London: Penguin, 1997, 21-2.
22. Maturana and Varela, *Autopoesis.*
23. Ibid., 38.
24. Villanova, *Rosarium Philosophorum.* http://www.rexresearch.com/rosarium/rosarium.htm
25. Hermes in ibid.

WormSign

Nicola Masciandaro

A writhing mass of words, spoken by many and none. A sermon in the sign of the worm.[1] Bless the coming and going of Him. May His passage cleanse the world.[2] My text is the first two minutes of Mgła's *Presence,* played over the space-folding sequence from David Lynch's *Dune.* Mystical advice for the voyage: You cannot do better than to place yourself in darkness and unknowing ... No need to call to Him from afar: He can hardly wait for you to open up: the opening and the entering are a single act.[3]

Dune, dir. David Lynch. Universal Pictures, 1984.

Worms, hungering for all the dimensions
Eat through my heart and form within my dreams
Spawn of Leviathan flows through my veins

To gracefully poison thoughts of men.[4]

The worm stands, for not standing, for anything.[5] The way of the worm stands in its hunger. Avoid at once the error of reducing the worm *to* its hunger, as if it were merely a hungering thing.[6]

Dune, dir. David Lynch (Universal Pictures, 1984)

Despite the interesting ontology that would entail—interesting because it might grow your status as philosopher-priest of the worm, as the other-than-worm that survives by occluding worms itself with names—understand that worm is prior to its hunger: *worms*, comma, *hungering* ... Not prior in the negative direction of being the subject of hunger, as if the worm would say *I hunger therefore I am*. Prior in the positive direction of being the agent of hunger itself, pure and infinite hunger. Absolute prepositionality. The *for* that tastes and moves in the absence of all the dimensions, that alone knows how to hunger for them. Note that Mgła does not say *all dimensions*, as if the number of dimensions were indeterminate, as if this were a nameless hunger for some unseen totality of dimensions, as if worm-hunger were a form of faith.[7] Mgła sings *all the dimensions,* indicating the volitional vermicular writhing as a form of dimensional knowledge, a feeling of the t( )tality, the ( )hole. There is no turning back, but only a pressing forward ... It never rests till it is filled with all being. Just as matter never rests till it is filled with every possible form, so too intellect never rests till it is filled to its capacity.[8] As worms is exactly what emerges in a body's *after,* so worms is precisely the corpo*realization* of hunger as body's *before*.[9] He can hardly wait for you to open up. Worm is sign of the hunger that takes flesh, the desire that instantly makes it as instrument. It is the self-movement of the essential *seizure* of embodiment, the spontaneous body of primordial needing.

Wormlust, *Wormlust* (Volkgeist, 2006)

Remember what happened, your happening—the slimy purity of self-originating appearance. It will be an inevitable memory of what never occurred, an impossible memory of something that still must. In the absence of body, soul could not have gone forth, since there is no other place to which its nature would allow it to descend. Since go forth it must, it will generate a place for itself; at once body, also, exists.[10] Must the sleeper awaken? Will something be born from this restless slumber? The question affirms its answer. The terrible fact of worm says *yes*. We now know the location of this narrow passage through which thought is able to exit from itself—it is through facticity, and through facticity alone.[11] Specimens longer than 400 meters have been seen in the deep desert.[12] Don't you see, *che noi siam vermi / nati a formar l'angelica farfalla*?[13] That we are worms? Like Augustine: *Omnes homines de carne nascentes, quid sunt nisi vermes? Et de vermibus Angelos facit.*[14] All men born from flesh, what are they if not worms? And from worms he makes angels. *Cadaver*, in the common medieval etymology, comes from *caro data vermibus*, flesh given to worms. So what. What is this monstrous birth, that is vermiformly at once from and to? To be born [says a dead phenomenologist] is both to be born of the world and to be born into the world.[15]

Zyklon, *World Ov Worms* (Candlelight Records, 2011)

The evolution of individualized corporeal form around the

integral cyclonic ( )hole of birth and death is the crawling of WORMS, something neither produced nor created *ex nihilo* but born from anything, from all things.[16] The worm is an animal that is commonly born from flesh, wood, or any terrestrial thing without any sexual union… There are worms of earth, water, air …[17] A something defined by its self-modulating movement, which is what *worm* signifies.[18] What is my life? That which is moved from within by itself. What is moved from without is not alive.[19] *Spontaneous,* from *sponte,* by one's own free will, by itself. The spirit blows where it wills, and you hear the sound of it, but you do not know whence it comes or whither it goes; so it is with everyone who is born of the spirit.[20] Such is the subtle slithering among forms, the *ex-per-ientia* or coming-out-of-going-through of individuated identity, the neither-this-nor-that *thing* for whom there is no distinction between life and being. [I]n due course, the soul experiences and feels that it is metal, vegetable, worm, fish, bird, animal, man or woman. Whatever be the type of gross form and whatever be the shape of the form, the soul *spontaneously associates itself* with that form, figure and shape, and experiences that it is itself that form, figure and shape.[21] A worm … unfolds its motion gradually, in direct line, stretching out the contracted parts of its little body and contracting those extended parts. So set in motion, it glides along.[22] The old doctrine of spontaneous generation is not only biologically incorrect but ontologically true of every entity—a figura or specular image of the life-event that is actually happening to you, a song sung by nothing, my sweetest vermin.[23]

Although the soul … is infinite and without form, this partially conscious soul actually experiences itself as a worm in the gross world. This is ignorance. This ignorance persists as long as the consciousness of the soul is not fully evolved, but even when the soul has come to full consciousness, it is still said to be enveloped by ignorance because this fully evolved consciousness does not make the soul Self-conscious instantaneously. On the contrary, when the consciousness of the soul is fully evolved the soul begins to identify itself as a human being.[24] You have made your way from worm to human, and much in you is still worm … Behold I teach you the overman … The overman is the meaning of the earth.[25] Thus it is that throughout the myriads of universes there are planets on which the seven kingdoms of evolution are manifested, and the evolution of consciousness and forms is completed. But only on the planet Earth do human beings reincarnate and begin the involutionary path to Self-realization. Earth is the centre of this infinite gross sphere of millions of universes inasmuch as it is the Point to which all human-conscious souls must migrate in order to begin the involutionary path.[26]

There will be flowing water here open to the sky and green oases rich with good things. But we have the spice to think of, too. Thus, there will always be desert on Arrakis … and fierce winds, and trials to toughen a man. We Fremen have a saying: 'God created Arrakis to train the faithful.' One cannot go against the word of God.[27] I beseech you, my brothers, remain faithful to the earth and do not believe those who speak to you of extraterrestrial hopes! … They are despisers of life, dying off and self-poisoned, of whom the earth is weary: so let them fade away! Once the sacrilege against God was the greatest sacrilege, but God died, and then all these desecrators died. Now to desecrate the earth is the most terrible thing, and to esteem the bowels of the unfathomable higher than the meaning of the earth![28] [So] I flung myself into the oily underground river that bubbled somewhere to the caves of the sea; flung myself into that putrescent juice of earth's inner horrors before the madness of my screams could bring down upon me all the charnel legions these pest-gulfs might conceal … [now] my dreams are filled with terror, because of phrases I dare not quote. I dare quote only one paragraph … 'The nethermost caverns,' wrote the mad Arab, 'are not for the fathoming of eyes that see; for their marvels are strange and terrific. Cursed the ground where dead thoughts live new and oddly bodied, and evil the mind that is held by no head... . For it is of old rumour that the soul of the devil-bought hastes not from his charnel clay, but fats and instructs the very worm that gnaws; till out of corruption horrid life springs, and the dull scavengers of earth wax crafty to vex it and swell monstrous to plague it. Great holes secretly are digged where earth's pores ought to suffice, and things have learnt to walk that ought to crawl.[29] Where was I?[30]

Lost in the black presence of *Worms, hungering for all the dimensions,* gracefully hammering the idol of my metal head with the poison thoughts of men. *Sermo,* a stringing together of words, from *serere,* to join. Regarding the particular opening I am tunneling, object all you want that evolution is not teleological.[31] The point is that you want to. Infinite teleology, terrifying all-willing ateleological teleology flies stratospherically far above plan, has no need for it, nesting only in the endless plan of realizing there is no plan, only the planless plan of which each insane breath coming out your worm-mouth is living, inhumanating proof. For so long as we persist as dammed-up reservoirs of labour-power [says a thirster for annihilation] we preserve our humanity, but the rivers flowing into us are an irresistible urge to dissolution, pressing us into the inhumane. Beneath the regulated exchanges of words we howl and gnaw at our fettered limbs [i.e. are our own worm]. An impersonality as blank and implacable as the sun wells up beneath us, a vermin-hunger for freedom: If I am inhuman it is because my world has slopped over its human bounds, because to be human seems like a poor, sorry, miserable affair, limited by the senses, restricted by moralities and codes, defined by platitudes and isms.[32] Reza Negarestani senses this when he identifies worm-space with the Whim: Nemat-space is an ultimate crawling machine; it is essentially cryptogenic and interconnected with Anonymous-until-Now... . *Incognitum Hactenus*—not known yet or nameless and without origin until now—is a mode of time in which the innermost monstrosities of the earth or ungraspable time scales can emerge according to the chronological time that belongs to the surface biosphere of the earth and its populations… . In *Incognitum Hactenus*, you never know the pattern of emergence. Anything can happen for some weird reason; yet also, without any reason, nothing at all can happen.[33] For *all* the dimensions.

This is the superlative craving, the supreme prepositionality according to which *anything* is a perfect event, the hunger that comes from *everywhere*, that unleashes each thing/being/entity as an all-eating void, a ( )hole. Our luminescent, naked bodies dissolve into a swarm of obscure creeping things, and we are a mass of glutinous coiling worms, endless.[34] Whoever walks in this way, whatever he does is all one; whether he does anything or nothing is of no account. And yet the least action or practice of such a man is more profitable and fruitful to himself and all men … than all the works of others who … are inferior to him in love.[35] This is the continual breath of the Outsider, the one whose heart-tablet is inscribed with the surviving invocation from the vermiform grimoire (*De vermis mysteriis*): *Tibi, magnum Innominandum, signa stellarum nigrarum …* To you, great Not-To-Be-Named, signs of the black stars. The one who says: Such a lot the gods gave to me – to me … And yet I am strangely content … I know not where I was born, save that the castle was infinitely old and infinitely horrible.[36] Eckhart names him: It is one, it has nothing in common with anything, and nothing created has anything in common with it. All created things are nothing. But this is remote and alien from all creation… If I were to find myself for a single instant in this essence. I would have as little regard for myself as for a dung worm.[37] All this market-driven herd-talk of 'turns' that now infects every culture, of this turn and that turn, is only deferred, perverted desire to become, to con*vert* to the worm you already are, to the multiple singular agency that is culture's very ground. When we behold a wide, turf-covered expanse, we should remember that its smoothness … is mainly due to all the inequalities having been slowly levelled by worms. It is a marvellous reflection that the whole of the superficial mould over any such expanse has passed, and will again pass, every few years through the bodies of worms.[38]

Stop fearing and worrying and fussing. Feast on the flesh that only you can eat, that you *will* eat. They want us to fear death so much, but we can inhabit it like vermin [says Land], it can be our space … we can knot ourselves into the underworld, communicate through it, cook their heavenly city in our plague.[39] Worms is not a self-grooming *we*. It is the only, unbounded community—a line of openness that slashes through the god, the human, the earth[40]—the unimaginable ever-present perfect abyssal consummation of all and one. A terrible thing is intelligence. It tends to death as memory tends to stability. The living, the absolutely unstable, the absolutely individual, is, strictly, unintelligible. Science is a cemetery of dead ideas, even though life may issue from them. Worms also feed upon corpses. My own thoughts, tumultuous and agitated in the innermost recesses of my soul, once they are torn from their roots in the heart, poured out on to this paper and there fixed in unalterable shape, are already only the corpses of thoughts. How, then, shall reason open its portals to the revelation of life?[41]

Eat the flesh of floating corpses / Heads converted to drinking bowls / Swallow the blood from these rotting skulls / Behold the ritual passage to the infinite / And mutilate oneself for him … Wretched flesh eaters / Unholy beggars / Meditate on TOTAL DEATH / Sacrifice of the body / Utmost annihilation of mind / All in the name of The Cursed One (Witchrist, 'Devour the Flesh,' *Beheaded Ouroboros*).[42] Baldasar Heseler, a Silesian medical student, was present at Andreas Vesalius's first public human anatomy at Bologna in 1540. He wrote: When he had detached it [the cerebellum], he showed us in its end towards the beginning of the medulla the vermis below which the duct leads to the medulla along the spine. And he took out the vermis, and it was as living, like worms that grow in wood and in flesh, *wie eyne made* [worm].[43] If a Toradja man sees a worm on the path in front of him, he places his head-cloth on the ground near to it. If the worm crawls on to the cloth, he then knows that it is his own soul-substance. He puts the worm into the head-cloth which he replaces upon his head, so that the soul-substance can enter his body.[44]

In the 14th-century Cambridge brain diagram illustrating Avicenna's *Canon of Medicine,* the cerebral worm is represented between the powers of memory (vis memorativa) and cognition or imagination (*cogitativa vel ymaginativa*). Mediating between the two, the worm works as a valve modulating the active and passive operations of thought, its movement translated in the human tendency to lower the head when thinking and raise it when recollecting.[45] Equipped by the artist with an oculus of its own, the vermis figure captures the identity of life and thought as theoretic, visionary movement, *sermo mentis,* the autophagous vermicular turning of inner conversation. All life is thought [says the sage of the One] ... Men readily distinguish the various kinds of life but do not do the same with thought: they call some things thought and others not because they do not try to find out what life really is ... all beings are contemplations... . contemplation (*theoria*) and its object constitute a living thing.[46] Up, abysmal thought, out of my depths! ... you sleepy worm: up! ... Once you are awake, you shall remain awake eternally... . I, Zarathustra, the advocate of life, the advocate of suffering, the advocate of the circle – you I summon, my most abysmal thought![47] The eye with which I see God is the same eye with which God sees me.[48] *Who* is the human being into whose throat everything that is heaviest, blackest will crawl? Meanwhile the shepherd bit down as my shout advised him ... Far away he spat the head of the snake ... Never yet on earth had I heard a human being laugh as *he* laughed! ... I heard a laughter that was not human laughter – and now a thirst gnaws at me, a longing that will never be still.[49]

The worm stands, for not standing, for anything. It even knows how to bite off its own head, to swallow itself whole. 'What should I do now?' And a Voice said, '*Eat! Eat Yourself!*' He had no choice but to eat, so He ate Himself! At that moment He found that He was EVERYTHING.[50] It knows how to bring forth from its very powerlessness to do so. The products of putrefaction are to be traced to the Soul's inability to bring some other thing into being.[51] Enter then into this ( )hole. Into the void within the planetary body, a place infinitely vaster than the space surrounding it. Man reaches the World only by way of transcendental darkness in which he never entered and from which he will never leave. A phenomenal blackness entirely fills the essence of man.[52] Enter the black you see. This thing cannot be taught ... I have passed forth out of myself ... I am no longer an object coloured and tangible, a thing of spatial dimensions; I am now alien to all this, and to all that you perceive when you gaze with bodily eyesight.[53] Fulfill the promise of the Reverend Mother: You will learn about the funeral plains ... about the wilderness that is empty, the wasteland where nothing lives except the spice and the sandworms.[54] Both are alive. Inhabit the interface and turn into the worm that you are. Convert to involution. Crawl through the blinding space of your own rot.

But You ... turned me back toward myself, taking me ... from where I had put myself all that time that I preferred not to see myself. And you set me there before my own face that I might see how vile I was, how twisted and unclean and ulcerous.[55] Embrace your blackening, the corpse bride of yourself. 'Any living form will suffer from the plague ... On this very day, He will chant through me / Anything great is built upon sorrow, through your eyes I see the thousand lives I could swallow' (Antaeus, 'Rot,' *Rot*).[56] In order to really fuck the passions of finitude, in order to actually pierce through the dark passage of facticity, it is necessary to weaponize the correlation, to behead your being-in-the-world. Speculating about the worm is not sufficient. Better to study than to be ignorant, better to feel than to study, better to experience than to feel, better to become than experience. Once when Merwan was banging his head on the floor at home, his mother heard a thudding sound coming from his room… . [he] had blood all over his face. Crying she asked, 'Merog, have you gone mad? Are you totally mad?' Wiping the blood off with a towel, he said, 'I am not mad! I have become something else!'[57] Bang your head into a black hole, make space for the worm to crawl. Black metal is the spice, boring into my skull. *Ego … sum vermis et non homo* (Psalm 22.6), For I am a worm and not a human.[58] As if he were to say [comments Eriugena], I who am more than a human penetrate the secrets of all nature, as a worm [penetrates] the bowels of the earth, which no one participating only in human nature can do.

Or turn away from the transi tomb, read no further in the body-soul debate, the words of the worms ringing in your ears: Wretched soul, go away. How long shall your quarreling last? / Worms are holding their own debate, binding fast their judgments; / Maggots are casting lots on my flesh. / Many a noble body will rot. I am not the last.[59] Do not mourn the earth.

Notes

1. The text is given here more or less as presented at the *Melancology* symposium. A few notes have been added for clarification and elaboration of ideas.
2. Frank Herbert, *Dune*. New York: Ace Books, 1987, 124.
3. *Complete Mystical Works*, trans. Maurice O'C. Walshe. New York: Crossroad Publishing, 2009, Sermon 4.
4. Mgła, 'I,' *Presence*. Northern Heritage Records, 2006.
5. A correction of bipedalism, the ideology of human superiority as scripted in the upright stance. The superiority of the human posture lies not in its standing or standing-for (that is the identitarian lie of the human to itself, of the

human-as-lie), but in the fact of uprightness as real form of evolutionary movement, a movement that overcomes the vermicular only by continuing it, by staying and remaining true to its squirmy, super-dimensional restlessness. The significance of uprightness is not in standing for anything, but in aiming at purposeless through the necessity of alteration—'Without change something sleeps inside us, and seldom awakens. The sleeper must awaken' (*Dune,* dir. David Lynch)—that is, in vitally moving beyond principle: 'Hoc enim proprie vivit quod est sine principio' [Only that which is without a principle properly lives] (Meister Eckhart). Just as the logical manifestation of hands and mouth is founded on their mutual positive becoming-uselessness (the freeing of forefeet from walking frees the mouth for talking and generates the hand as grasper-feeder), so the evolution of consciousness itself occurs through the abandonment of form and the death of prior capital directionalities: 'I died as mineral and became a plant, / I died as plant and rose to animal, / I died as animal and I was man. / Why should I fear? When was I less by dying? ... Oh, Let me not exist! For non-existence / Proclaims in organ tones, 'To Him we shall return!'' (Rumi). The evolutionary birthing of consciousness follows a *rotational* path—'the roots of plants are analogous to the head in animals' (Aristotle)—around the 'heaviest weight' of the 'new gravity: the eternal recurrence of the same,' a path following the negative essence of the infinitization of will: 'Do you want *this* again and innumerable times again?' (Nietzsche). Reiner Schurmann coordinately explicates the process, via Eckhart, as an alchemical 'rotation of forces [that] terminates in singularization,' in the theotic production of a pure *this*: 'The alchemist reduces metals by liquefaction so as to produce one piece of the most excellent metal; likewise the soul's forces must return to indistinction in God's ground so it may become excellent in being singularized … Nothing less than God's being is distilled in my singularization … His Godhead depends on it, which is to say that the ineffable extensivity of being is identical to the equally ineffable intensivity of the singular' (*Broken Hegemonies*). The central idea and feeling of my Mgła-*Dune* mashup (see <http://youtu.be/7uTrobzzodY>) is likewise one of taking inner flight by intensively going nowhere and standing for nothing, by *negatively staying*, that is, standing not in neutrality, but in the nigredic, self-liquefying resting in the depth of one's own ground, with the vermin that 'eat through my heart,' where my 'worm does not die, and the fire is not quenched' (Mark 9:48).

6. That would be the way of immanence-without-transcendence, the false promise of the reductive (as opposed to creative) 'this is it' that claims knowledge of and identity with one's own hunger—surest way to ruin a meal.
7. I am thinking 'faith' here particularly in its (post)modern deferring form of belief (as opposed older idea of faith as perception of the invisible). The distinction between hungering for *all dimensions* and hungering for *all the dimensions* captures the difference between desire and will, between simply wanting, needing something to be the case, to arrive, and the more desperate and deliberate volition that asserts what it lacks through sheer negation of its negation. Cf. Georges Bataille's 'desire to be everything': there *is* an everything and I *will* be it. *Inner Experience*. New York: SUNY Press, 54.
8. Eckhart, *Complete Mystical Works*, Sermon 4.
9. The idea is played out in Aristotle's *De Anima*, in which the essential intersection of life and feeding is examined on the basis of self-similar continuance as imitation of eternity: 'Since no living thing is able to partake in what is eternal and divine by uninterrupted continuance … it tries to

achieve that end in the only way possible to it ... so it remains not indeed as the self-same individual but continues its existence in some *like* itself' (*De Anima*). I, however, am installing this life-hunger before life, in the sense of a hunger that life itself feeds and never satisfies.

10. Plotinus, *Enneads*, 4.3.9.
11. Quentin Meillassoux, *After Finitude: An Essay on the Necessity of Contingency*, trans. Ray Brassier London: Continuum, 2008, 63. i.e. facticity is wormhole of the absolute.
12. *Dune*, 529. The citation of the sci-fi data here aims to expose the sheer orchestral beauty and brutality of actual existence, to restore the scholastic preciousness of 'facticity' to the gargantuan domain of logic-squashing entity. Cf. 'He was strangely convinced that the marking was the print of some bulky, unknown, and radically unclassifiable organism of considerably advanced evolution' (Lovecraft, *At the Mountains of Madness*).
13. *Purgatorio* 10.124-5. Birth is not only production, but something from which something else it born; birth births.
14. *In Joannis evangelium tractatus*, 1.13; PL 35:1385.
15. *Phenomenology of Perception*, tr. Colin Smith (London: Routledge, 1962), 527.
16. Worm is not thus simply a specific life-form peculiarly proper to panpsychist reflection on the life/matter interface. Worm is rather the real concept of corporeal life, its elemental idea, as Leibniz's meditations on the cheese and the worms show. This is due to the way worm is differentially essential, at once a non-atomistic pure minimum of body always capable of containing/being-contained in others of itself and a body always other than itself, something born from other material and always moving into new forms. Worm itself is the real self-othering of matter and the actual formlessness of form.

17. *'Vermis est animal quod plerumque de carne, vel de ligno, vel de quacumque re terrena sine ullo concubitu gignitur; licet nonnumquam et de ovis nascuntur, sicut scorpio. Sunt autem vermes aut terrae, aut aquae, aut aeris, aut carnium, aut frondium, aut lignorum, aut vestimentorum' Etymologiae,* 12.5, 'De vermibus'.
18. 'Worm. As. *wyrm,* G. *wurm,* Lat. *vermis,* worm ; Goth, *vaurms,* serpent; ON. *ortnr,* serpent, worm. Sanscr. *krmi,* a worm; Lith. *kirmis, kirminis, kirmele,* worm, caterpillar; *kirmiti,* to breed worms; Let. *zirmis,* maggot, worm. The origin, like that of *weevil,* lies in the idea of swarming, being in multifarious movement, crawling. Pl.D. *kribbeln, krubbeln, krcmelen, krimmeln, kriimmeln,* to be in multifarious movement, to swarm, boil. 'Idt was daar so vull, dat idt *kremeled* un wemelde:' it was so full that it swarmed. *Up kribbeln*. Hanover *krimmeln, la/en:* to let the water boil up. Du. *wremelen,* to creep ; Da. *vrimle,* to swarm ; *vrimmel,* a swarm'. Wedgwood & Atkinson, *A Dictionary of English Etymology*.
19. *Complete Mystical Works,* Sermon 13a.
20. John 3:8.
21. Meher Baba, *God Speaks,* 5.
22. *'Vermis non ut serpens apertis passibus vel squamarum nisibus repit, quia non est illi spinae rigor, ut colubri, sed in directum corpusculi sui partes gradatim porrigendo contractas, contrahendo porrectas motum explicat, sicque agitatus perlabitur. Etymologiae,* 12.5, 'De vermibus'.
23. The reference is to Le Chants de Nihil, *Ma plus Douce Vermine*. Dernier Bastion, 2009. As time is the 'moving image of eternity,' generation is the purposeless image of the purpose of life: 'The Goal of Life in Creation is to arrive at purposelessness, which is the state of Reality'. Meher Baba, *The Everything and the Nothing*.
24. Meher Baba, *God Speaks,* 20-1.

25. *Thus Spoke Zarathustra*, trans. Adrian del Caro. Cambridge: Cambridge University Press, 2006, 6.
26. Meher Baba, *God Speaks*, 292-3. This is a difficult idea to get one's head around. It is one thing to think Earth as simply where I happen to be (life happened on earth and I happened to be among its living at this point in its history), or more abstractly and generically, to think earth as radical thisness or plane of immanence. It is another to think that this very particular planet, however replaceable by another 'Earth' when this one dies, happens to be *the* singular turning point for the initiation of involution, a kind of cosmic receptacle and interchange into which all human-conscious souls throughout the universe must flow. The possibility is not any more absurd than the general temporal-topological senselessness, less so if the fact of one's being here somehow attests to it. There is no reason not to subject all events of arising, birth, sudden acontextual self-presence etc., every deep condition for asking 'why am I *here*?' to scientific inquiry (other than the false correlational reason of preserving the human 'we' as object of scientific discourse) and transmigrational planetary geography offers a real domain for doing so. For me the attractiveness of Earth as cosmic center lies precisely in its universal Ptolomaism, a reinvention of medieval intuition that offers a scientistic ground for the Nietzschean imperative: remain faithful to the earth – a faith that the space-folding flight to Dune effects.
27. Herbert, *Dune*, 488.
28. Nietzsche, *Thus Spoke Zarathrustra*, 6.
29. H.P. Lovecraft, *The Festival*.
30. Not standing on the earth, certainly. Has any who are here ever really been here, in the open air, as it were? Rather it seems we are all being swallowed. Cf. 'Earth: a sacred temple, godless and unbuilding / Cooking consciousness

into something it is not' (*Event of Oneself*).

31. There a subtle semantic gesture here to the relation between objection and object, the discursive throwing down of an obstacle and the older sense of that to which a power is related. Objecting is an appetitive act.
32. Nick Land, *Thirst for Annihilation*, 257.
33. Negarestani, *Cyclonopedia*, 49.
34. Eugene Thacker, *An Ideal for Living*, 13.
35. Eckhart, *Complete Mystical Works*, Sermon 4.
36. H.P. Lovecraft, *The Outsider*.
37. Eckhart, *Complete Mystical Works*, Sermon 57.
38. Darwin, *The Formation of Vegetable Mould*, Chapter 7.
39. Nick Land, *Thirst for Annhilation*, 93-4.
40. Reza Negarestani, *Cyclonopedia*, 207.
41. *Tragic Sense of Life*, trans. Anthony Kerrigan (Princeton: Princeton University Press, 1972), 100-1.
42. (Invictus Productions, 2010).
43. *Andreas Vesalius's First Public Anatomy at Bologna*, 1540: An Eyewitness Report, trans. Ruben Erikson (Uppsala, Almqvist & Wiksell, 1959), 289.
44. William James Perry, *The Megalithic Culture of Indonesia*, 150.
45. See Mary Carruthers, *The Book of Memory: A Study of Memory in Medieval Culture*, 2n ed. Cambridge: Cambridge University Press, 2008, 68.
46. Plotinus, *Enneads*. 3.8.8, cited from *The Essential Plotinus*, trans. Elmer O'Brien and *The Enneads*, trans. Stephen MacKenna.
47. Nietzsche, *Thus Spoke Zarathustra*, 173-4.
48. Eckhart, *Compelte Mystical Works*, Sermon 57.
49. Nietzsche, *Thus Spoke Zarathustra*, 127.
50. Bhau Kalchuri, *The Nothing and the Everything* Manifestation, 1981, 11.
51. Plotinus, *Enneads*, trans. Stephen MacKenna, 5.913.
52. Francois Laruelle, 'Du noir univers.'

53. *Hermetica*, trans. Walter Scott, Boston: Shambala, 1993, 239.
54. Herbert, *Dune*, 30.
55. Augustine, *Confessions*, trans. F.J. Sheed, Indianapolis: Hackett, 2006, 8.7.
56. Battlesk, 2004.
57. Bhau Kalchuri, *Meher Prabhu: The Biography of Avatar Meher Baba*, 14 vols Manifestation, 1980, 1.251-2.
58. John Scotus Eriugena comments on Psalm 22.6: 'For none of the material things in nature is more lowly than the worm, which is conceived from simple earth. Nevertheless, through this is represented the incarnation of the Word of God, which transcends every sense and intellect [Phil 4.7]. 'Who will explain his begetting?' [Acts 8.33, from Isa 53.8, cf. Augustine, *Expositions of the Psalms*: 'In what sense 'no man'? Because he is God. Why then did he so demean himself as to say 'worm'? Perhaps because a worm is born from flesh without intercourse, as Christ was from the Virgin Mary. A worm, and yet no man. Why a worm? Because he was mortal, because he was born from flesh, because he was born without intercourse. Why 'no man'? Because In the beginning was the Word, and the Word was with God; he was God (Jn 1.1)'] It can also be understood thus: 'I am a worm and a human is not,' that is, I am a worm and human is not a worm. As if he were to say, I who am more than a human penetrate the secrets of all nature, as a worm [penetrates] the bowels of the earth, which no one participating only in human nature can do. With the sense agrees that which is written in another Psalm, 'and my substance in the depths of the earth [PS 139.15], that is, and my substance, which is wisdom in itself, subsists in the depths of the earth, that is, the innermost folds of created nature. 'For the divinity beyond being is the being of all.' Thus the worm that penetrates the hidden things of all creation is the Wisdom of the Father, which, while human,

transcends all humanity'. *Commentary on the Dionysian Celestial Hierarchy.* [Addam, *inquit, praedictis imaginationibus illud symbolum, quod omnium vilius esse visum est, et magis significare, vel ut expressius* [Col.0168C] *transfertur, magis obscurum vel dissimile. Divini siquidem sapientes, id est theologi, tradiderunt, ipsam sapientiam in specie vermis seipsam formasse, eo loco fortassis, ubi per prophetam loquitur: «Ego sum vermis et non homo». Hoc enim intelligitur de Christo, qui de virili semine non est natus, sed sicut vermis de simplici natura terrae, ita ipse ex visceribus perpetuae virginis et incontaminatae carnem assumpsit. Nihil itaque in natura rerum materialium vilius verme, qui de simplici limo concipitur, et tamen per ipsum incarnatio Dei Verbi, quae superat omnem sensum et intellectum, imaginatur. «Generationem ejus quis enarrabit»? Potest et sic intelligi: Ego sum vermis et non homo, hoc est, ego sum vermis, et non homo vermis.* [Col.0168D] *Ac si diceret: Ego, qui plus quam homo sum, secreta penetro totius naturae, sicut vermis viscera terrae, quod nullus alius humanae naturae particeps* [Col.0169A] *potest agere. Cui sensui arridet, quod in alio psalmo scriptum est: «et substantia mea in inferioribus terrae», hoc est, et substantia mea , quae per seipsam sapientia est, in inferioribus terrae, hoc est, in intimis naturae conditae sinibus subsistit. Esse enim omnium est, superesse Divinitatis. Vermis itaque, qui abdita totius creaturae penetrat, sapientia patris est, quae dum est homo, omnem superat humanitatem. Audi Apostolum de se ipso loquentem: «Paulus apostolus, non ab hominibus, neque per hominem, sed per Jesum Christum, et Deum patrem, qui suscitavit eum a mortuis». Nonne ipse est mysticus ille vermis, in cujus imagine quingentesimo semper anno transacto de cinere arabicae avis, phoenicis dico, proprii sui pectoris* [Col.0169B] *flamma consumptae, vermis nascitur, et ad pristinam viriditatem revocatur? Christus siquidem ardore passionis, quam sponte sua susceperat, consumptus est, et descendit ad inferos mirabilis vermis. Sed mox post triduum reversus est, suique apostoli, qui eum in cruce ardentem viderant, in spirituali corpore resurgentem conspexere, virtutumque pennis volantem, ad Patremque suum ascendentem mirati sunt.]*

59. 'Wrecche gost, thou wen away, hou longe shal thi strist laste? / Wormes holdeth here mot, domes byndeth faste; / Maked he habbeth here lot on my fleyshe to caste, / Mony fre bodi shal roten, ne be y nout the laste' (In a thestri stude y stod [In a dark place I stood], MS. Harl. 2253, fol. 57r)

Shuddering: Black Metal on the Edge of the Earth

Steven Shakespeare

And the feeling body shudders and lurches on the edge quaking with dead inertia, a caged oak. Suppressed from the instant that seed took root. In earth that promised of a monolith. All I see are saplings shackled to stone. A genocide of all we have sown.

Skagos 'Anamnesis II: A Dry, Sterile Thunder Without Rain', 2010.[1]

Just as no evil spirit dares name the holy name, so every good spirit shudders before the empty space, before the equality of annihilation, and this shudder that is productive in the life of nature is impelling in the life of spirit.

Søren Kierkegaard[2]

Trident-ine Rites

In December 2010, an advance party of the Black Metal Theory Symposium and friends attended a gig in Liverpool. The headliners were Watain.

Watain roadies don't just set up the musical equipment. Like servers in church, they are also responsible for laying out the sacred space: the altar complete with skulls; the sacrificed animals stuck on spikes; the candles and cloths. This was to be a ritual performance, and the band duly reverenced the altar before they played.

The crown of the set consisted of two large tridents. During the performance, these were impressively wreathed in flame. Beforehand, however, they looked less imposing.

The unlit Tridents looked a little like foam cut-outs. Every time a roadie walked across the stage, they shuddered precariously as if they were going to flop over at any moment. Not so much Satanic majesty as Spinal Tap. One of the symposium members present at this event perfectly summed up the effect afterwards with a Facebook status that read simply: 'wobbly flaming tridents'.

Black metal bands can rely on many things for the atmosphere and effect of their performances. Rawness is mediated through ritual, the visceral through the artificial. The threat - or the promise - of absurdity haunts these borderlines. With absurdity comes the sense of vertigo, of a world out of joint, of a radical instability which is the watermark of being. Black metal takes us screaming down the rabbit hole.

On the Edge

Where do we shudder? On the edge, always on the edge. Between life and death, nature and spirit, where one infests the other. Black metal finds a kind of rapture in this horror. No doubt it will always spawn cartoonish Satanism, rabid nationalism, and pathetic declarations of kultish orthodoxy. But the evolution of its disgust outpaces such congealed forms. It buries its way into the earth, despising human parasites.

What it finds there is not always simple. It finds the 'inner contradiction', which for Schelling is the source of all life: forces which belong to one another in their very antagonism. It finds the absolute in duplicity. What we once called: evil.

The bands of the Pacific Northwest or Cascadia, and associated bands further south in California, often tread this path towards the heart of the earth. With Skagos and Panopticon, they call for the 'acceleration of industrial collapse' and the eruption of an anarcho-primitivist for of life. In one sense, they follow the call of Rousseau and the Romantics - or, closer to their home, of Thoreau and Emerson. To reject the artificiality of civilisation, to cultivate self-reliance, and so to touch once more the infinite spirit which animates nature: we can follow these tracks through the work of Wolves in the Throne Room, Skagos, Fauna, Echtra, Alda, Fell Voices, Leech, Mania and so on.

However, we should not mistake this for a mere return to nature as a pure state of being. Something other is going on: a meeting of extremes without unification: 'Skagos is misanthropy and apotheosis. Skagos is love, Skagos is hate, Skagos is hope and is fear'.[3] Machine and nature are the two faces of a ritual by which an inhuman, monstrous spirit is born, a promise and a hatred for humanity whose ambivalence will never be dispelled. The edge between life and death, the shudder of horror runs through the veins of black metal's earth. It is part of its geology.

The feeling body is sickened by its confrontation with an earth that promised much, but delivered only captivity and death: 'All I see are saplings shackled to stone.' The songs of these bands are often raging psalms of lament. They want to rip meaning from the dead hands of the earth, but can only do so by surrendering to the earth's own dead, frozen core:

> I behold the world through cold, dead eyes.
> The womb is barren and infertile.
> The sun grows shy and the night grows strong.
> We are all cast down and enslaved by the ripping cold. The field is a frozen corpse, but life seems to linger in the air, a mist both rich and void. Skagos, 'Caliginosity' (*Ást*, 2009)[4]

This lingering life, rich and void, is crushed by the artifice of civilisation, but something remains, something escapes. There is a desperate ambiguity as the song continues:

> Cloaked in the skin of a beast,
> we embrace the Leviathan as a necessity.
> We assemble in caves;
> we cower and wait.
> My bones grow stiff and cold.

Rigor mortis begins to take hold, a living death. Becoming animal, we still subject ourselves to the Leviathan - the artificial beast which Thomas Hobbes held up as the model of sovereignty. Only by embracing the Leviathan, handing power to an absolute authority, are human beings freed from the endless war that is their state of nature. But this necessity, this artifice only pre-empts our death. It is the oblivion of earth and blood.

And so we enter a time of waiting, shrouded by animal skin, sheltered in the earth's rocky interior. But no light arises at the end of this Advent ... only a hidden fire, and fog and silence:

> The glorious breath of flame keeps the blood from freezing.
> The earth is suffocating within the ice, in a deep, cold sleep, with dreams of finality.
> The freezing moon washes the world azure,
> with the fog, the endless fog,
> and the world grows fucking silent...

The song replays a kind of ritual of rebirth, entering the earth's liminal spaces to be born again. Wolves in the Throne Room express a similar sentiment:

> I will lay down my bones among the rocks and roots of the deepest
> hollow next to the streambed
> The quiet hum of the earth's dreaming is my new song
> When I awake, the world will be born anew
> Wolves in the Throne Room,'I Will Lay Down My Bones Among the Rocks and Roots' (2007).[5]

However, whereas the Wolves celebrate the ending of the work of the beast and look for a purifying rain, Skagos remain the dark, in the fog, shuddering on the edge of the end. Will it be annihilation or rebirth?

> I am waiting for the great abate. Thunder claps, But no water falls. Thunder claps! And no water will fall. Shattered ouroboros. I feel the mountain within: the sea, the soil, the sky. Suffocating under eight millennia coils. Shattered ouroboros.
>
> Skagos, 'Anamnesis II: A Dry, Sterile Thunder Without Rain'

The ouroboros, the snake consuming its tail, is an image of eternity, or at least the eternal return of the same. Skagos mourn its breaking: and yet unless its totality is disrupted, life is impossible. The folding back of the all into the one is both performed and disrupted by black metal. Seeking apotheosis and unity, it uses disruption and discordance as its weapons.

> Devoid of metamorphosis. Twisted larvae starve. Megaflora extinction. An era of gynocide. I call thee, hark, Ares! I call thee, hark ... apocalyptic atavism! Here one can neither stand nor lie nor sit. There is not even silence in the mountains, but dry sterile thunder without rain. I await the flood in rusting chains For a fertile thunder, that reeks of rain.

Skagos takes us to the place that is no place, unhinged and unthinged: an echo of the phrase of Roger Caillois, quoted by Ray Brassier, about the experience of a schizophrenic: 'He feels himself becoming space, *black space where things cannot be put*.'[6]

The music itself is a kind of dry sterile thunder, performing its own collapse into the earth, into its black space. It waits for rain, for the stench of life: the cycle is renewed, but only through breaking the dead grip of self-reflection. This is larval music, in a process of becoming without clear ends.

Rituals of Earth

It is worth noting that Skagos use the term 'anamnesis' in the title of the song we have been discussing. Anamnesis is the Platonic recollection of the eternal forms. It is the Christian remembering of the passion of Christ ritually re-enacted in the eucharist. Anamnesis is the paradoxical entry of the eternal into time: a painful incarnation. Skagos' anamnesis revolves around a ritual internalisation of the inhuman: 'I feel the mountain within: the sea, the soil, the sky.' What is remembered and embodied is the geology which outstrips the human condition.

The ritual element of black metal can hardly be doubted, but should we understand it as inverted Christianity, as Gnosticism, as animism? Without rejecting the validity of these interpretations, I agree with the approach that it is best conceived as alchemy.[7] The alchemical ritual brings together technology and artifice with a spiritual force that treads the line between reverence and blasphemy. It the transmutation of metal made intimate with the transfiguration of the soul. It is an exertion of will, a creation though chaos as much as a recognition of an absolute unity underlying all things. Alchemy resolves the cosmos into its original forces in order to co-opt, compress and intensify the act of creation.

As Mark Taylor points out, alchemy is intimately linked to the sacred role of the miner.[8] The search for gold beneath the ground would be the search for the pure substance earth wishes to create. The earth finds itself impeded, producing various lesser metallic abortions. The miner/midwife aids in the process of birth.

However, mining is not enough. The metallurgist must create an artificial womb in which to purify the contaminated gold, a womb which prefigures the alchemical crucible, where purification gives way to conception. Even base substances can be made gold, but only after they have been resolved into nigredo, the abject black matter. Putrefaction and decomposition occur for the sake of new birth, the release of powers.

Nigredo names black metal's self-production through ritual decomposition. It is the power of chaos and blackness without which the formed, lustrous object could never be produced. Alchemy is both the veneration of original substance and its technological repetition, the revelation that substance was always already decomposing. Black matter curled in the heart of gold. Who can tell where one ends and the other begins?

Black metal must live in paradox: unable to get clear of the dying, malformed earth which both binds it and births it, unable to articulate nature and purity except through the contaminated machine of its technology and dissemination. What Derrida writes of faith applies just as forcefully to anti-faith: it is only possible because the original substance is not simple, because originality is always the effect of a repetition: 'No faith, therefore, nor future, without everything technical, automatic, machine-like supposed by iterability'.[9] Black matter takes nothing from materialism - except its finality and finitude.

Alchemy is nature on speed, seeking a still point. Black metal finds its roots in the accelerated mayhem of thrash and death metal, but ironically it tends towards a kind of immobility. Consider the increasingly stretched out songs or concepts which dominate a certain black metal scene in the US; from Weakling through to recent releases such as those by Fell Voices, Ash Borer, Leech, Echtra works, Fauna and Blood of the Black Owl. Songs or ritual compositions of 20 to 40 minutes are becoming normal. The trance-like effect of these recordings witnesses to a kind of stasis within motion. It recalls a passage from Baudrillard:

> Speed is not a vegetal thing. It is nearer to the mineral, to refraction through a crystal, and it is already the site of a catastrophe, of a squandering of time. Perhaps, though, its fascination is simply that of the void. There is no seduction here, for seduction requires a secret. Speed is simply the rite that initiates us into emptiness: a nostalgic desire for forms to revert to immobility, concealed beneath the very intensification of their mobility.[10]

Perhaps it is no accident that this passage comes from Baudrillard's book on America, which he argues that the US embodies 'a primary, visceral, unbounded vitality, springing not from rootedness, but from lack of roots', that it is 'the *only remaining primitive society*'.[11] Lacking a deep past, the US is characterised by 'a ritualism that is ferocious but whose superficial diversity lends it beauty'. Primitivism here means not the recovery of authentic ancient roots, but the rootlessness which forces the ideal into material reality, abolishing the distance between nature and culture.

According to Baudrillard, this ritual search for identity and origins encounters two things. First, the fact of the original inhabitants of the North American content, whose existence must be expunged in favour of the myth of wilderness. As Baudrillard puts it, 'The dead Indian remains the mysterious guarantor of these primitive mechanisms, even into the modern age of images and technology.'[12]

The second confrontation is with the 'Geological - and hence metaphysical - monumentality' of the desert, echoed in the canyons of the metropolis. This is why Baudrillard refers to the mineral nature of speed. The forward rushing motion of the car in the desert hardly gets it anywhere. Speed only underscores the indifference of the earth - a temporary compression and acceleration of forces which exceed our grasp. Speed as pointless expenditure, 'senseless repetition' fleeing all centres and origins, to the point where it meets unimaginable slowness. For Baudrillard, America's 'primitivism has passed into the hyperbolic, inhuman character of a universe that is beyond us, that far outstrips its own moral, social, or ecological rationale'.[13] In the wilderness we meet 'the remorseless eternity of a slow-motion catastrophe ... Among this gigantic heap of signs - purely geological in essence - man will have had no significance'.[14]

Black metal mines this catastrophe, distils its frozen metallic core even in the lush forests of the northwest, revels in the putrefying reduction of its elements, rails against the pretensions of human ambition to be at the centre of the world.

In this context, the nature-centred ritualism of a project like Fauna takes on a different dimension. Fauna's *The Hunt* (2007) is a conceptually linked set of pieces lasting 71 minutes in total. The hunt appears to be a metaphor for a return to lost origins, a Gnostic ascent from the dust and stone of earth to the original fullness of the Great Spirit. And yet as the hunt is consummated, the narrator is bound to the earth in new ways:

> My arrow is a seal
> A covenant with life
> My spear is a seed
> I plant in our womb
> Turning outward to seek the gift
> That will stake me to the earth …
> In its centre
> Blood in the tracks
> Assent begets assent
> I feast on glory
> As two become one again

Two become one: union. But the consequences of this are anything but a simple escape to spiritual purity. The narrator is staked to the centre of the earth. The womb of the earth, of the animal, is our womb. Two become one only through an impossible gift, a turning outwards, an inevitable taint. The music rides on metallic waves, verging on drones, towards a kind of discordant serenity, without harmonic resolution.

To use Skagos' words, the sapling remains shackled to stone, to the geology and the technology which makes it possible. The catastrophe which flings us from our origins is not merely resolved by the ritual of the hunt: it is repeated, and received again as artifice and as glory.

It is all too easy to oppose nature and culture, organism and machine, originality and artifice - and, these days, perhaps even easier to conflate them. The USBM of the west coast seems to offer something different: a rootless primitivism which refuses to evade the horror and indifference of the earth. Of course, this lends it a deep ambiguity: to what extent is USBM another expression of colonising power, of the eradication and expropriation of indigenous territories and rituals? Is this another Western projection of the wilderness as the blank canvas for its hegemony and desire?

There is no direct answer to this question. Native American ritual finds a kind of afterlife in some of the projects we have mentioned, but it would miss the point to look for authentic roots. Rather, the ritual is a configuration of space, time become space, the space of the earth; it repeats the colonising fascination with wilderness, but also evokes an unruly, monstrous atavism.

The apocalypticism which results might be seen as no more than a symptom: a regressive fantasy of spiritual conflict which masks the real and mundane contradictions of US hegemony over global capitalism, the very driving forces of conformity and environmental degradation lamented by the bands we are dealing with. However, these 'real conditions' are themselves produced and enforced through simulation and apocalyptic religious narratives. Apart from the overt political statements of a project like Panopticon, the resistance of black metal to this dominant ideology is through the creation of rituals of gravity, which hurl us towards the mortal, material underground of culture and nature.

Black metal thus ungrounds itself by going to ground, always recreating its fall, the gravity that pulls it toward the zero point of the earth's frozen core. In other words, the return to the earth is not the recuperation of a stable foundation in thought or being. It is a journey towards an unsettling abstraction, formed of decomposition. Black metal is 'theoretical' in its visionary descent into this quality of abstraction. It is an experience echoed uncannily in Baudrillard's encounter with the silence of Death Valley:

> And the silence is something extraordinary, as though it were itself all ears. It is not the silence of cold, nor of barrenness, nor of an absence of life. It is the silence of the whole of this heat over the mineral expanses that stretch out before us for hundreds of miles .... A silence internal to the Valley itself, the silence of underwater erosion, below the very waterline of time, as it is below the level of the sea. No animal movement. Nothing dreams here, nothing talks in its sleep. Each night the earth plunges into perfectly calm darkness, into the blackness of its alkaline gestation, into the happy depression of its birth ... one may speak of the abstraction of the desert, of a deliverance from the organic, a deliverance that is beyond the body's abject passage into carnal inexistence, into that dry, luminous phase of death in which the corruption of the body reaches completion. The desert is beyond this accursed phase of completion, this humid phase of the body, this organic phase of nature.[15]

Here alchemy is itself transmuted into 'alkaline gestation', a reversal of life towards leaden death. It is this fleshless earth to which black metal returns us, even when draped in the verdancy of Cascadia, or wedded to the rhetoric of primitivism. In this sense, the abstract earth is the real condition of life and thought, an abstraction which (echoing Hegel's philosophy of nature) becomes fruitful only insofar as it is already divided against itself. To fail to reckon with this reality is to remain stuck within humanist and spiritualist delusions.

Consider Mania's tape (*s/t*, 2010), which echoes the anti-civilisation, anti-agriculture, anti-machine views of anarcho-primitivists such as John Zerzan, but it is mixed with a healthy dose of sheer hatred for humanity: 'When civilization crumbles and none of this is left, won't hesitate when must stab this knife into your chest' ('Primal Instincts'); 'I don't want to feel part of this machine, anything seems better than this numbing' ('Numbing'); 'Behold your impenetrable useless machine, frozen solid ... man cowers under the immense power of nature' ('Ice Covered Sphere). And what is left when nature returns and the machine of civilization is dead? Not a paradise of foraging and play, as Zerzan would have us believe, but another kind of numbness - 'Globe immersed in eternal frost, eternal frost, eternal cold, eternal void, all encompassing for all time' ('Ice Covered Sphere').

At the end of the tape the call to awaken seems to merge with a call to despair. Until the sun burns, the earth and the machine run together, interlocking mechanisms of monstrosity: 'The same course repeats the last ten thousand years. It's the same machine with your earth friendly gears you can't change this globe' ('Awaken'). Machine and nature are the two faces of a ritual by which an inhuman, monstrous spirit is born, a promise and a hatred for humanity whose ambivalence will never be dispelled. The strange hope of this appeal is that it at least names the inevitable complicity between the earth and the machine, rather than - as Zerzan does - opting for a purified noncultural nature, which turns out to be the fulfilment of our humanity after all: earth as our playground, earth as our unbroken immediacy, earth as the untainted primitive - the constant fantasy of advanced capitalism and the society of the spectacle.[16]

In contrast to this voyeuristic dream, black metal ritual is not the mere enforcement of cultural codes, but the obsessive exposure of culture's contaminated reproduction of itself: a dangerous memory. A sacrament of black matter.

In 'Smoldering Embers', Skagos envisage the evisceration of an 'artificial beast' which echoes the political thought of Thomas Hobbes. As noted earlier, for Hobbes, the war of all against all which is the human state of nature, could only be ended by the erection of a sovereign power, which he likens both to the Biblical mythical monster of chaos (Leviathan) and to an artificial animal. In contrast, Skagos appear to welcome the overthrow of this beast (which previously we saw them embrace as a cold necessity), and the rekindling of ancient fires. However, the final words of the song reveal a tension between retrieving a buried past and the possibility of something radically new:

> The drought earth thirsts for man's blood. Nefarious whittling in the worship of progress. The last communities dance with the guile of wraiths, drowning in a miserable rebellion, wading through the entrails of an artificial beast. Ancient fires are eclipsed but never are they extinguished. Tongues of flame lash out as the embers of atavism smolder. Redemption is a ship sunk thousands of years ago. New beginnings must be found.[17]

The earth in which redemption has been buried is not a pure savior, but a thirsty consumer of human vitality. The question is open: does salvation lie in unearthing a past, natural form of consciousness? Or does it depend upon turning one's back on salvation as such - letting the earth be the indifferent earth, so that new beginnings, divorced from all scenes of primal origins, may be fashioned?

The Unassimilated

The matter which fuels alchemical ritual and the emergence of consciousness is, as Schelling reminds us, the darkest thing of all; not because it is a hidden substance, but because it is the potency of the becoming of being, the shattered ouroboros: 'The earth is darker than conception and yet the lights never fade'.[18] Repetition, but never of the same.

The machinic structure of repetition, of speed as monumental slowness, defines much of the sound of the US bands I have touched on here. Black metal, as an alien European import, is both a promise of origins and a free-floating technology. Shuddering between the two, and sometimes despite itself, USBM exposes us to nature as machinic, originally repeated, always inhuman, inorganic.

In an essay on the nature of film, Esther Leslie (drawing on Adorno) argues for a recovery of shuddering. A sign of technical failure, the jarring of the image is exactly what cinematic mechanisms attempt to eliminate. As cinema attempts to suppress its mechanical infrastructure, we are held in thrall by images which offer a human coating to the void.

Leslie continues:

> If we could discern it, we would shudder at the unmediated exposure to the abyss of emptiness that those filmic shadows, those 'living and non-living' effigies, impersonating us and ours, in the guise of humans, represent. We would be chilled by the horrible truth they display, which is the actuality of cinema's efforts to mechanize even us, as it conspires to make all of life a matter of industry, a technical lethality. Were the shudder to come, occasioned by the music's fall out or the stuttering of the filmstrip in the projector, it would itself be a hopeful sign, standing in for the very principle of life itself.[19]

As Leslie notes, the association of shuddering and life recalls the experiments of Galvani, who created movement in dead animals though the manipulation of electric currents. His discoveries fascinated idealists and naturephilosophers. Hegel saw in galvanism the transition point from the tension of electricity to the real interaction unity and difference in chemical processes - a stage on the way to the emergence of organisms, a decisive break with merely mechanical modes of explaining phenomena. Galvanism prepares the way for spirit, spirit conceived of as organic, holistic self-consciousness.

However, Galvanism also unleashed a more discomposing fantasy: that of reanimating the dead or creating life anew. Remember the moment of crisis in Mary Shelley's Frankenstein:

> It was already one in the morning; the rain pattered dismally against the panes, and my candle was nearly burnt out, when, by the glimmer of the of the half-extinguished light, I saw the dull yellow eye of the creature open; it breathed hard, and a convulsive motion agitated its limbs.[20]

Later Frankenstein succumbs to dreams:

> I thought that I held the corpse of my dead mother in my arms; a shroud enveloped her form, and I saw the grave-worms crawling in the folds of flannel. I started from my sleep with horror; a cold dew covered my forehead, my teeth chattered, and every limb became convulsed: when, by the dim and yellow light of the moon, as it forced its way through the window shutters, I beheld the wretch – the miserable monster whom I had created.[21]

Under a yellow moon which reflects the yellow eye of the monster, Frankenstein shudders at the horror he has brought into being - a horror that exposes his own twitching mortality to light.

We can happily remain seduced by this horror, and black metal is adept at creating such aesthetic moods, moods which feed a gnostic desire for escape. I suspect black metal demands more of us, however: an incorporation which provokes an agony of will, an agency, even a resistance. Not one which floats free of material conditions in a human fantasy of subjectivity, but one which is born out of the shuddering, of its lurching on the edge of something other. Paradoxically, it is Mania's hopelessness, its acceptance of the evil we are part of, which signals the possibility of an 'outside' to our current situation: 'A never-ending, all encompassing, urban sprawl of technological infrastructure will engulf all life and there is no fighting it, only embracing it and using it to further your immediate needs until it collapses...'[22] To employ a Mania song title (from the 2008 *Endless Hunger* release), we experience 'a collapse of spiraling iteration': deeper into the complicity, the unsleeping, undead filth of the machine.

As Leslie puts it:

> The shudder, then, is on the cusp. It inaugurates the attempt to master nature, to overcome all that is different. But it also marks the point of an afterwards that might still – if only bodily, unconsciously, involuntarily - remember what it was like to once be touched by something different, unassimilated.[23]

Zerzan would have us reject all symbolism and ritual, as the formalisation and alienation of our emotions under hierarchies of domination and control.[24] Ritual inaugurates and maintains cultural order. To abandon ritual is also to abandon culture and inequality for the sake of an aboriginal spirit, our natural humanness. Black metal is therefore unfaithful to the anarcho-primitivist creed. Resolutely symbolic and ritual, cultic even, it refuses Zerzan's dream of Eden even as it reaches out to grasp it. It is a twisted, crackling version of the rootless primitivism Baudrillard sees at the heart of US culture.

Cascadian Black metal's spirit is therefore less the organic holism of Hegel, more the irritability, through which, according to Schelling life is stimulated and reproduced: 'a galvanism that reproduces itself'.[25] In its sound, form and deformity interact mechanically to make 'spirit' tangible aurally and lyrically. Spirit is both rooted in natural unity, and longs to return to it; but also and at the same time, spirit is the irritated will, which needs and is repelled by its natural ground. In a sense, spirit is this mechanical friction but also its enduring, the strange fidelity it evokes.

Why speak of fidelity at this late hour? In black metal's return to the earth, the possibility remains of embracing a simplistic ideology, whether its form be primitivist or nationalist/national socialist. Such ideologies, with their claims to an unsullied natural identity, offer an escape from the incalculable demands of responsibility. As Dominic Fox has argued in relation to the depressive black metal music produced by US artist Xasthur, the freezing sound world constitute a set of exercises detaching the soul from 'worldly attachments'. However, these exercises can become 'purely narcissistic and self-salving if they do not also release the soul *for* new worldly commitments'. The sound world remains a 'simulacrum – a spiritualization – of malcontent' rather than 'the focused displeasure of the militant'.[26]

Something similar could be said about the trance-like effect of the nature-oriented black metal of Cascadia (in which 'Cascadia' itself can easily become a simulacrum, a constructed image used to regulate narratives and ideals of salvation). The productive impulse which shudders through the music occurs when the simulacrum exposes its own inadequacy to the real, to the unassimilated, contradictory earth.

For Kierkegaard, merely standing at the graveside is not enough. The aesthetic mood of melancholy is just another mask for indecision, for the forgetting of the moment when we become nothing, which is also the moment of crisis, of decision. As he writes, 'The vacillating person is only a witness to the continual boundary dispute between life and death'.[27] The point is not to evade the shudder or aestheticise it, still less to 'talk oneself out of death'; it is rather to allow thinking to be convulsed by materiality, to allow the spirit to be impelled and irritated to earnestness, a militant grave worm enmeshed in the shrouds of the black earth:

look down upon this nothing-dead-place ...
i call forth my future weapons ...
i stab the pain of your white stare ...
though you will change and change again ...
i will not relent
Blood of the Black Owl, *A Banishing Ritual,* 2010.

Notes

1. Skagos 'Anamnesis II: A Dry, Sterile Thunder Without Rain' (*Skagos/Panopticon* split, 2010).
2. Søren Kierkegaard, *Three Discourses on Imagined Occasions* (Princeton: Princeton UP, 1993), p. 89.
3. www.myspace.com/skagos
4. Skagos, 'Caliginosity' (*Ást,* 2009)
5. Wolves in the Throne Room, 'I Will Lay Down My Bones Among the Rocks and Roots' (*Two Hunters,* 2007)
6. Ray Brassier, *Nihil Unbound. Enlightenment and Extinction,* London: Palgrave Macmillan, 2007, 43-4. In context, Brassier is discussing Caillois' description of the 'thanatropic mimicry ... whereby the organism is driven to disintegrate into the organic', 43. Organisms seek to dissolve themselves into 'de-individuated space' – a trope we find repeated in Cascadian black metal.
7. As suggested in the description used by Nicola Masciandaro on the Black Metal Theory website: 'Not black metal. Not theory. Not not black metal. Not not theory. Black metal theory. Theoretical blackening of metal. Metallic blackening of theory. Mutual blackening. Nigredo in the intoxological crucible of symposia.' http://blackmetaltheory.blogspo t.com/
8. Mark C. Taylor, *About Religion. Economies of Faith in Virtual Culture,* Chicago: University of Chicago Press, 1999, 122ff.
9. Jacques Derrida *Acts of Religion,* London: Routledge, 2002, 83.

10. Jean Baudrillard, *America,* London: Verso, 1988,7.
11. Ibid., 7.
12. Ibid., 99.
13. Ibid., 7.
14. Ibid., 3. The specific reference is to the region around the Grand Canyon.
15. Ibid., 71.
16. 'Instead of the coercion of work—and how much of the present could continue without precisely that coercion? — an existence without constraints is an immediate, central objective. Unfettered pleasure, creative endeavor along the lines of Fourier: according to the passions of the individual and in a context of complete equality.' John Zerzan, 'On the Transition' http://www.primitivism.com/transition.htm
17. Skagos, 'Smoldering Embers' (*Skagos/Panopticon* split, 2010)
18. Skagos, 'Smoldering Embers'. On Schelling, see Iain Hamilton Grant, *Philosophies of Nature After Schelling* (London: Continuum, 2006, 67.
19. Esther Leslie, 'Shudder – Shutter – Shatter', *Animate Projects,* 2009, http://www.animateprojects.org/writing/es say_archive/e_leslie_2
20. Mary Shelley, *Frankenstein,* London: Penguin, 2003, 58.
21. Ibid., 59.
22. Mania, 'Ideas', *Eternal Warfare* http://www.eternalwar fare.org/?page=ideas
23. Leslie, 'Shudder-Shutter-Shatter'
24. John Zerzan, 'Language: Origin and Meaning' http:/ /www.primitivism.com/language.htm; 'Time and its Discontents' http://www.primitivism.com/time.htm; 'Running on Emptiness' http://www.primitivism.com/emp tiness.htm
25. F. W. J. Schelling, *First Outline of a System of the Philosophy of Nature,* Albany: SUNY press, 2004, 128.
26. Dominic Fox, *Cold World. The Aesthetics of Dejection and the*

Politics of Militant Dysphoria, Winchester: Zero Books, 2009, 56.

27. Kierkegaard, *Three Discourses*, p. 84. Cf. Steven Shakespeare, 'Books About Nothing. Kierkegaard's Liberating Rhetoric' in George Pattison and Steven Shakespeare (eds), *Kierkegaard: The Self in Society*, London: Macmillan, 1993, 97-111.

Black Metal in the White Tower: Metal's Formless Presence in Contemporary Art

Amelia Ishmael

Black metal is a language of contemporary visual art.[1] Since its inception in the late 1980s as an extreme and experimental underground metal subculture in Norway, the black metal genre has developed sophisticated ideologies and discursive systems of communication effected both sonically and visually. The language of black metal is often signified by rich archetypal symbologies, histories, and mythologies. It is accented by heaviness, dark mysticism, obscurity, and distortion. Within the past twenty years, significant recognition of metal's cultural impact has prompted publications, conferences, and exhibitions—yet black metal's presence in contemporary art has previously been inadequately explored.[2]

This essay focuses primarily on examining black metal's presence in photographic images, drawings, and sculptural installations by three American artists: Grant Willing, Terence Hannum, and Banks Violette. It argues for a black metal art history that may be used to articulate how the language of black metal is used by artists to construct meanings. Within each of the artworks I'll discuss, black metal exists as an essential subject matter; it elicits a spatial atmosphere, *stimmung*, or melancology constructed by establishing a specific perimeter where black metal is referred to, evoked, and experienced.[3] Its presence is signified by environmental, compositional, and architectural spaces that are formless, undefined, seemingly empty, or void—appropriate for black metal: a language frequently defined by its negation. The neologism 'melancology' joins together the concepts of 'black' and 'ecology,' and may be used to describe black metal's vital atmosphere, which was defined succinctly by *Terrorizer*'s former editor Jonathan Seltzer as an integral quality of black metal.[4] As a location within these artworks, black metal is experienced temporally, spatially, phenomenologically, nostalgically, and psychologically. Yet, because black metal's signifiers are steeped within the subculture's own underground histories and are communicated transmodally through sonic and visual means, a familiarity with its iconographies, sounds, and ideology is essential to the viewer's recognition of black metal's presence within.

The attribution of a black metal language in contemporary art raises at least three initial problems. The first issue comes from dissidents of subcultural and popular culture studies: many fans and musicians find academic study of their culture inappropriate and, simultaneously, some institutions are sceptical of the value of subcultures.[5] Secondly, metal has long been a music genre associated with the working class and belonging neither to a 'high' nor popular culture: thus, without mass distribution, much of black metal's history is unpublished or based on rumours and bootlegged copies—troubling concepts of authority, fact, and authorship.[6] Finally, black metal's influence within these artworks takes place primarily within the artists' private art studio, a transitional site typically separated from finished artistic productions. All three of these problems are rooted in historically constructed scholarly and social boundaries that enforce misassumptions. By practicing an expanded art historical methodology, my research navigates between the academic library, the concert venue, and the artist's studio; my methodology is rooted in art history, yet accented by journalism, visual culture studies, and musicology.

Grant Willing, Terence Hannum, and Banks Violette each express a fluency in both the languages of art history and black metal. As these artists refer to the previously established visual and sonic systems belonging to black metal, they also force reassessments of the melancology of black metal by exposing its presence within unexpected locations: Willing finds black metal within the mountainous landscapes of the American West, Hannum finds black metal within transformed religious cathedrals and concert venues, and Violette creates a location for black metal within the white walls of the contemporary art gallery or museum. Their works are not mere surrogates manifested in response to the lack of Norwegian geography in America, but are re-evaluations of the language of black metal itself, instigating the viewer's relationship to concepts they find in black metal such as the sublime, transcendence, and the void.

Relocating black metal to the American West

Grant Willing's *Svart Metall* (2008-2010) is a series of fifteen photographic prints, self-published in the format of a limited-edition Metal fanzine.[7] It features images gleaned from black metal albums alongside original landscapes and still lives shot primarily throughout the American West. The format of *Svart Metall* refers to the prominent international black metal zine culture—including *Slayer Magazine* of Norway (1985-2010), *Mortician Magazine* of Holland (1991-1994), and *Descent Magazine* of North America (1994-1999)—that transported the subculture across the globe. It borrows the aesthetic, iconography, and modes of black metal's ephemeral culture and rediscovers them within the American landscape, which becomes redefined through *Svart Metall* as a location where the *stimmung* of black metal may be found.

are re-photographed directly from black metal album covers and inserts and refer to iconic aspects of the black metal genre. The photographs feature, respectively, a cloaked figure trudging through a mountainous snowstorm, and a historical stave church. The troll-like figure in 'Untitled (Mannduad)', holding a rake and obscured by a thick cloak, makes reappearances on black metal albums, such as Burzum's *Svart Dawn* (1993). His character affirms the Norwegian isolated rural countryside, natural mysticism and mythology, and desolate ecological mood exemplified by black metal bands such as Darkthrone, Mayhem, and Burzum. The image of the stave church in 'Untitled (Fortun)' is a reoccurring motif in black metal as well. These heritage landmarks incorporate unique wooden facades mixing Christian and Norse iconography, simultaneously symbolizing both Norwegian nationalism and the invasion of Norse culture. The stave church earned a unique stature on June 6, 1992 when, amongst a series of arson crimes targeting similar sites, the twelfth-century Fantoft stave church was burned to the ground.[8] Though no one was convicted, it is commonly believed that the culprit was affiliated with the black metal subculture. Since the burning of Fantoft, stave churches—particularly this site, before and after it was reduced to a charred skeleton—have frequently reappeared in places such as the album cover of Burzum's *Aske* (1992) and in Banks Violette's 2004 installation in the Whitney Museum of American Art.

Though these images are sourced directly from black metal ephemeral materials, they are not a documentation of black metal but rather an investigation of the underlying qualities that initially inspired the use of blizzard-worn figures or stave churches as a visual means to communicate black metal. The reproduced images undergo new syntactical processes through Willing's re-cropping and re-printing and visual noise or texture is introduced and amplified by digital and analogue feedback, echoing the lo-fi production techniques used within black metal. As the images move further away from their indexical source, they tease out concepts related to origins, making an affinity to the integral mythic speech taking place through the ever-changing retelling of black metal's history.

Referential images such as these two are integral to the series, yet the majority of *Svart Metall* presents Willing's unique photographs. As the opening image for *Svart Metall*, 'Untitled (Moon)' sets the timbre for the entire publication.

This photograph is completely pitch-black except for a full gleaming moon rising above a field of trees. Here, a ray of moonlight in the centre foreground seems to sweep briskly over a brief clearing in a dark wood before fading back to black along the photograph's edges. This black area is formless, but it is not empty. Unlike an unexposed negative, it is a developed space seething with the unknown. The illuminated layers of leaves and branches create a dense rhythmic texture of highly detailed surfaces, yet due to the image's extremely high contrast the depth of this foliage is indistinguishable and dizzying. This visual texture echoes the sonic texture of a black metal composition; the guitars and drums are frequently densely layered, indistinguishable notes play on top of each other, creating an audible depth. The photograph 'Untitled (Moon)' provides a glimpse of illuminating comfort, amplifying the threatening wilderness hiding beyond what cannot be seen. Similarly, black metal music is often disharmonious, eerie, sounding untuned or like the victim of screeching amplifier feedback. The vocals are witchy, foreign, like some creature from this wood. In this landscape, as within a black metal soundscape, active listening promotes an acute awareness of senses and anticipation for unpredictable disruptions within ambiguous surroundings. By immersing the viewer within this environment Willing's evocation of black metal approaches Edmund Burke's description of the Sublime. There is a terrific pleasure in confronting this scene and immersing oneself within an obscure surrounding. As Burke describes, 'to make any thing very terrible, obscurity seems in general to be necessary. When we know the full extent of any danger, when we can accustom our eyes to it, a great deal of this apprehension vanishes.'[9] The senses become elevated to compensate for what cannot be seen; indefinable sounds disrupt silence; the possibility of danger heightens perception, heightens pleasure.

The chorus, that is so common in classic rock, is rejected in many black metal songs in favour of a symphonic quality of alteration that forces the listener to constantly renegotiate their experience. Riffs repeat, but transform over the length of a track—which commonly reigns closer to ten minutes than the three minutes of pop music, long enough to build a dense and complex sonic landscape. The double bass drum frequently sounds like a racing heartbeat or blood rushing through my body. This experience of listening is an experience of a musical mood that resonates with 'Untitled (Moon).'

Unlike the sourced photographs, images like 'Untitled (Moon)' do not represent Norway; these images are an American nationalization and localization of the *stimmung* that black metal historically found within the Norwegian landscape. Willing's images testify that the language of black metal transcends the authoritative concept of a True Norwegian black metal (TNBM); his black metal is nomadic, exportable, transferable. It is the visual manifestation of United States black metal (USBM), a genre that describes—quite simply and without any other qualifiers—any black metal coming out of the US.[10]

Willing's images seem steeped in a similar fascination with individualism, the occult, serious play between the boundaries of life and death, and a relationship to the danger and violence prevalent throughout black metal.[11] But rather than Norse mythology, the accent that he brings to *Svart Metall* appears informed by the nineteenth-century paintings made by artists of the American West.

This tendency echoes a phenomenon in contemporary American black metal bands. Rather than borrow Norwegian history and culture, and attempt to transpose TNBM's Scandinavian references to pre-Christian culture, Atavism, and Vikings, American black metal artists of the twenty first century are uncovering their own identities within America's pre-

Western culture. The musicians themselves have talked about these interests with the New York-based music critic Brandon Stosuy, who is currently developing a book on USBM. The musician Wrnlrd from Virginia described that his music explores:

> ...this idea of connecting to the past and the spirits of one's ancestors. Viking metal, war themes. In the U.S. I think it's the idea of the individual that resonates more powerfully, the strong individual with his own agenda: The pioneer, the entrepreneur, the lone gunman.[12]

Willing's *Svart Metall* series are an intentional reflection on original TNBM images, yet they also tap into the rich history found within his own locality. I am proposing that concepts of the Viking may be compared to that of the Indian or pioneer; that the Norwegian mountains could relate to the Rocky (or even further east, the Appalachian) Mountains; Atavism could share qualities found in Transcendentalism. To be sure, these comparisons are not an attempt to imperialistically replace Norwegian cultural identity, but to suggest that qualities of American culture can be used to explore an evolving language of black metal that goes beyond forms. There is an established history in America for a black metal *stimmung*. It can be found in nineteenth century paintings by social outsiders such as John Quidor (1801-1881) and Albert Pinkham Ryder (1847-1916) which display a similar attraction to the terrific dangers within America; the natural mysticism found within the sublime landscapes of dessert, mountain, forest, or sea; and the horrors of America's own nationalist history. Encroaching on contemplations of the individual's experience in the Modern age, Quidor and Ryder's paintings also express a dissonance to organized religion and capitalism, and a romanticism of the wilderness over urban environment, ideologies prevalent within black metal.[13] Visually, these nineteenth century American paintings describe 'a dark style, characterized by gloomy tonalities, deep shadows and glaring highlights, grotesque figures, and claustrophobic or chaotic spaces' and are layered with symbols of the artists' personal difficulty and inner turmoil felt as they struggle with concepts of individualism and freedom within America.[14] This comparison exposes the notion that black metal has revitalized a new spirituality among American artists. Yet, this is not the type of communal teenage identity of the 1970s that Dan Graham explored in his film *Rock My Religion*, but rather an individualist pang to thrust oneself against and transition through limitations and obstructions, to use the American landscape as a means to challenge and self-actualize.[15] Constantly lost in the dark wilderness, occasionally glimpsing the sun or moon, looking for passage, confronted by obstacles at every turn, Willing's images convey the spiritual and existential frenzy black metal communicates sonically.

Exploring transcendence at a black metal concert

The *Recent Drawing* series (2010) by Terence Hannum demonstrates how black metal has evolved from its previous location within a geographical landscape to a melancologic soundscape individually experienced by audience members of the black metal concert.[16] Metaphorically immersing the viewer, the site of many of Hannum's drawings from this series is a synthesis of the cathedral and concert venues: a metaphysical blending referencing the spiritual and ritualistic events shared by both music and religion.[17] A black metal context is established for this series through Hannum's use of white and grey-toned gouache paint on black paper—a high contrast, lo-fi aesthetic that echoes black metal album covers and zines. Hannum's exploration of a formless black metal *stimmung* is discernable within the undefined areas surrounding three iconographic signifiers: the vast architectural area of a cathedral's interior, the towers of amplifiers framing a performing space, and a lone head-banging audience member who is immersed in the concert experience.

In Hannum's drawing 'Descension', an architectural location for Metal is defined by brilliantly backlit stained glass cathedral windows located in the top third of the drawing, high above a stack of amplifiers.

Designed to resonate sound, the cavernous space of the cathedral reinforces the sonic experience where traditionally a sermon or choral performance would fill the air to create a sensorial experience for practitioners as they visually reflect on mediating religious iconography. Here, the Gothic architecture restates the sustaining power of the amplified electric instruments. Natural human scale and acoustics are abandoned in a transcending surge as the heightened volume resonates throughout the chambers.[18] This architectural scene, with its overarching capacity to amplify sound, establishes a ground or framework for the sonic atmosphere Hannum implies. It stands in place of the concert stage setting Metal bands perform in today, and indicates a boundary for a soundscape to occur within.

The possibility for an *extreme* volume beyond the natural acoustic resonance of the cathedral's architecture is indicated in Hannum's drawings, through the addition of, not just one, but *stacks* of electronic amplifiers spanning the entire lower border of the drawing. Giving the amplifier an iconic stature that continues throughout this series, 'Descension' appears to include a homage to this technology of the late twentieth century which introduced a sheer volume of sound previously impossible.[19] Yet this is not a memoriam to defunct vintage amplifiers. The active electrified vibrations of air are extremely present. Attempts to visually represent the sensation of sonic phenomena moving through amplifiers are a difficult accomplishment. As anyone who has been to a loud metal concert can attest, Hannum's compositional technique of providing an architectural boundary in 'Descension' could not autonomously frame sound. The sound leaking outside of the architecture of the music venue is often just as loud as inside; the venue indicates the location of sound, but fails to contain it. It would seem then that the only way to visually document its literal presence would be to show its effect on other objects.

A physical and sonic encounter with black metal is implied in Hannum's 'Black Diadum' by a figure standing in front of two towering rows of amplifiers receding along a single-point perspective.

Seen only from the back of the head, her hair is messed in a head-banging nod to the speakers. In the distance where the two rows of amplifiers might meet there are no musicians mediating between the amps and the single audience member. In fact, the details between the individual and the technology in both 'Black Diadum' and 'Descension' appear to sink into the material of the pitch-black paper itself. It is formless: it looks like empty space. Yet here, exemplified by the texture within the ground of the paper substrate, Hannum allows the physicality of the media to resonate throughout the drawing, suggesting the artwork itself as a space charged with intense sonic activity. We cannot *see* the sound, but Hannum evokes its presence through his references to specific iconography and concepts: the aesthetic references to black metal's ephemeral materials, the amplifiers, and the subject's wildly animated hair.[20]

Hannum's inclusion of the individual's experience does not only function to give an audience to the sonic activity. To further attune the drawings' viewers to their own presence in front of this scene Hannum frequently shifts vantage points: in 'Descension' the viewer shares a place in the presence of this lone figure, yet in 'Profane Sepulcher' Hannum offers the viewer a position as the solitary audience to black metal.

Here, rather than excluding the viewer from a private ritual, Hannum invites the viewer to activate her own subjective experience in relation to black metal. Unlike in 'Descension' which is lit by the stained glass window casting light down from above, the light source in 'Profane Sepulcher' is front-lit, as though emanating from the viewer herself.

Freed from implied architectural boundaries, the depth of the site described in 'Profane Sepulcher' is unknowable: the pitch-black space is seemingly infinite in all directions. Candles stagger in succession throughout the composition. One long, narrow, white, vertical candle comes to the eye, a second immediately succeeds and enforces the impression of the first—its slight alteration in height creates a rhythm, like notes on a music staff, implying an expansion beyond the paper's edges. Simultaneously, the wall of amplifiers is like a towering wave building over the viewer. Their potential loudness is thunderous and overpowering; like a terrific storm it awakens me.[21] Fully immersed in noise I am no longer able to process my experience. I am in awe. Through art history, one other image comes to mind that fills me with a relatable response: Caspar David Friedrich's 'The Wanderer Above a Sea of Mist' (1818).[22] As Kant's writings on aesthetic reception describe, this painting does not represent the sublime, but rather the Wanderer's sensitivity and apperception of the sublime.[23] 'The Wanderer above a Sea of Mist' confronts the viewer with their own apperception. Standing on this cliff one inhales the blurred boundaries of the tumultuous fog as it streams across the mountains, sky, and rocks. The Wanderer illustrates a forced admission of an inability to know, a threshold of comprehension that has no other way out than through transcendence. This solitary journey taken by Friedrich's Wanderer is a courageous expression of individuality and self-reflection also beckoning within Hannum's 'Profane Sepulcher.'

Throughout *Recent Drawings,* Hannum's emphasis of the subject and the individual's active experience allows him to overcome the nihilism typically associated with metal, in favor of the Transcendental. The formless spaces, or voids, Hannum depicts are not empty or silent, they are potential, active, creative spaces seething with metal. The possibility of transcendence through black metal is similarly explored in Hunter Hunt-Hendrix's manifesto 'Transcendental Black Metal.'[24]

'Transcendental Black Metal' is an exploration of black metal's sonic intensities that relates to concepts of self-overcoming expressed by the philosophers Burke and Georges Bataille, and the composer Glenn Branca. Hunt-Hendrix's description of the first stage of encountering black metal is phenomenological experience marked by the fortification of boundaries or rules: 'a certain muscular clenching, a constriction of the jaws, fists, arms and chest.'[25] This exercise of tightening is one of terror, and is present in Burke's description of how the sublime is produced, marking 'an exertion of the contracting power of the muscles' resembling pain.[26] Actual violence is necessarily foregone in this experience; rather, this stage is defined by a will to confront limitations. This exercise is 'capable of producing delight; not pleasure, but a sort of delightful horror, a sort of tranquility tinged with terror; which as it belongs to self-preservation is one of the strongest of all passions. Its object is the sublime.'[27]

As Hannum's *Recent Drawings* affirm, this sublimation is achieved in part through the mere power of volume.[28] This concept is similarly communicated through Branca's album *Ascension* (1981), a forty-minute-long acoustic composition for guitars that immerses the listener within difficult layers of voluminous, seemingly impenetrable, walls of sound that must be temporally navigated to achieve a Bataillean transcendence by the act of listening *through* rather than listening *to* music. But just as *Ascension* does not end with a sonic assault, the experience of transcendental black metal does not end with the viewer transfixed—standing next to Freidrich's Wanderer, at the peak, staring out, into the abyss. This standing-still at the edge is an inactivity, a nihilistic pause, an atrophy 'It is a fissure, a crack, a lack of being. An insufficiency compared to the promised plentitude.' Transcendental black metal reacts to this delight of heights with a 'complementary dissatisfaction—as through no brutal breakdown can be quite brutal enough.'[29] The intensity of the experience ruptures the individual, 'we lose ourselves, we forget ourselves and communicate with an elusive beyond.'[30] Here the individual must enforce her own will and shatter through boundaries by way of 'sacrifice; an auto-destruction, a self-overcoming whereby the initial rules, having been fully digested and satisfied, are thereby mutilated.'[31] This is not a suicide, but a transformation, a sublimation of the sublime that is the means to insatiable creativity and experimentation. This undergoing overcomes the viewing of the emptiness spaces within Hannum's *Recent Drawings* as a sort of stagnancy, encouraging rather a creative evolution that requires 'a total expenditure of power' and 'fosters growth and increase of strength.'[32]

Sculpting black metal soundwaves

Encounters with the formless melancology of black metal are further explored in Banks Violette's untitled exhibition at the Whitney Museum of America Art in 2005, his performance/installation at Maureen Paley in London in 2006, and his installation at the Barbara Gladstone Gallery in New York City in 2010.[33] These sculptural installations convey the intense phenomenological experience of an individual being confronted with black metal. Rather than repositioning black metal within the Western landscape, or the concert venue, Violette initiates the art gallery's potential to be transformed into a location that can elicit a black metal experience. Violette's untitled exhibitions in 2005, 2006, and 2010 demonstrate key shifts in his exploration of black metal as his art moves further from illustrating specific events within the genre's historical subculture and towards interacting with the language of black metal behind, under, and beyond its established references.

Before delving into Violette's installations, it is important to note that since 2002 his artwork has existed alongside a complicated lineage of critical reception, coming from both the fine arts community and the black metal subculture. This issue is largely due to codal incompetences and interferences: when black metal is incorporated as an integral aspect of the artwork, many gallery visitors and art critics seem to find Violette's messages largely indecipherable. Instead of gleaning meaning from the artworks, interpretations are faultily redirected to emphasize his biography, the sensationalist aspects of black metal's paramusical history, or Violette's art historical influences alone.[34] Simultaneously, Violette has ruffled the feathers of many participants in the black metal community by perceivably offering vital aspects of the underground subculture as attractive and commodifiable by avant-garde culture.

These misreadings are part of a larger historically contingent interference occurring within contemporary art history's reception of artworks that incorporate sonic and visual influences—it is as if the interdisciplinary artworks of Steven Parrino, Robert Rauschenberg, and Dan Graham in the late twentieth century have been victim to a selective art historical amnesia. As this essay asserts, metal's influence within contemporary art is not an occurrence in the peripheries of contemporary art. Rather than continuing to elude engagement with interdisciplinary artworks, this observation of Violette's fluency in art history *and* black metal affirms the need for a more interdisciplinary art history that recognizes how artists like Violette creatively maneuver to bring these two spheres together. Like Parrino, Violette has been upfront about his musical influences, stating in an interview for *i-D* magazine, 'my relationship with metal far, far precedes any relationship with the art world.'[35] By considering the installations themselves as the essential source of interpretation, and introducing an articulation of Violette's use of the language of black metal, this essay works towards revising Violette's critical reception.

Banks Violette's 2005 installation at the Whitney Museum of American Art presented a stark 12-foot-tall architectural framework cast out of salt, which stood in the centre of a black painted room atop a glossy black stage.

This skeletal structure was a direct reference to both the Fantoft stave church's burning in 1992 and the photographic representation of its charred ruins featured on the cover of Burzum's 1992 album *Aske*.[36] Violette's invocation of a stage setting—rather than an art pedestal—directly referenced the performance space of black metal concert backdrops, a sonic reference further emphasized by an audible musical score commissioned from Thorns Ltd.[37] The melancology of this installation was exemplified by the salt glistening across the sculpture's surface, visually echoing the frozen ecological conditions of Scandinavian winters, and the ninety-minute-long minimalist-drone soundtrack, a sonic and tactile anaphone which Violette described as 'an attempt to give snow sound' and 'as a kind of landscape painting in sound that evokes the cold, harsh Norwegian terrain.'[38]

This installation's relationship to space and time creates a phenomenological location that must be navigated and actively experienced by viewers for comprehension. Like the Robert Morris's installation 'Untitled L-Beams' (1965-7) or LaMonte Young and Marian Zazeela's 'Dream House' (1979), the viewer's presence is entangled in the artwork: she is both integral to the actualization of the installation, and yet the installation introduces a situation that is wholly independent of her.[39] Here, Violette creates a potential mediating space between reality and fantasy, between the subjective and anti-subjective, between the location of black metal within the Norwegian geography and its situation within the art gallery.

'Untitled' (2005)'s direct incorporation of literal references to black metal's historical events and musicians seemed to present viewers with a single meaning accompanied by a key—provided by gallery texts—to be decoded.[40] This tendency was overcome in his 2006 and 2010 installations. In this departure, Violette allowed his artworks the freedom to suggest new complexities, which the viewer could engage and create various meanings from.

Violette's 2006 exhibition at the Maureen Paley gallery was initiated with an hour-long performance by the drone metal band Sunn O))) which took place on the ground floor of the gallery during opening night.[41] As though partaking in an ancient ritual, musicians Stephen O'Malley and Greg Anderson were cloaked in black-hooded robes and surrounded by a dense fog of dry ice. Though Gallery visitors could only imagine these details because the space was veiled with a white sheet, and entry was prohibited until after the performance. Sunn O))) has built their reputation and nomenclature upon their devotion to the technology of their Sunn O))) brand amps which they activate in a low-tempo, distorted, voluminous drone with guitar and bass. To attend a Sunn O))) performance is to experience a deep, pressure-filled amplifier massage penetrating your entire body as the band builds a dark, atmospheric, resonating sonic landscape felt long before and after it is heard. Adding to Sunn O)))'s performance at Maureen Paley was a vocal performance by Mayhem's Attila Csihar, conducted entirely from within a sealed coffin made by Violette out of salt and resin. When the concert ended the musicians exited unseen and viewers were finally admitted, like forensics, to witness the afterbirth.

On the ground floor, where the performance occurred moments before, stood the empty set an installation of eight of Violette's short glossy black stages—now hosting evidential footprints—and four tall backdrop panels.

In front of the stage, the busted coffin Attila performed within lay in the centre of a black epoxy circle on the floor.[42] In the upper gallery the musician's guitars, keyboards, and towering amplifiers were transformed into pallid salt and resin casts that, abandoned and installed on short stage platforms that mimicked and reversed the black epoxy in the gallery directly below.

In front of the salt stages, above a circle of white salt, lay the black epoxy coffin: smashed to bits.

Rather than offering spectators a performance, Violette's exhibition provided only its residues or traces. It presented the location of a black metal performance, after the event. For the next month visitors to the gallery seemed to take the role of audience members who, long after the last band has played, hover in the concert venue holding on to their recent experiences as if suspended in post-concert awe. Violette's 2006 installation was an exhibition of an empty stage and musical equipment: once primed for use, once activated but now exhausted, abandoned and turned to salt.

Two years later, in an interview with Christopher Bollen, Violette spoke to his musical influence in a mode that prefigured a shift in his work. Citing his experience working with O'Malley he implored, 'how do you take a discrete object that is placed pretty much on a pedestal and make it radiate out into the environment? We fill it up with the sound equivalent of the sculpture.'[43] Violette seems to be asking *How can sculpture make the experience of sound?* prodding an intermedia question of translation that has occurred throughout modern art. A self-proclaimed sculptor of sound waves, Michael Brewster writes:

> Sound has a physical size, an actual dimensions in feet or meters, as well as density, vibrancy, rhythms and textures. Walking through it in its resonant state provides an experience similar to perusing a landscape but from the inside, with all of your body instead of from the outside with just your eyes. It shows us the *near field*. Like a solid it has volumes, edges, planes, fullnesses, flatnesses, roundnesses, and hollows: the works. It comes *fully equipped* to elaborate our experience sculpturally.[44]

This statement further explores the relationship that sound has to sculpture, it stresses that sound is experienced in the round, prompting an 'expanded sculptural experience.'

By inquiring into the potential to manifest sound sculpturally, Banks Violette effectively manifested the *stimmung* of black metal in an installation at the Barbara Gladstone Gallery in 2010.

This achievement was accomplished in spite of the art criticism surrounding the exhibition and the gallery's checklist, which declared that the inclusion of four independent art objects. Here, the ominous florescent tube chandelier 'throne' (2010) nearly touched the floor, connected to the ceiling by a thick metal chain. Wires from the illuminating tubes string across the cement into a large music gear case. Nearby, are two large sculptures, 'blackouts/blackholes (and all the things inbetween)/ for DS Snow' (2009-2010)—frequently referred to by critics as 'screens.'

Their flat, black, epoxy painted, fiberglass surfaces are highly reflective, allowing the florescent light radiating from 'throne' to 'project' onto them. Recalling a concert stage set, the screens are installed on metal scaffolding and stabilized with black sandbags. Installed around the gallery's perimeter, the sculptures leave a large, open void in the center of the gallery where the set design suggests a stage would have been. At first, I recall what Sonnenborn described in her profile of one of Violette's earlier installations, 'We are left wanting [...] for the sculptures raise expectations of sound, movement, fury, fame, only to render such prospects void by the absence of any.'[45] The space is so charged with potential; it seems to be anxiously yearning for some hint of extreme metal, but the only audible sounds are the receptionist on the phone and the faint sound of traffic outside. It is a standardly sanitized, silent, white-walled, Chelsea gallery space. The din of its attempt to be unobtrusive is annoying.

Surely Violette had intentionally chosen not to include sound. Yet why would he do this? The review by Linda Yablonsky on the *New York Times* blog described the crumpled surfaces of the 'screens' as referencing 'the remains of the stage at a rock show disrupted by stampeding fans. Or the walls of a nightclub after a bombing.'[46] Both descriptions seemed to beg my desire for sound here. I find myself continually drawn to the empty space in the gallery's center, which each sculptural unit seems to face and direct as their point-of-focus. Here allowing my relationship to black metal to inform this experience—in the same way that I habitually exercise my knowledge of visual art to inform any other art experience, I am able to recognize how Violette created my desire for sound. In this open space in the center of the gallery the sound quality does not have to be literally some sort of black metal soundtrack piping from hidden speakers in the gallery walls. Instead, what Violette evokes is the *stimmung*, the potential for sound. Like the pitch-black wilderness of Willing's photographs or the ground of Hannum's paintings, black metal is present. It is signified by the attractive glossy black material covering the 'screens' and the bright glaring glows of the florescent lights which resemble the type of lo-fi grainy, high contrast Black metal photos evidently inspiring Violette's work. Rather than a display of four independent sculptures, Violette's 2010 exhibition was one immersive art installation.

These screens construct a particular parameter—a location where a metal soundscape is referred to, evoked, and experienced. To bring back Seltzer's quote from the introduction of this essay: 'the most important thing to black metal is the atmosphere. It has a very, very potent atmosphere. And that is the first thing that defined black metal when it came out.'[47] And it still is. Indeed it is the atmosphere that Violette's 2010 installation evoked and allowed to swell from the visual works. The ecology of sound that established a space for metal to exist. This prominent 'emptiness' hovered in the center of the space—represented sonically by the silence of the gallery and, in Violette's case, physically by the denotation of a formless space in the center of the installation. Overpowering the white walls of the Barbara Gladstone, Violette's 2010 installation reimagines the contemporary art gallery as a site for black metal to occur. Black metal in the white cube. The gallery does not contain black metal, but Violette evokes it—like Willing's photographs, like Hannum's paintings—the mood of black metal is lured from the ether and collected within contemporary art.

Conclusion: Open the Gates

In its third wave, the language of black metal is completely untethered. It is no longer exclusively a music genre or a subculture. It is no longer temporally or spatially contained within the perimeters of Norway, the mountains or woods, the concert venue, or even an artwork, black metal is a formless language that may be conjured across disciplines, modals, visual and musical media. It is locatable, yet any attempts to define it by location will fail. It displaces itself as soon as the concert floodlights switch on, thickening in the darkness. It is as the lightening which gives 'a dense and black intensity to the night it denies:'[48] *Not here!* It cries. *Not that!* The lightening flashes, and is gone, and the pitch-black night sky rejoices; primordial order, status quo. In the methodology of black metal then, in imagining a black metal art history, it has been integral to define the sonic and visual language of black metal by its absence, by its formlessness, its crevices, and its voids.

By exploring black metal's presence in the artworks of Grant Willing, Terence Hannum, and Banks Violette this essay introduces black metal's existence as a language used by contemporary artists. It analyzes the pitch-black wilderness in Willing's 'Untitled (Moon),' the seemingly infinite atmosphere in Hannum's 'Profane Sepulcher,' and the disruptive void of Violette's untitled 2010 installation to recognize how each of these artists are exploring the *stimmung* of black metal in different ways, grasping spaces where nothing is, and manifesting them as seething with the loud frenzy of potential sonic activity. Reaching outside of black metal to twentieth and twenty-first century visual art and music, this essay also works towards contextualizing a black metal art history within a larger history of the syntheses between subculture, music, and art.

To conclude this essay I evoke and synthesize statements by black metal vocalist Gaahl and visual artist/musician Mike Kelley to proclaim—*Black metal art history needs warriors*.[49] To be sure, the American artists Grant Willing, Terence Hannum, and Banks Violette are not the only contemporary artists incorporating and evolving the language of black metal in their artworks, yet this essay marks the first significant step in, I hope, many that will emerge and contribute to a historical consideration of the meanings that artists create by incorporating the language of black metal within contemporary art. This feat is not only one to advance black metal theory but to recognize the depth of the cross-disciplinary cultural significance that the iconography, sound, and ideology of black metal has throughout our worlds.

Notes

1. In my definition of language I am referring to linguistic, mythic, and musical language. See Ferdinand de Saussure, *Writings in General Linguistics*, Oxford: Oxford University Press, 2006; Roland Barthes, *Mythologies*. trans. Annette Lavers, New York: Hill and Wang, 1972; and Philip Tagg, *Introductory Notes to the Semiotics of Music* (http://www.tagg.org/xpdfs/semiotug.pdf, July 1999).
2. For key writings on metal see Ian Christe, *Sound of the Beast: The Complete Headbanging History of Heavy Metal*, New York: HarperCollins Publishers, 2003; Gabriel Fischer and Daniel Ekeroth, *Swedish Death Metal*, Bazillion Points, 2008; Garry Sharpe-Young, *Metal: the Definitive Guide*, London: Jawbone Press, 2007; Karl Spracklen, Andy R. Brown, and Keith Kahn-Harris, eds. *Metal Studies: Cultural Research in the Heavy Metal Scene* Special Issue *Journal for Cultural Research* 13.3 (2011) Taylor & Francis Routledge; Robert Walser,

Running with the Devil, Middletown, Connecticut: Wesleyan University Press, 1993; and Deena Weinstein, *Heavy Metal: A Cultural Sociology*, New York: Lexington Books, 1991. For key works on black metal specifically see Aaron Aites and Audrey Ewell, *Until the Light Takes Us* (DVD, n.p., 2008); Gabriel Fischer, *Only Death Is Real: An Illustrated History of Hellhammer and Early Celtic Frost 1981-1985* Bazillion Points, 2010; Nicola Masciandaro, ed. *Hideous Gnosis: Black Metal Theory Symposium 1* CreateSpace, 2010; Michael Moynihan and Didrik Søderlind, *Lords of Chaos*, Los Angeles: Feral House, 2003; Brandon Stosuy, 'A Blaze in the North American Sky,' *The Believer* 6.6 (July/August 2008), 7-22.

3. The German word *Stimmung* is the noun formed from the verb *stimmen*, 'to harmonize,' and related to the word *stimme*, 'voice.' The concept of *stimmung* comprises of a mode of experience/perception, an atmospheric dimension and a communicative efficacy, a mood, and an attunement. It is used as both a concept or aesthetic. Friedrich Nietzsche describes the *stimmung* as a formlessness that elicits an artistic concept or creation when discussing Schiller's poetic process. Martin Heidegger describes the *stimmung* as a mood or atmosphere of 'being in the world,' which both a priori and in public has several meanings, including 'tuning' and 'mood.' See Nietzsche, *The Birth of Tragedy*, Random House, 1967, 49; and Heidegger, *Being and Time* Harper and Row Publishers, 1962, 175. I am using *stimmung* here to propose a particular mood that is a where the potential for black metal expressions may be found.
4. Selzer, former editor of the British Extreme Metal magazine *Terrorizer*, stated 'the most important thing to Black Metal is the atmosphere. It has a very, very potent atmosphere. And that is the first thing that defined Black Metal when it came out.' Jonathan Seltzer, *Murder Music*, directed by Malcolm Dome and David Kenny (Rockworld.TV, 2007) http://

www.youtube.com/watch?v=VhNUj-o_pXE&feature =player_embedded#!

5. Scott Wilson, 'Pop Journalism and the Passion for ignorance' in *Hideous Gnosis*, 247-250; and 'blog comments reprinted from the *Black Metal Theory* website' in *Hideous Gnosis*, 267-275.
6. Refer to 'Home of Metal' the 4-day conference, taking place September 1-4, 2011 in the birthplace of Metal: the industrial city of Birmingham, U.K., http://www.homeofmetal.com
7. 'Svart Metall' takes its name from the Norwegian for 'Black Metal.' Grant Willing was born in Castle Rock, Colorado in 1987. He received his BFA in 2009 from the Photography department at Parsons the New School for Design in NY. *Svart Metall* has been exhibited at Foam Fotografiemuseum in Amsterdam (2011), Capricious Gallery, in New York (2011), Best of the NY Art Book Fair at PS1 MoMA at Long Island City (2010), and the Photographer's Gallery in London (2010).
8. According to Norway's *Aftenposten* newspaper, 37 fires occurred between 1992 and 1994, as cited in Moynihan, *Lords of Chaos*, 106.
9. Edmund Burke, *A Philosophical Enquiry into the Origins of our Ideas of the Sublime and Beautiful*, edited by Adam Phillips, Oxford University Press, 1990, 54.
10. Stosuy, 'A Blaze in the North American Sky,' 7-22.
11. Grant Willing, interview with author, Feb. 7, 2011.
12. Brandon Stousy, 'Meaningful Leaning Mess' in *Hideous Gnosis*, 152.
13. See Jason Forster, *Commodified Evil's Wayward Children: Black Metal and Death Metal as Purveyors of an Alternative Form of Modern Escapism* (Dissertation, University of Canterbury, 2006) http://ir.canterbury.ac.nz/bitstream/10092/966/1/essay_fulltext.pdf and Keith Kahn-Harris, *The 'Failure' of Youth Culture: Reflexivity, Music, and Politics in the Black Metal Scene*

(Dissertation, Goldsmiths, 2001) http://SOC-Kahn-Harris2004a.pdf

14. Sarah Burns, *Painting the Dark Side; Art and the Gothic Imagination in Nineteenth Century America* (University of California Press, 2004), xix.
15. Dan Graham, *Rock My Religion*, video (Electronic Arts Intermix, 1984). For the script and text for *Rock My Religion* see Dan Graham, *Rock My Religion: Writings and Projects 1965-1990* (Cambridge, Mass: MIT Press, 1994), 91-125.
16. Terence Hannum was born in 1979 in Somers Point, New Jersey. He earned a BA in Studio Art, Religion, and Philosophy from Florida Southern College in 2001, and an MFA from the School of the Art Institute of Chicago in 2004. Hannum has shown in solo exhibitions at Depaw University, Indiana; PeregrineProgram and Gallery 400, Chicago, IL; Invisible NYC, NYC; Light & Sie, Dallas. His band Locrian was formed in 2005, and consists of Hannum, Andrè Foisy, and Stephen Hess.
17. Shannon Race, 'From Seminary to Slayer,' *fNews magazine*, November 11, 2010. http://fnewsmagazine.com/wp/2010/11/from-seminary-to-slayer/
18. Robert Bork, 'Stairways to Heaven: Gothic Architecture, Heavy Metal, and the Aesthetics of Transcendence,' *Medieval Academy of America*, Sept. 27, 2010. http://www.medievalacademy.org/medacnews/news_bork.html Bork and Hannum's exploration of a cathedral's interior architecture as a site for extreme metal volume is echoed in Robert Longo's cover art for Glenn Branca's *The Ascension: The Sequel*, Systems Neutralizers, 2010.
19. These painted representations of amplifiers are composites sourced from photographic images found in vintage amp catalogues such as *Acoustic*.
20. The physicality of the ground of the paper in *Recent* Drawings reminds me of Adorno's description of the 'hear-

stripe' that exists under and behind any recorded sound. The 'hear-stripe' is that minute intervention of background noise or hiss that hi-fi production struggles to absolve. Though barely audible its presence is a constant reminder, that listeners are barely conscious of, that this is not 'real.' See Theodor Adorno, 'The Radio Symphony' in *Essays on Music,* translated by Susan H. Gillespie, edited by Richard Leppert, University of California Press, 2002, 251-270. In black metal this lo-fi quality is used to affirm human intervention, in Hannum's *Recent Drawings* this tactile noise is an affirmation of sound.

21. Burke, 75.
22. The USBM band Wolves in the Throne Room attribute a song title to this painting in their album *Black Cascade* (2009).
23. Immanuel Kant, *Critique of Judgment,* translated by Werner S. Pluhar, Hackett Publishing, 1987.
24. Hunter Hunt-Hendrix, 'Transcendental Black Metal,' in *Hideous Gnosis,* 53-66. Hunt-Hendrix studied musical composition and philosophy in Columbia University's bachelor's degree program. He is the frontman of the band Liturgy, formed in 2008.
25. Hunter Hunt-Hendrix, 'Transcendental Black Metal' in *Hideous Gnosis,* 56. See also Liturgy's album *Aesthethica* (2011).
26. Burke, 121.
27. Ibid, 123.
28. See 'Power' in Paul Hegarty, *Noise/Music: A History*, London: Continuum, 2007, 117-130.
29. Hunt-Hendrix, 56.
30. Georges Batille, *Inner Experience,* Translated by Leslie Anne Boldt, NY: SUNY Press 1988, 11.
31. Hunt-Hendrix, 54.
32. Ibid, 60.
33. Banks Violette was born in Ithaca, NY in 1973. Violette went

to the School of Visual Arts, NY, where he earned his BFA in 1998, and his MFA at Columbia University in 2000. His work solo exhibitions, including those at Museum Dhont-Dhaenens in Deurle, Belgium; Kunsthalle Wein; the Modern of Art Museum of Forth Worth, Texas; Kunsthalle Bergen, Norway; and the Whitney Museum of American Art, New York.

34. Randy Kennedy, 'Master of the Dark Arts,' *The New York Times*, May 15, 2005.
35. Alex Needham, 'Art: Banks Violette,' *i-D* (the horror issue) 2.267 (June/July 2006), 189-190. See also Parrino, 'The Road to Electrophilia' in *The No Texts*, 31-34.
36. Taking its title from the Norwegian word for 'ashes,' Burzum's *Aske* is one of the most infamous covers from black metal history, referencing black metal musicians' alleged association with church burnings across Norway in the early 90s.
37. Thorns Ltd. is an experimental music project begun in 2003 and includes Finn Olav Holthe, Jon Wesseltoft, and Snorre Ruch—the infamous former guitarist from black metal band Mayhem.
38. Shamim M. Momin, *Banks Violette* (New York: Whitney Museum of Art, 2005): 20.
39. Susan Best, 'Minimalism, subjectivity, and aesthetics: rethinking the anti-aesthetic tradition in late-modern art,' *Journal of Visual Art Practice* 5.3 (2006), 127-142.
40. Katie Stone Sonnenborn, 'Displaced Histories: The Art of Banks Violette,' *The Brooklyn Rail*, September 2005: 10; Momin, *Banks Violette*.
41. Unable to attend this performance, I take my analysis from a Sunn O))) concert I attended in Chicago in July 2009, and accounts from Needham, 'Art: Banks Violette' *i-D*, Michael Wilson, 'Subcultural Capital.' *Artforum.com* June 6, 2006. http://artforum.com/diary/id=11138 ; Skye Sherwin, 'Banks

Violette.' *Art Review* 3 (September 2006): 134, Maxine Kospa, 'Elegant Bareness: Banks Violette's Death Metal' *Metropolis M* 5 (October/November 2006): 101-102.

42. The installation of the coffin in the gallery later became the album cover for Sunn O)))'s 2007 LP *Oracle* (Southern Lord, 2007).
43. Christopher Bollen, 'Banks Violette,' *Interview*. (December 2008), 160.
44. Michael Brewster, 'Where, There or Here?' in Brandon LaBelle, and Steve Roden, eds. *Site of Sound: of Architecture & the Ear*, Errant Bodies Press, 1999, 101.
45. Sonnenborn, 'Displaced Histories.'
46. Linda Yablonsky, 'Artifacts, Banks Violette,' *New York Times Blog*. February 17, 2010.
47. Dome, *Murder Music*.
48. Michel Foucault, *Politics, Philosophy, Culture,* edited by Lawrence D. Kritzman (London: Routledge, 1988), 326, as quoted by Scott Wilson, 'BAsileus philosoPHOrum METaloricum,' in Masciandaro, *Hideous Gnosis*, 36.
49. In Aites, *Until the Light Takes Us*, Gaahl, formerly of Gorgoroth, described, 'You do not play Black Metal if you are not a warrior.' The artist Mike Kelley stated in his introduction to the *Poetics Project* that the historicization of minor histories between music and art 'will be perceived as a war for control of meaning.' As quoted in Branden W. Joseph, *Beyond the Dream Syndicate: Tony Conrad and the Arts after Cage*, New York: Zone Books, 2008: n1.20.

In the Abyss of Lies
A Short Essay on Failure in Black Metal

Liviu Mantescu

I will not crush the world's corolla of wonders
and I will not kill
with reason
the mysteries I meet along my way
in flowers, eyes, lips, and graves.
The light of others
drowns the deep magic hidden
in the profound darkness.
I increase the world's enigma
with my light
much as the moon with its white beams
does not diminish but increases
the shimmering mystery of night –
I enrich the darkening horizon
with chills of the great secret.
All that is hard to know
becomes a greater riddle
under my very eyes
because I love alike
flowers, lips, eyes, and graves.
(Lucian Blaga, 1919; Translation by Andrei Codrescu)

Writing about black metal is *wrong*. And this is why I persist in doing it. Writing about black metal is an imprisonment in lucidity, in a permanent and yet tiresome state of lucidity, stretching your mind between the incomprehensible pulse of life (and therefore *death*) and the act of writing.

Can you empathize with Jackson Pollock? Imagine feeling

like him but not having the great fortune of painting tools at hand. Shouting your existence is not enough, you want to leave some *signs* behind you, not for those that sooner or later will follow you, but as traces of memory. Eventually these signs dissolve themselves in the *world of words* without *any voice*. I understand that one can play black metal, sing black metal, paint black metal, act black metal, but to write about black metal is … an act which starts honestly, but stretches regard between two caves: the chasm of impulses, and the deep-dark cave of reflection. You are alone, forlorn, naked! The only point of reference is your own history, of which you actually want to be rid. People don't have nature, people have history (Ortega y Gasset). … you permanently remember that you are. People want to get rid of their nature. The result of such a journey most probably will be dishonesty. And here you are, in the true failure, falling between the two caves in the abyss of lies.

One more illustration to add here for is in my way, I can see him laughing – Cioran! Why you didn't kill yourself, you Satanist! You, that played football with skulls in graveyards and ripped all saints! Until … until you saw the skull of the beautiful girl that you loved when you were a child. Until … instead of the beautiful blue eyes there were two black holes filled with dust. I always wanted you to die in the *Seine* hit by a boat just before sinking! Instead, you also fell in the abyss of lies.

Wrong death signs
World of words
Any voice
Remembering… Seine

Blaga's poem is a starting point for *our* (black metal is not that individualistic as the narrow minded fans think) endeavor here - to speculate and exacerbate on 'melancology'. I want to say the following: the main characteristic and novelty of black metal is indeed *not* to bring the world's mysteries to light but to increase them '*much as the moon with its white beams does not diminish but increases the shimmering mystery of night*'. If we accept this, then we are immediately connected to the transcendental realm. Does melancology relate to this ethos? I will proceed by recapitulating black metal's most obvious tendencies not to reveal, but to conceal.

Starting from band's logos, voice, the acidic distortion of the guitars, the nicknames, the native language used in the lyrics, what are all these? Are they a reaction to the commoditization of the extreme metal scene? Are they a way to avoid censorship because of the extreme messages? Or is something else behind? The fact is that black metal is the first metal genre which is born outside of the US or the UK.[1]

Although a form of metal, black metal's *Lebenseinstellung* (philosophical underpinnings and sensibility) is different from everything that has stood *under the sign of metal* before. It emphasizes the locality to which it addresses, but has at the same time a permanent state of lucidity that goes beyond, further beyond from humane troubles. Acquiring *Lebenseinstellung* in black metal is, as any other form of transition, made in two steps: decodification of the initial (black) metal, and creation of a new form of black metal. This is how vedic metal came about, just to give an example. Politically speaking, black metal came to represent a *resistance* through locality *to the hegemony* of US-UK metal. Spiritually, it reconnected urban culture to transcendental realms.

People expressing their localities contributed to a fulminous propagation of unarticulated mystery. This mystery springs from a confined heliotrope ecology and erupts in uncontrolled and unpredictable forms of expression of mixed sensibilities. Once articulated these sensibilities will be re-dedicated to the new locality which was just born - the small community that shares the same sensibilities and that has the *keys to the gate*, placed in a specific ecology. This space will be destroyed immediately through reinterpretation and recreation. Like an offspring eating its procreator, this re-location leads to a metabolism with no ultimate authority and *no Panto-creator*. This creative-destruction dialectic amplifies the sensation of the unknown and speeds up into a synergistic creativity. This synergistic creativity is both on horizontal and vertical, and is spatio-temporal.

> *Aprins-a focu!/ Si-n foc sa ardza!/ Din-napoi spre vesnicie!*
> (Thus lighted the fire!/ And in fire shall burn!/ From beyond into eternity!) Negura Bunget, 'Vînt dă Rău Pîn Valea Iadului'

Now let's see if, and how, melancology relates to the above described ethos. From the beginning I want to make it very clear that is my judgment of conviction that *there is no entity without identity*. There is no meaningless human intellectual activity. Following Kierkegaard, Iain Thomson points that 'life is made more meaningful when you respond to meanings that are independent of you (...) If you think that all the meanings come from you, then you can just take them back, you are a king without a castle, you are a sovereign of a land of nothing. It has to be something in the world that pushes back, that has some force over you'. (I recommend to the ignorant Tao Ruspoli's documentary film *Being in the world*, 2010). Herbert Dreyfus and Sean Kelley in their recent book *All Things Shining* point to how the Western polytheism gradually became more and more monolithic until everything was understood in relation to a single god, and then this synthesis fell apart and left the Western culture with a choice between nihilism or a return to polytheism.[2] black metal is the prototype answer to these phenomena...

This is to say that there is no solitude in black metal. Therefore, the plane of immanence for melancology as a possible conceptual reference for black metal is not, in my opinion, extinction and is not non-being. The foremost characteristic of black metal is the defense of a mystery which is organically linked with a defined locality. The heliotrope ecology is at the basis of the synergistic creation of new affective fields, of new never-ending unknowns.

Our
Lebenseinstellung under the sign of metal
Resistance to the hegemony
Keys to the Gate
No Panto-creator
There is no entity without identity

Alone in the forest ... So dull to say: I am alone in the forest; or: I want to be alone in the forest! Where is your transcendental sensitivity, you *Almighty..., Count..., Necro-..., Winter-, Brutal-..., bla, bla, bla...-ness?*

Alone in the city, what mastery! What a great ability to stay alone when you are surrounded by ... human beings! Alone walking... in the city, and cheering with the birches on the way: oh ... brothers, how you thought me to stay alone when I am surrounded! Oh ... unnamed brothers and sisters bushes, how grandiose you are here surrounded by these... already ruins. Oh ... how black metal you are!

Alone walking, in thought planning,
And sore sighing, all desolate.
Me remembering, of my living,
My death wishing,
Both early and late.

(Alone Walking - Old Funeral, Hades, Hades Almighty)

If we talk about desolation, loneliness, individualism, misanthropy, these real feelings you can only encounter them in the ruined civilization of cities, or of the civilized villages. One cannot get in touch, develop and express these sentiments in an 'uninhabited' forest. The bourgeoning image of forest as a spiritual refugee is only the production of the spoiled, wealthy kids, who, when coming back from the 'forests unknown', they go in the kitchen and eat from the shopping that mama and papa did in the supermarket.

But here in the city ...!, how proud the birches stand, like white candles in the grandiose ceremony of *the marriage between the sublime and death*. When You runaway in the forests You are just a bunch of bags of genetically modified potatoes that cannot feel the majesty of real desolation that the city is, of this necrotic swarming of cars on the streets; your brain is a smashed plastic bottle that cannot resonate these beautiful hymns from *the symphony of destruction*. Here you need to stay alone! Here you need to stand-up and fight! When the forest from the margins of the city is invaded by tourists, what will you do next? You will go to a more faraway forest, using probably a car. And when this one will get 'polluted by tourists' as well, what is next? You get the plane to go to untouched grounds, flying probably with borrowed money. And then ... What is your relation with the forest from Malaysia where you are now? None. But you are black metal, and because of you the forest is black metal as well: this untouched forest, the most black metal of all... What a pathetic sense of colonialism...! You got your black metal boots to foreign ground, got into delirium tremens because you forgot *Lord of the Rings* in the airport, and die by a spider bite. Hahaha... Bon voyage!

In the forest one cannot be alone. Searching for loneliness in the forest is absurd for someone who claims to be connected to a transcendental realm through music. If black metal started as the transcendental expression of metal music, it clearly needs to disembarrass the childish desire for trolls in the middle of the wilderness in order to stay honest and achieve the nihilist stance that it is preaching. The *child's laughter in the asphyxiated city* is the most insulting act alive. *What is more black metal than this?*

Alone in the forest…
Almighty…, Count…, Necro-…, Winter-, Brutal-…, bla, bla, bla...-ness.
Alone in the city, what mastery!
The marriage between the sublime and death
…this symphony of destruction -
A child laughs in the asphyxiated city
What is more black metal than this?

Melancholy is related to memory. Melancoholism is drinking beer *alone!* In a rainy morning on a kerb in the city. This is when you realize how clear your mind is: the only ones that know the truth in this world are the prisoners and the prostitutes. The rest of the people are swarming to consolidate their hypocrite castles. You, yes, you! You are the point of reference for two reasons: you revolt against them (you want to crush them forever); and you posses transcendental knowledge. Transcendental knowledge is different from memory, from remembering. It is superior because it has nothing to do with individual human beings, with diversity. It comes from someplace else: where everything stays still, where there is no desolation because there is no ambition, where there is no shape because there is no identity, where NOTHING constantly calls for you in a monotone tune for you know *vatitas vanitatum et omnia vanitas*. Dasein – being in the world, means acknowledging where you are and what you stand for. What do you stand for?

Melancology is useless.

Wrong death signs
World of words
Any voice
Remembering… Seine.
Our
Lebenseinstellung under the sign of metal

Resistance to the hegemony
Keys to the Gate
No Panto-creator
There is no entity without identity.
Alone in the forest…
Almighty…, Count…, Necro-…, Winter-, Brutal-…, bla, bla, bla...-ness.
Alone in the city, what mastery!
The marriage between sublime and death
…this symphony of destruction -
A child laughs in the asphyxiated city
What is more black metal than this?
alone!
vatitas vanitatum et omnia vanitas

Notes

1. I do not take into consideration Venom here because I see them more as a violent irruption which stayed as the basis for other metal genres as well.
2. Hubert Dreyfus and Sean Dorrance Kelly. *All Things Shining*. Free Press, 2011.

To The Mountains: The implications of Black Metal's Geophilosophy

Dominik Irtenkauf

What interests most about the role of mountains in black metal is this question: what does rock sound like? Of course we find a metallic sound in black metal, one of the most extreme genres at the fringes of the metal world. Black metal theory asks for a certain reflection on documents, on writing and theory rather than sound itself. Moreover, it seems to me that mostly the process of black metal theorizing is grounded in the subjective inner experiences of the writing person, or should be.

For a start, melancology catapults the writer into a shivering self-reflection as to find a meaning to this neologism. It seems to be comprised of the old brother melancholy and the new sister ecology which then combines the qualities of the two into a new creature. So, it is an ecology more concerned with a bleak outlook on environment and human interactions.

Ecological concerns ask for a description of the world we live in and then what should be improved in order to guarantee healthy and wealthy lives for everybody. However – and that is a great but – black metal yearns for destruction and annihilation. You could delve through any interview with a black metal group and find some sentences aiming at self-destruction or world collapse.

At the same time, black metal has always in spite of claims to the contrary had its decent share of life-sustaining measures. The aggressive and rude appearance in terms of sound can be understood as an emotional strategy. Ecologically speaking, black metal asks for a world that is akin to extreme expressive eruptions. The worlds that are being described in those lyrics seem to be quite hostile to human life. Immortal's descriptions of their fantasy realm Blashyrkh for example. This realm might seem unbearable to the lay in metal yet the band's members as well as their followers seem to rejoice in developing such a world of its own. 'Older mountains sleeping in my sight / By chilling woods I stand / A grimly sound of naked winds / Is all that shall ever be heard from here' (Immortal, 'Blashyrkh (Mighty Ravendark)', *Battles In The North*, 1995).

It is not all about destruction but on the contrary, by rocking against melancholy some bands reach out for a certain kind of life-sustaining attitude. That attitude is strongly connected to a specific perception of wild untouched nature which is located far from common human dwellings. As a revolt against the modern world, black metal musicians develop an anti-modern imagery in their lyrics even to the point of glorifying parts of history rarely esteemed nowadays. In that approach black metal reaches back to epochs about which we have only vague knowledge. Further, some describe a realm where actually only a select few can enter and survive.

When black metal theory enters a melancological terrain, only the most intrepid explorers find the right sound, entering those hidden realms behind the wall of rabid drums and shrieking guitars. As with Immortal, when they try to emulate natural phenomena in their music. In Immortal's seminal record *Battles In The North* (1995) can be heard acoustic elements that closely resemble the natural sound of blizzards and cracking snow avalanches rolling down the mountain slopes.

In geophilosophical terms black metal tries to get rooted in the soil of the earth, exiled from civilisation. As Keith Kahn-Harris shows, hostility to the latter pushes black metal to the extreme limit of what is socially acceptable. For the same reason, black metal lyricists tend to stress nature's disinterested forces: man is weak and puny in the face of overwhelming nature. One can best experience man at his puniest when standing on a mountain slope gazing down at the villages and towns far below in the deep valley. This attitude shows an incipient Romanticism to black metal thought, in its desire to identify with nature in seeking out high-peak experiences. Black metal reverberates most of all to emotions, it seems to me, rather than to the library consciously studying staples of books and papers to find their forms of musical expression. Through direct encounters with their environment, the Norwegian generation were inspired to occupy themselves with natural forces, be they inside or outside their bodies. In the British daily *The Guardian*, Gaahl, ex-singer for Gorgoroth, tells the journalist: 'My family owns three mountains. There's not much else around there. Love of nature is a big part of Black Metal. It's easy to feel isolated in nature. And solitude and distance from everyone else is very important to us.'

Most of the time, black metal is concerned with opposing what it sees as comfortable, wealthy and healthy. In my experience working as a journalist for various magazines, interviewing several black metal groups over the years, a certain tenor is clearly evident: we opt for elitism and we don't want to intermingle with average men too much. We stand out – musically as well as intellectually. Yet there is a certain peer group black metal musicians maintain relations with. Persons of dubious character, anti-social, even homicidal – such incidents can be found in several private biographies of this social group. The company of wolves gathers around blackened sacraments that build a centre of worship in those circles. Their anti-social and anti-establishment philosophy is based on an extreme individualism.

Yet it seems to be more revealing to focus on black metal's 'materiality': what kinds of matter build the phenomenon known to us as black metal? Frost – wood – rock – stones – earth – and some kind of blackness. These elements interact with and pertain to an ecological system that black metal aims at. Ecology is about taking influence on the world and thus effecting personal decisions in nature as well as in social surroundings. Despite the topics of wreckage in this sub-genre of metal, there is a line that supports a definite emotional upheaval: giving vent to accumulated energized feelings, trying to flee from chthonic forces and rotten soil. One strong picture for this process are mountains, respectively a mountainside. They are implemented into black metal concepts for reaching out to the skies. Yet black metal is far from turning into an airy condition – the solid rocks will guide this metal's way up to the peak where snow covers the stones. It stays heavy and most of all black. What does that actually mean? Black metal sleighs its materiality all along the path – to any places it will decide to conquer. So there's always blackness and most of all matter included. Blackened earth, blackened mountains, blackened sky.

To put it in a nutshell: black metal's core is reduction – reduction of sound (evidently), reduction of shape (visually) and reduction of expression (whole concept). So when mountains appear as geophilosophical icons in black metal, they are understood as graphic contours of elitism. Black metal musicians delve into a mountainous monumentalism reaching by doing so a higher perspective on man's state of mind. There is a certain trait in mountaineering, respectively mountains's conquest that could be perceived as parallel to some black metal lyrics. Yet it is not the aim of this chapter to deliver an exhaustive overview of these images. One interesting example comes from a German band called Bergthron, often associated with pagan metal because of their songs about woods and runic illuminations. Their most recent album, *Expedition Autarktis* (2010) combines an imaginary polar expedition with Norse mythology and its pantheon. Interestingly enough, *Autarktis* refers to the German name of Antarctica yet also includes the adjective 'autark' meaning independence. The long history of polar explorers (that can be somehow compared to mountaineers in aspects of exhaustion and deprivation while on an expedition) is linked to a genuine black metal interest: Scandinavian mythology. To persevere in an environment under highly extreme conditions could sum up the whole album's concept. Under these circumstances the explorer realizes Norse gods in their capacity of meaning and potential.

Black metal's fascination with mountains is obvious. There is enough literature on this sub-genre's history and its main subjects. You can of course talk about black metal if you participate in the whole process of producing extreme views and sounds from the margins of culture. Recently, there has been much talk about extreme metal's history. That is due to several reasons: one of the most evident might be the personal careers of this style's musicians and followers. They try to combine their different interests. Extreme metal has crossed the anniversary of 25 years, so there's enough space and time now for retrospective.

To get to the core of black metal philosophy one needs to explore the inner sectors of the genre and its activists, many of whom take the philosopher Georges Bataille as an inspiration:

> I call experience a voyage to the end of the possible of man. Anyone may not embark on this voyage, but if he does embark on it, this supposes the negation of the authorities, the existing values which limit the possible. By virtue of the fact that it is negation of other values, other authorities, experience, having a positive existence, becomes itself value *and authority.*[1]

A frequent metaphor for this voyage to the limit of the possible in black metal is mountain climbing. When climbing up mountains lost its exclusive role for aristocracy, the lure of mountainsides was advertised more generally and published reports spoke of the wonders of conquest. At the same time, intrepid alpinists strove for ever higher peaks and distinguished themselves by resorting to more and more challenging modes of scaling. To scale means to be ambivalent: to climb up and to register uncharted territories. There is an appeal of challenge that goes with rock climbing.

There is a seminal sequence in a video documentary on former Gorgoroth frontman Gaahl who now entertains the music project Godseed. US-American journalists visited him in his Norwegian wilderness and then he suggested to them a day trip to an outstanding place which he regarded as sacred. They were dragged high to a snow-covered mountain peak where Gaahl's grandfather had built a wooden shed long ago. They had to carry any plank of wood to the peak because up there was only barren land and no trees. Then there is the rather famous videoclip by Immortal showing them bare–chested, man-handling their axe guitars (which can apparently function without electricity), their performance hundreds of meters above average habitat for human beings. In the bright sun and blinding snow you cannot hide except for some narrow gaps in which you can fall by chance and get missed. This mass of stones and rocks, covered by some layers of snow, stands up for the right of persistence. Solid as a rock, bulwark against all liquid and fluid and airy non-beings. However, any monument can be eroded, any pillars can be sleighed (down) and crushed, torn down to earth and made to dust. Black metal thought is about perseverance, the sound of perseverance to conquer death and his capricious complices. One never knows what happens next. Dealing with human life's inconsequence, some black metal bands find truth in the outer surroundings of our planet's ecological system. Hitting extremes means to re-shift the world's centre to a new position or to strengthen relations to the founding chain that leads back in due course of time to the '*urszene*', to a place in space and time where it all began.

Black metal bands have been continuously referring to mountains as their medium of transcending inherited borders. To conquer the world and by doing so, they evolved an ecological approach to nature, the latter being preferred to the lousy doings of stupid fellow men.

While for some bands mountains are little more than a superficial metaphor, others have a more profound approach to these landmarks of landscape. At the same time this apparently profundity can become imprisoned in the codes of dogmatic texts.

> *In der Psyche sind die Grundqualitäten der Wirklichkeit, die Götter der Erfahrungsreligion, weiterhin Realitäten. [...] Aber die geschichtliche Wirklichkeit läßt sich nicht mehr mit olympischen und chthonischen Charakteren der Göttergeschichte beschreiben, d.h. sie ist nicht mehr Spiegelung der Wirklichkeit der menschlichen Archetypen. Sie ist eben deshalb auch nicht mehr innerlich verständlich.*[2]
>
> [The actuality's basic qualities, the gods of any empirical religion, turn out to be still realities in the psyche. [...] However, you cannot describe historic reality by olympic and chthonian figures of gods's history, i.e. it is no more representation of the actuality of human archetypes. For the very same reason, it can no more be inwardly understood. My translation]

Black metal still tries to understand human archetypes in inner reflection. That leads to a highly emotional expression in all their works. Geophilosophical criticism aims at understanding the position of places and tropes in aesthetic contexts like a musical sub-culture. Any trope in black metal carries an energetic transgression of borders and limits. For some, this effect is mitigated by commercial considerations but the true deep raw edge of black metal wants to shock and shift borders.

While for some bands the chthonian earthing of man's existence abounds, for still others seek to oppose this gravity and fly with the skies, rather than the earth, at their feet. They push it into the opposite direction – into altitude. They build mountains in their songs. Maybe this is a sound way to escape the musty innards of our planet. 'Black Lava, drifting down the mountainside / Black Lava, you can't fight' (Satyricon, 'Black Lava', *Volcano*, 2002).

The more 'melancological' groups reflect on changing emotional reactions to mind and matter, raising awareness of life's ever-present decaying process. We realize that all nature has to grow and fall, to bloom and wither and is integrated into a cycle; and we must change with it. On black charts some musicians draft a different understanding of their style: instead of surrendering their bodies and souls to the void and extinction, they confess their sympathy with tortured nature. This is the case with Satyricon's classic 'Mother North' which deals with an ecological consciousness: 'Mother north – how can they sleep while their beds are burning? / Mother north – your fields are bleeding // [...] A Future benighted still they are blind / Pigeonhearted beings of flesh and blood / Keeps closing their eyes for the dangers that threat ... ourselves and our nature / And that is why / They all enrage me'. Wolves In The Throne Room from the United States admit their involvement in environmentalism. Perhaps explicitly environmentalist groups are exceptions to the rule, but the fascination with awesome nature is pervasive, leading sooner or later to moments of self-transcending quality. Figuratively or literally, black metal musicians find strength in walking through awe-inspiring nature or in idolizing monuments of rock, vulgo: mountains. Their fascination with bleak landscapes can be explained as a sort of metal heritage, yet aiming at landmarks made of stone and ice could be deduced from a different approach: the will of power and knowledge, the elitist exclusion from human habitats, the passionate and therefore heavily emotional reaction to totalization of earth's discovery. Black metal bands in my understanding hunt for white spots in mind and territory. Therefore they venture to places at the extreme rim of this known world – just like mountain peaks and snow-covered slopes in thousand meters of altitude. They seek elevation and gather momentum in monuments of solid rock – to overcome melancholy.

According to Robert Burton's seminal treatise on the *Anatomy of Melancholy*, a man lost in melancholy should be entertained by his friends and be distracted from the source of his sorrows. In black metal it is a bit different: most musicians indulge in pain, sorrow, depression and suicidal states of mind, at least lyrically and when performing on stage. However, my argument underlines the will to fight against lethargy, passivity and apathy in order to aim for an elitist approach. On the one hand, self-wreckage abounds on black metal records and in the scene, on the other hand being harder to one's own drives and desires than average men – there is an asceticism and discipline to the whole thing of getting involved into the allure of black metal and becoming true to the cause. ('I am the beast in passionate pain / I am the grim being of the highlands / Of the other side ... / I am winter when you freeze [...] // Seems like I dwell in a circle / Somewhere in the Nordic Hemisphere // Where the howling winds rage / And the mountains are majestic / I can breathe and where there is / Human flesh I feel strangled' (Satyricon, 'Immortality Passion' *Nemesis Divina*, 1996). Only in nature is there breath for black metal musicians, away from the stink of 'human flesh' and civilisation.

One danger, of course, with using geophilosophy as a tool to explain black metal's evolution is the tendency for some writers to over-stress ethnic localizations of attitudes and mental characteristics, as if only a Norse man could possibly produce black metal because of the specificities of his environment. Further, adherence to nature and the soil can easily be dismissed as a proto-fascist ideology. Then again, one's social environment and upbringing can be seen to hold the key to explaining black metal's generation. For me, far more illuminating than focussing on certain nations and world regions is to look for the characters of landscape which are likely to be found in several different places. Mountains are indeed one ideal feature in black metal landscapes that can be compared between different localities. Perhaps, through referring to such landmarks black metal musicians actually evade being tagged as politically conscious, but then again, can ecology really be advocated for without any political stance? I believe so. Geophilosophy should restrict its focus to questions of geological reflection, on tropes and topological links between location and culture. Black metal belongs to a global sub-culture and thus cannot be thought about without a clear specification of the places in consideration in each article. For a melancological approach, in my view, nature's materiality should be considered first, its influence on music creators. Mountains deliver impressive scenery for black metal. Yet only the faint-hearted keep their flock at this level. Explorers venture higher and deeper into the rock, the material of which black metal is built.

Rocking against melancholy means to find a cure in following black metal's code: no pain no gain, no rock no mountains, no rock no shock. Stone turns into music. Solidity into flow. Solitary existence into social awareness. There are more people who dig black, so they accumulate an eco-system with according gravity centres and fringes. The mountains that take a part in black metal's imagery refer to functions of self-strengthening and transcending peer group orientation. We must not forget the sheer rage and disgust in this kind of music. This is a strong emotional statement against giving up. Black metal cannot be possibly overheard. So why is there a tendency for ruin if there is so much power behind the instruments? In these kinds of interrogation it is essential to disconnect psychoanalysis and the likes from intruding into argumentation. Of course there is a certain malaise towards the world and an inability to line in socially accepted behaviour. Melancology asks for a start to the end. Instead of falling into a winternight's depression, a black metal musician might leave the house for a walk up the mountains.

Landscapes of mental extinction turn into landscapes of power sources. It remains a man's task anyway yet the direction of perspective changes. Mountains aren't only described as the place in which man can find solace but as the naturally built monument inciting movement and opposition against lethargy.

Some might recognize Satyricon's track title in this geophilosophical chapter's name which is indeed titled 'To The Mountains'. It hints at a mythology of the self because peak-conquering mountaineers provide a role model for protagonists in black metal lyrics. Besides the figure of warrior there is the figure for the mountain conqueror, a man who wants to dominate or oppose nature. There is the desire to confirm the warrior's strength and the will to conquer, to stand above fellow men. In mountaineering this desire is more directed to scientific exploration and later on to recreational activity. Just imagine a concept album by some black metal group dealing with Mount Everest's long history of reaching to the top. These are acts of civilisation. Black metal musicians really or metaphorically climb up mountains because of escaping from any civilisation. Plus there is a strong physical exhaustion involved in it as well. 'Lies, deceit / Fright, escape / Caught, burdened / Gone, trapped / Get up, on your feet / Give me, your very self / It's time to Rise!' (Satyricon, 'To The Mountains', *Now, Diabolical,* 2006).

Geophilosophically, mountains stand out in landscapes, they reach for the sky, they build the surface on which philosophical loners like Nietzsche's Zarathustra can find their self-expression. Besides, they seem solid and can confront any catastrophe. Maybe mountains stand for the search of peaks to survive emotional surges swapping over musicians of this specific style, reaching for a vantage point in order to persist high above. Why does a follower of the black metal kvlt find so few images of man's flying in the lyrics? Wandering on a mountain and even climbing up strongly binds the experiencing man onto the surface. Black metal, in my understanding, never loses touch with earth, in a chthonian sense. Its roots dig as deeply as into the underworld and find their echoes there. However, implementing mountains into their imagery implies a sentiment of grandeur, despite melancholy and depression tearing down the blackened souls. Satyricon deal with this state of mind in their already mentioned song: 'I lost touch with me / I was and still am fire / Ignite! To the mountains // Live breath sense move / I know it pains me too / Ignite! To the mountains'. A lost touchstone to creativity must be erected to great heights again. So the image of mountainside erupts; it is a strong image for strong warriors who want to prove to themselves and most of all to the world that they still have enough power in them to get to the top.

Satyricon's mainman Satyr answered in one interview with a Finnish web magazine:

> When I wrote "To The Mountains" for *Now, Diabolical* I was up in the mountains and I had spent some hours getting to the mountain top and when you get up there you can see many other mountains of Norway – you look in one direction it's that mountain or in the other directions it's this mountain. It was very impressive. And after I went back I wanted to write about something that gave me that grand feeling I had on top of that mountain. That's very hard. But seeing all this made me make other stuff also gigantic. So I thought let's try to make a song that has the gigantic feeling that I was seeing and how the mountains made me feel inside.

Scaling mountains inside one's own soul takes black metal to a new level of understanding geophilosophy. The ever-prevalent melancholy is driven under the rocks and their sound could be heard in rock music in general, and black metal adds a special element to this sound: sheer despair and black bile that can corrode even rocks; like a ferment in the underground, it feeds black metal's ferocity and provides as much force as to build whole mountains. The tip of an iceberg that reaches far beneath the surface it swims on.

Then leaving old trodden paths brought those black metal musicians to a new understanding of mountains, step by step they scaled a new height in metaphor. Of course, there are still dozens of groups dealing with mountains as lyrical clichés for their pagan landscapes, but Satyricon's 'To The Mountains' goes further and stands for a more intellectual approach. It is a symbol of strength, a metaphor of transgression, of overcoming the average self on the way to the *Übermensch*. Instead of focussing on specific spiritual mountains like the alleged entrances to hell (the vulcano Hecla on Iceland for example) or some hosts of heavenly pantheon, black metal bands use mountains in their materiality as expressive tools for their emotional ups and downs. This sort of metal ponders upon the contingent decadence of matter, that is, decay by using shapes and patterns. While working on taboo topics, black metal erodes itself. In French bands like Blut Aus Nord and Aosoth, can be heard shredding guitars and virtually no catchy song structures, only a vile experimentation with sound that leads to the fading of the material black metal is built of. Rooted in the soil and exiled to the fringes of corporeality – both tendencies are simultaneously involved in those bands's attempts at eradicating the borders to the beyond, the inexplicable, the one-without-words-and-articulation.

> We are not fascinated by the blast beat parts and we hate [generic] boundaries when we are talking about art and creation, we want to explore new sounds and new musical territories, we need to create a particular atmosphere, sometimes extremely macabre (on *MoRT* for example) or ethereal, epic etc. ... we need to touch the extremities of every sensations. Certainly not versatile but in quest of the necessary equilibrium, our discography represents this

> equilibrium, the light calls the darkness and the darkness calls the light.[3]

Black metal is most resistant to decay because it fully embraces processes of degeneration, decomposition and last but not least deconstruction. So what can the imagery of mountains deliver to this direction?

They can hardly be overlooked. Mountains fill whole horizons and to get to the top, you have to be persistent enough and physically healthy. That seems to be in complete opposition to melancholy and lethargy. Black metal might be perceived as a totally nihilist stance against life. Yet the bands in this chapter prove that this is only one side of the medal. There is as strong an urge to combat against melancholy as to sink into utter depression and decay of matter. Mountains geophilosophically stand against black metal's draining movement into the gulf of annihilation. Symbols of pride and natural grandeur express themselves in amplitudes of guitars and altitudes of mountains. As told, only by inner experiencing the emotional household, a reading close to black metal sound experience can be delivered. The sheer vehemence of the sound leads into an opposition to melancholy. Black metal bands find those monuments of rock appealing enough to build a line against the melancholical implications in this genre's self-consciousness. Mountains deliver a wake-up call to the genre if we read and listen closely enough. They raise the listeners' eyes high enough to see something more than black bile and pale moon-coloured faces with small traces of tears dropping their heads to the ground. Heed Satyricon's call: It's time to ignite. To the mountains![4]

Notes

1. Georges Bataille *Inner Experience,* trans Leslie-Anne Boldt, NY: SUNY Press, 23.
2. Reinhard Falter: Natur prägt Kultur. Der Einfluß von

Landschaft und Kultur auf den Menschen: Zur Geschichte der Geophilosophie, Munich 2006: Telesma, 525.

3. Interview with Blut Aus Nord in December 2010 for *Legacy* magazine issue #70
4. From an interview with Satyr @ www.freemagazine.fi./interview-with-satyricon/ last accessed on: 01/04/2012)

The Hot, Wet Breath of Extinction

Evan Calder Williams

Hans Hörbiger's *Welteislehre* (World Ice Theory), dreamt in 1894, elaborated in 1898, published in 1912, known previously as *Glazial-Kosmogonie* (Glacial Cosmogony) before he felt the need to further Germanize it, is an extravagant, crystal bleak, obstinately unfounded, and gorgeous theory. In short, the basic substance of the solar system is ice: ice moons and ice planets move through global ether made of ... ice. The frosty, scraping motion of winter rendered infinite. No big bang, just the wet *thwup* of a sodden dead star smacking into an immense burning sun, sizzled vapor spray, splattering out into empty space. Radially drifting slow, freezing into elementary matter, to found and give foundation for structure to come.

It should be initially qualified twice. First, it is, obviously, a theory with no empirical ground whatsoever, a musing thought cut loose and re-sutured to the apparatus of looking-like-science, even as it purports to be an authentic *kosmotechnische Weltanschauung* (a cosmotechnical world view).

Second, there's its nasty introduction to the ranks of melancholic Nazi pseudo-science. It was employed both as a counter to 'Jewish' science (of things such as experimental verifiability and observable phenomena) and as a cosmically grounded racial climatology. Hörbiger's followers were fond of heckling other astronomers ('Out with astronomical orthodoxy! Give us Hörbiger!') and made the racial associations of the theory unmistakable: 'Our Nordic ancestors grew strong in ice and snow; belief in the Cosmic Ice is consequently the natural heritage of Nordic Man.'

For the time being, I hold this second qualification to the side, even though its future destination is never truly aside, let alone gone or mediated. It can only be placed askance for a slippery moment because the linkage between its order of worlds and the attempted ordering of this world in accordance with Nazi anthropological thought is neither accidental nor surpassable. (Elsewhere, we should think further and better about the fundamental melancholy of the aesthetic that underpins much of far-right and Aryan-supremacist iconography and cosmology, with its black suns and gloom ice ether – that is to say, what looks very much like a proto-melancology. On this occasion, I do not venture a claim of the 'fundamental politics' beneath the intent to talk about melancology nor to jibe at the fact that similar ecological-aesthetic inheritances run very close to a fascist political-aesthetic inheritance. All the same, it must be held in the air. It does not mean necessarily that melancology is fascistic. It does mean that fascist aesthetics are melancological.)

My present question concerns how Hörbiger's whole enterprise (his 'astronomy of the invisible') is a prime instance of speculative thinking reaching its peak, beginning from a near lyric moment of potential misprision - *weird, I just realized that the moon looks like a bunch of ice stacked together* - that unfolds to the horizon. Rather than saying *yes, many things look like ice when the sunlight hits them correctly, for example, that car windshield or, for example, that icicle, yet I know it not to be eternal, order-founding ice,* the cosmological is built teetering, toppling out, telling science to *fuck off* while clinging to its hems, all to bind the universe as such to a solitary judgment. Like the cosmic pendulum of which Hörbiger dreamt, swaying and growing longer and longer with each stroke through the windless void until it broke, world ice theory lengthens from an untethered fulcrum. An instance of total intentionality (all must be objectively as it seemed to me at that moment) produces an entire system and consequently threatens such a first thought, such a cosmopolitics, such a nostalgia, such a fading illumination.

How does it threaten it?

(A mid-stride note: what follows borrows the same principle or remains tentatively faithful to Hörbiger's reasoning. That's to say: stretch the pendulum, throw the fragments out to see what else they gather, and circulate amongst the declining returns of such thinking, in its breakdowns and autophagy.)

Halted, gloomy, and falsely eternal as it is, the system undoes its apparent stasis - *be ever faithful to the originary ice!* - on its own terms: as an instance of the accelerating motion of thought itself, as a fantasy cosmopolitics, and as an acceleration which cannot be contained by the trappings of eternality. In short, the gap between a frozen thought and a thought to which clings the aura of frozenness, with fallout on all sides. In this system, matter (the matter we access and see, of this solar system, of what binds our experience) takes form in accordance with the action of condensation and freezing. The ground of our experience is the crystallization of a flung chunk of that 'first' wet star, some foundation granule around which vapor can recondense, harden, and become the Earth.

Two things follow from this. First, the binding is temporary and dependent on coldness as a negative value: the basic condition for this genesis of what knowably exists is passage through what it is not and what threatens it. The cold is not flaming gas or the friction of impact, and this *not* alone gives shape to the scattered material. And what is it giving shape to? Not the genesis of all form out of what could be, but *this* particular arrangement, *this* solar system. There lies the second point: this is not an origin story of the universe. The universe prefigures, predates, and exists independently of our ice-worlds. Stars burn and die, stone melts into liquid and cool again. And the rules still apply here, in this corner of it, even as the order is exceptional, founded through a confrontation with the prime figure - a gigantic star - of that other order. The dominance of ice, as organizational and generational principle, of hardening into shapes solid enough to stand and think on, comes about through the collision with the exorbitant, auto-consumptive, heat-producing center of simultaneous expenditure and transfer. (And we then ask: what happened to that other star, the one slammed with the wet dead sponge? Does it keep burning a little quieter now, by the vaporization that made all this possible? Was it fully consumed and splattered in that instant, now part of the rain of ice across the dark? Or did it matter not a whit? Its scale so large: like spitting in the desert, a soft hiss and nothing is changed? Except for Hörbiger, who could see in that petty drool's evaporation the possibility of crystal spheres, dark masses racing toward other collisions...)

The half-step to the politics of this, and its allure to the Nazis, is an easy one, and it has little to do with the simple equation of *Nordic = ice*, even as such a commensurability remains the initial operation of linkage. It's more than just the sense that it is extremely convenient to have the meteorological standards of your chosen lineage reflected in the solar system more broadly. Instead, it resides in the sense both of voluntary decision and of interruption that rests on the back of an eternalizing realism which it nevertheless dismantles. That's to say: beyond the lingering rhetorical play of eternal ice and thousand year Reichs, a fascist cosmology - or even one simply accessible to deployment by Nazis - requires an unprecedented event (the dead star collision) to which one has to adhere and work to protect. One must do so all the more because it is opposed to both general opinion founded on principles of 'proof' and observation and, moreover, because it is opposed to the general laws of the universe, which constantly threaten ice. The theory, and the cosmos it describes, backs itself willfully into a corner, hackles up, and declares itself under siege. As Hörbiger told Willi Ley, 'Either you believe in me and learn, or you will be treated as the enemy.'

To take on its related politics: in spite of the founding of a total correlation (people from 'pure' icy lands = 'pure' icy solar system), the event that makes it come into being is entirely opposed to this. It is a violent, annihilating confrontation that results not in the arid cold shards of Northern sentiment, but a warm, wet spray of *filth* that can only take pure ice shape because it is not, and never was, pure, because there are particles around which the water can form. (Or worse, for the Nazis, God forbid that water picked up some other dirt floating around the cosmos: what if the ice moons and ice planets aren't even direct, clean descendents of that first dead star!). This engenders the simultaneous thought that this white ice is the rule of the cosmos and that it must be asserted as such because it clearly isn't. Born of the possibility of its own undoing, the exceptional ice gathers its forces to reconvene a first moment dark to it, when ice as dominant principle was not there. It aims to produce new, icier dead stars, far colder than that damp becoming, so that the next time, that gigantic star, center of exorbitancy and threat to white eternality, wouldn't survive the encounter. The dead white sun returns home harder, and the outcome is the snuffing out of light and heat itself.

Of course, such a confrontation, doomed to fail, dimly aware of this as it speeds headlong toward the apathy of total negation, is only local. A further lengthening of the pendulum, then, away from the inane murderous fantasies of the last century, toward general law of entropic distribution: the heat death of the universe. (Or, at least, the approach towards heat death through cold death: first, the unsustainability of life, then the impossibility of motion itself, the grinding to a halt of the entire enterprise.)

Two options.

The flourishing and buttressing of ice worlds into bridged, halted shapes, a dead city of the solar system, an extension of its logic out to other parts of the universe. Tenuous, spider-silk thin linkages, previously too weak to hold now bind harder into connective glacial tissue. The storms of icy ether firm up, become blocks. Negative space itself becomes whitely solid, oceans of milky nothing with no room for movement. The general thermodynamic rules still apply, and so the principle that brings life to an end, the promise of extinction, becomes the guarantor of the extension of this other lifeless way of being. The reign of ice spreads wider. The frozen decay it sustains, that spins beneath us, is not a hold-out against what may come but a precursive image, the eye of the permafrost ice storm.

Unless it's all inverted. Taking on Hörbiger's speculative gesture - as it inverts known laws in order to occasion that moment of the pendulum's snapping off - deserves an impossible thermodynamics in reverse, the extropic swelling of heat. As if cold was a positive value, leeched away to nodes of thermal energy.

Starving, consumptive anti-suns that suck the cold right out of it all.

And everything will melt.

And this too, we should insist, is the real figure and task of speculative thought, which must not think that it is enough to speak immediately of decay or sludge or to think that the ice-bound will remain in its binds and that such a static landscape isn't comforting. To think that either outcome would be a shock to thought, a threat to the ego's heights. Rather, we need not the *formless from scratch* but the decohering as such. The wet topple. Which means: we begin with building this frozen architecture, these towering, impossible arcs of ice, these isolated states, these economies that cohere. And we do so not to let them stand, to imagine their inhuman purity across the ages. We do so to make them rot, to sniff out their breaks. We build so to see *how* they fall.

We speak of ice to speak of thaw.

And *everything* will melt. All the shapes on which our knowing seemed possible, which we thought formed in our judgment, which we thought guaranteed by warmth and light, finds itself betrayed. Not a warm fire to which we cling, but a leech of our potential coldness and coherency. It's the opening of all out to deformation. It's back to vapors one and all, across the board flung and drawn. Being becomes a fogged and inconstant hothouse. Those ancestral bacteria buried deep in the ice are warmed, by the theft of cold, and woken. They come to be, teeming, at the very moment that there is no ground to stand on, as the globe ends, just a trailing trail of steam. The wet, hot, panting breath of incoherent life as the solar system falls apart. Existence's last collapse, the slow hissing gasp of all that is solid melting into fuming slush.

Sound of the Abyss

Eugene Thacker

'Music is the last enunciation of the universe.'
E.M. Cioran

1. Sub-Bass from Deep Space

In January of 2009, scientists at NASA's Goddard Space Flight Center announced receiving transmissions of an unexpected and unexplained cosmic sound. The NASA team's huge, balloon-like satellite, which is immersed in approximately 500 gallons of ultra-cold liquid helium, was originally launched in 2006, ascending some 120,000 feet into the atmosphere, where it was to detect subtle heat emissions from very early star formations. Instead, it became a receptacle for a kind of cosmic sub-bass. As one of the scientists noted, 'instead of the faint signal we hoped to find, here was this booming noise six times louder than anyone had predicted.' A NASA press release noted that 'detailed analysis ruled out an origin from primordial stars or from known radio sources, including gas in the outermost halo of our own galaxy. The source of this cosmic radio background remains a mystery.'

While radio emissions from space are not uncommon, what makes these sounds a mystery is not just their magnitude, but an apparent lack of point of origin. In short, there do not seem to be enough galaxies around to possibly produce a sound of such magnitude. Neither supernovas, aliens, nor the Death Star are capable of generating such a sound. Perhaps we were witnessing what alchemist Robert Fludd once described as the 'celestial monochord'.

INSERT FIG 27

In the early seventeenth-century, Fludd produced a diagram

linking the Ptolemaic universe to musical intervals, providing a means not only of viewing the cosmos as sonically ordered (a principle of sonic reason, as it were), but of comprehending the possibility of a divine superchord that was responsible for all other sounds.

While the NASA report makes no such occult claims, it remains interesting because it hints at a theme that is, I think, at the center of extreme music genres today, and that is the relationship between *sound* and *negation*. Now, we commonly think of the relation between sound and negation as the negation of sound. And this in turn, relies on the well-worn dichotomy of sound and silence.

One can explore all sorts of combinations within these relationships. But that is not my aim here. What I'd like to suggest is that, when thinking about sound and negation, negation is often understood as something that happens *to* sound, or, alternately, that happens *in* music. By contrast, we can take a different approach and ask: can music or sound itself be a negation? That is, is there a negation that is not something that one does *to* sound or music, and that is also not something that simply *produces* silence?

In a way, this is what black metal genres do, presenting us with forms of negation that are co-extensive with music and sound. For instance, old school Norwegian black metal, with its intentional use of low-fi recording equipment and stripped-down song structures, presents a music whose separations between individual instruments ends up in decay and indistinction, melody that melds into anti-melody. The 'necro' sound presents music as a negation of the soundness of sound, an encrusted, distorted music that is about to rot, not only the musical foundation of melody, but the physical substrate of music itself. Similarly, doom metal and funeral doom metal takes the most basic element of music – its temporal flow and its existing in time – and negates that by making music that is grave, *gravitas*, leaden and weighted down with the gravity of melancology and pessimism. Doom metal presents a music of tempo that is so *grave* that it negates tempo. Finally, drone metal, with its minimalist dissipation of all music into a monolithic, dense line of sound, presents us with the whittling away of all harmony into a single, thick, absolute tone, collapsing the musical spectrum into a dense black hole.

In each of these examples, black metal presents a music that negates some aspect of musical form – a song against all melody, a rhythm against all tempo, and a harmony against all tonality. What results is not an absence of music per se, but rather a form of anti-music expressed through music. At its limit, black metal brings us back to an even more basic distinction – that between music and sound – the former continually threatening (or promising) to dissolve into the latter.

2. Philosophy, Music, Sound

Let us return briefly to the NASA report of cosmic sound. One idea evoked in the report is the notion of a sound without a point of origin. We know that sound is a physical phenomenon. The basic physics of acoustics necessitates an origin of sound production – say, the vocal chords or a woofer in a speaker – that then produces, or radiates sound waves through the air. Such waves physically move us, brush up against us, and pass through us, and a portion of those waves are registered by our ears – but also, on occasion, in our chest, or in our breath. In philosophical terms, the physics of sound production looks very much like a Neoplatonic emanation of immaterial forms. This is a Plotinean sound, the sound of radiation, emanation, the sound that is outpouring and outflowing.

But what the NASA report seems to indicate is that there is a sound that has such magnitude, such density, that there is no point of origin that can contain it, much less produce it. Taking some liberties here, we might say that the sound is so much sound, so much in excess of itself, that it is a sound that paradoxically has never been produced. This is a Kantian sound, a sound that is dynamically sublime in relation to its point of origin. This sound exceeds itself and thus eclipses its own point of origin. The result is an enigmatic sound that is so much sound that it negates itself, becoming... what? Silence? Noise? Or something else altogether?

And from here we move yet another step, to a third type of sound. As one of the NASA scientists notes, in order to have enough galaxies in the universe to produce this sound, 'you'd have to pack them into the universe like sardines ... There wouldn't be any space left between one galaxy and the next.' Now, aside from this rather Lovecraftian image of cosmic sardines sonically descending on the Earth, what is interesting here is the notion of a sound without any point of origin, a non-directional sound. This is different from the Neoplatonic sound (a sound that radiates from a point of origin), and different again from the Kantian sound (a sound that exceeds and eclipses itself). This is the sound of Schopenhauer, a Schopenhauerian sound. This sound does not have an origin to negate, because there is no origin to negate. But it is also not simply a positive sound, a fecund sound that continuously pours itself forth, continuous sound as a gift of the heavens. Rather it is a sound that is, at the same time, pure nothingness, a presence that only asserts its absence.

Schopenhauer, that curmudgeon from Danzig who once called Schelling 'a windbag' and Hegel 'a monument to German stupidity' – this most 'doom metal' of philosophers also, curiously, possessed a fine collection of wind instruments. As Nietzsche reminds us, a pessimist in his public life, Schopenhauer himself was fond of, philosophically speaking, 'playing the flute.'[1] But high winds are hardly what we would think of as cosmic bass. In Schopenhauer's philosophy we find a slightly different view, a view that contains a nascent theory of the subsonic, one that is intimately related to his philosophy in general.

Even though Schopenhauer frequently rallied against his Idealist contemporaries, a look at Schopenhauer's philosophy reveals a sustained, in-depth engagement with the work of Kant. In particular, Schopenhauer returns again and again to the Kantian split between the phenomenal world as it appears to us, and the logically necessary, but ultimately inaccessible, noumenal world, or world-in-itself.

For Kant, this division between phenomena and noumena was an absolute limit, an impasse that constrained thought within the structural confines of the sensibility, the understanding, and reason. The most one could do was to assert the logical necessity of the noumena; beyond that, the noumena must remain unavailable to the senses, inaccessible to thought, and literally 'nothing' in itself.

Schopenhauer was deeply committed to overcoming this Kantian impasse, but doing so in a way that was different to the German Idealists. In so doing, Schopenhauer returned to the materiality of the body as his starting point. The body is at once that which is most familiar and yet the most alien; we are bodies and we have bodies; bodies are embodied, but also possessed and dispossessed. In a move worthy of H.P. Lovecraft, Schopenhauer argues that the noumenal world-in-itself is not an inaccessible, nothingness 'out there', but that the noumenal inhabits my very body as well. From this, one can deduce that the noumenal – inaccessible, empty, unknowable – is also in me and inseparable from me. In the differential between the body that I am and the body that I have, there lies the dark metaphysics of the noumenal world. I am the empty noumena that remains forever inaccessible to me.[2]

Such a move requires one to question philosophy's self-authorized ability to adequately think everything that it thinks, a sort of blind spot of philosophical thought: '... the principle of the world's existence is expressly a groundless one, namely a blind Will-to-Life, which, as *thing-in-itself,* cannot be subject to the principle of sufficient reason ..."[3]

In this strange collapse of phenomena and noumena, Schopenhauer differentiates between two aspects of the world. There is, first, the world taken as 'Representation' and second, the world as 'Will'. If the world as Representation is the world as it appears to us – that is, the world as sensible and intelligible – then the world as Will is, quite simply, the world as it does not appear to us – nonsensical and unintelligible. Sometimes Schopenhauer suggests that the world as Representation is one manifestation of the world as Will (in which we would think of the Will as source, and Representation as product). But this is tricky, because Schopenhauer is also adamant that the Will has no substance, has no Being, and thus 'is not'. Sometimes the Will is depicted as a kind of primordial force that determines Representation; but at the same time the Will is always, in itself, 'nothing'.

Thus for Schopenhauer the Will is not a personal, individual, or agential will, much less the motor of an all-too-human desire and lack. Instead, the Will is blind, anonymous, indifferent, and, ultimately, unhuman. At its limit, the Will not only is manifest as Representation, but also as the negation of Representation – indeed, as the negation of the very possibility of Representation. The furthest limit of the Will is the Will that is its own negation, what Schopenhauer enigmatically calls 'Willlessness'.

3. Schopenhauer and the Unsound

For Schopenhauer, the Will is never experienced as such; instead it is through the arts that we experience the Will at a distance. But not all the arts are alike for Schopenhauer. There is the Platonic model of art, as in painting and visual art. Here art represents things, that are themselves manifestations of the Will, which is in itself, nothing.

Music is different for Schopenhauer. Schopenhauer often comments on the enigmatic character of music and its relation to the world. On the one hand, music is, certainly, part and parcel of the human world. It is deeply mytho-poetic and speaks to the human condition of living in the world. But on the other hand, because most music is not representational, it appears to have a strange, almost alien autonomy – it almost exists out of the world, or at least harbours in itself a certain refusal of the world.

For Schopenhauer, the Will's most profound manifestation is in music. Music does not represent the world, but is itself a world, is itself a manifestation of Will:

> Thus music is as *immediate* an objectification and image/copy (*Abbild*) of the whole *Will* as the world itself is ... Therefore music is by no means like the other arts, namely an image/copy of the Ideas, but an *image/copy of the Will itself*...[4]

If visual art is representation, then music – in Schopenhauer's argument – is manifestation. If art represents things that represent the Will, then for Schopenhauer music directly reveals the Will – *in its nothingness.* And this is the key point. Schopenhauer likes music, not because it is the most adequate or the fullest expression, but because it is a self-negating movement, a manifestation without Being, an assertion of an absence, the expression of nothing:

> As our world is nothing but the phenomenon or appearance of the Ideas in plurality through entrance into the *principum individuationis* ... music, since it passes over the Ideas, is also quite independent of the phenomenal world, positively ignores it, and, to a certain extent, could still exist even if there were no world at all, which cannot be said of the other arts.[5]

While we may question Schopenhauer's sometimes dubious philosophical logic here, it does lead him to the fascinating suggestion of music without the world – literally, music without Being. For Schopenhauer music is directly indirect, in that it is not the Will in itself, but the manifestation of the nothingness at the heart of the Will. He goes so far as to say the following: 'Accordingly, we could just as well call the world embodied music as embodied Will ...'[6]

But what is it about music that gives it this character? What is it about music that enables it to present itself as this enigmatic manifestation of nothingness? What is the sound of this nothingness? Schopenhauer provides a suggestion by way of a basic analogy between music and the world, and it is here that bass sound becomes important:

> It is well known that all the high notes, light, tremulous, and dying away more rapidly, may be regarded as resulting from the simultaneous vibrations of the deep bass-note ... Now this is analogous to the fact that all the bodies and organizations of nature must be regarded as having come into existence through gradual development out of the mass of the planet. This is both their supporter and their source, and the high notes have the same relation to the ground-bass (*Grundbaß*).[7]

For Schopenhauer bass sound is enigmatic. On the one hand, he views it as the ground and origin of all other sounds, and yet he also claims that it is the most undeveloped, the most crude of sounds. In every sense bass sound is *primordial*.

> I recognize in the deepest tones of harmony, in the ground-bass, the lowest grades of the Will's objectification, inorganic nature, the mass of the planet ... Therefore, for us the ground-bass is in harmony what inorganic nature, the crudest mass on which everything rests and from which everything originates

> and develops, is in the world.[8]

But as Schopenhauer notes, it is precisely the inaudibility of bass sound – to human ears, at least – that indicates its profound intimacy with the unhuman, anonymous Will. As the bass sound recedes into inaudibility, it begins to touch the Will in itself:

> There is a limit to the depth, beyond which no sound is any longer audible. This corresponds to the fact that no matter is perceivable without form and quality, in other words, without the manifestation of a force incapable of further explanation...[9]

This receding of bass sound into inaudibility is an example of a particular type of negation. It is not the negation that results in silence, since the subsonic is only inaudible to human ears (that is, it can still be reproduced and measured). It is also not the negation that results in quietness, since the subsonic remains inaudible whether or not the volume is turned up to '11'. It is not the negation that produces noise, where all distinct sounds are dissolved into an indistinction, since the subsonic also has no distinction, except our own human range of relative audibility.

Essentially, what Schopenhauer is positing here is a kind of sound that is absolutely subsonic. It is a negation of a sound that negates itself, while it never is totally absent. It is a negative sound that is omni-present and yet un-manifest. In short, Schopenhauer's cosmic, primordial ground-bass is less the negation of sound, and more like the sound of negation – a sound that is, of course, indelibly self-negating. Thus the sound of the abyss is not silence, or quiet, or noise, but an *unsound*. That which is unsound – like a building, or a mind – is always unstable, continually about to collapse. But an unsound is also different than the opposition of sound and silence (an anti-sound), just as it is different from the relativity of all sound phenomena (super-sonic or sub-sonic). An unsound is akin, perhaps, to the term 'unknowing' in the apophatic mystical traditions, where the 'un' prefix is an undoing or unraveling, denoting both the negation of the ground of knowledge, as well as the paradoxical apprehension of an absolute limit.[10] This more than the knowing of what one doesn't know, but the apprehension of the ungroundedness of all thought, be it of knowledge or the knowledge of ignorance. In a similar vein, an unsound is more than the hearing of silence, or the listening to all the sounds that compose silence; an unsound is the possibility of sound becoming something other than acoustic or sonic.

To give us an idea of how this unsound is different from an anti-sound or a super-sound, we could consider a number of examples in contemporary sound art, examples that cross genres, from black metal to avant-garde to dark ambient. Each can be understood as effecting different strategies that point to, but never, of course, arrive at, the unsound. Each strategy is also a kind of physics of unsound, an acoustics that has as its ultimate aim the delimiting of the boundaries of the sonic domain.

In one group would be works that utilize what we might call a strategy of invocation. Lustmord's *Black Star* (from 2000 album *Purifying Fire*), Keiji Haino's *Milky Way* (1973), Striborg's *Spiritual Catharsis* (2004), and Darkspace's *Darkspace II* (2005) might be cited as examples. In each there is a use of sound to call up or to raise up something existing at the edges of the sonic. That invocation may certainly be vocal, but it can also simply be sonic, in which sound is its own invocation. In each of these examples, the abyss is a black backdrop from which sound is invoked, sound emerging from the abyss.

In another group would be works that utilize a strategy of darkening. Raison d'Être's *Metamorphyses* (2007), Nurse With Wound's *Soliloquy for Lilith* (1988), Francisco Lopez's *Untitled* series, and Thomas Köner's *Permafrost* (1993) are examples. Here, instead of calling up or raising, the work of sound is that of dismantling, dissipating, and withering the sonic domain. Either the music is so leaden and stretched out – as in doom metal – that the music disintegrates into sound, or, the so-called music is itself composed of what Lopez calls infrasonic' sounds that hover at the edge of audibility. In such works, the abyss is a black backdrop that is also sound, such that sound produces the abyss.

In a third group would be those works that use a strategy of density. Sunn O)))'s *Grimm Robe Demos* (1988), Wold's *Screech Owl* (2007), Winterkälte's *Structures of Destruction* (1997), and Merzbow's *Merzbuddha* (2005) are examples. Rather than adopt a subtractive approach, these works do the opposite, condensing, congealing, and clustering sound beyond its audible, or indeed, acoustic, capacity. All aspects of sound – tone, harmony, melody, rhythm – are maximized in their density, rendering sound opaque and inertial. In these examples, the abyss is a sonic black hole, the absolute density of non-being, absorber of all sound ... sound as the density of the abyss.

A final group would comprise works that utilize a strategy of writhing. Iancu Dumitrescu's *Medium II* (1978-79; for double-bass), György Ligeti's *Ramifications* (1968-69), Iannis Xenakis' *Syrmos* (1959), as well as the spectralist work of composers such as Tristan Murail, and Gérard Grisey, might be cited as examples. In these works sound becomes sculptural, writhing, indefinite, flailing and formless. While the techniques may range from 'micropolyphony' (Ligeti) to stochastic mathematics (Xenakis), the result is that of acoustic metamorphosis, the continual un-doing of sonic form. Xenakis's scores, in particular, display this forming and de-forming quality of sound (indeed many of his sketches for sound installations look like the black avatar of Fludd's celestial monochord). Here the abyss is the absolute writhing of sonic form, sound as the writing of the abyss.

In all these different sonic strategies, negation is less something done to sound (or to music), and more a negation that is indissociable from sound itself, as if inhabiting the very physical or acoustic materiality of sound. In their own way, each of these works makes of sound a philosophical problem, something that is central to Schopenhauer's aesthetics as well. In his metaphysics of the 'ground-bass', what Schopenhauer proposes is a type of sound that bears an indelible, almost inevitable relation to negation. Here the subsonic is more than just a sound at a certain frequency. For someone like Schopenhauer, 'the subsonic' is neither the absence of sound, nor is it the relativity of the audibility of sound. As a metaphysical principle, the subsonic is the expression of an empty sound, the sound of negation that is manifest but not apparent, real but not empirical, the sound of the abyss that is not silence, or quiet, or noise, but an *unsound*.

Notes

1. Nietzsche calls Schopenhauer out for his choice of instrument: 'Schopenhauer, though a pessimist, *really* – played the flute. Every day, after dinner: one should read his biography on that. And incidentally: a pessimist, one who denies God and the world but *comes to a stop* before morality – who affirms morality and plays the flute – the *laede neminem* morality – what? is that really – a pessimist?' (*Beyond Good and Evil*, trans. Walter Kaufmann, [New York: Vintage, 1989], §187).
2. It is no wonder that Schopenhauer had a statue of a gilded, beatific Buddha in his bedroom.
3. "On the Vanity and Suffering of Life," in *The World as Will and Representation II*, trans. E.F.J. Payne (New York: Dover, 1966), p. 579.
4. *The World as Will and Representation I*, trans. E.F.J. Payne (New York: Dover, 1966), p. 257.
5. Ibid.
6. Ibid., pp. 262-63.
7. Ibid.

8. Ibid.
9. Ibid.
10. 'But now as we climb from the last things up to the most primary we deny all things so that we may unhiddenly know that unknowing which itself is hidden from all those possessed of knowing amid beings, so that we may see above being that darkness concealed from all the light among beings' (*Pseudo-Dionysius: The Complete Works*, trans. Paul Rorem [New York: Paulist Press, 1988], 2.1025B).

Irreversible Sludge: Troubled Energetics, Eco-purification, and Self-Inhumanization

Ben Woodard

Introduction or Negative Ecology and The Ecology of Negativity

The aim of this chapter is to address the theoretical-aesthetic coherence of ecological black metal and, in particular, how such a project is enacted by bands such as Wolves in the Throne Room and Botanist. I will focus on how Wolves in the Throne Room's aesthetic construction of a natural world is separated from both energetic (or dynamic) ecological models as well as from the blackening or darkening of black metal as a genre. Similarly, Botanist creates an aesthetic isolation which, while less overtly political, is as separatist as Wolves' program, though in a more aesthetically directed (or self-reflective) sense. Or, to put it otherwise, I wish to argue that the aesthetic of greenness constructed by both Wolves in the Throne Room and Botanist relies on an uncritical concept of nature opposed to an equally uncritical concept of negativity (or blackness).

Both these separations/oppositions question the localizability of both nature as it is employed aesthetically/poetically and negativity as it is practiced, specifically in terms of the assumed connectivity of positivity (philosophically and politically) as well as the assumed isolation of negativity (philosophically and politically). In attempting this investigation I will rely mostly on the work of Timothy Morton, Reza Negarestani, Benjamin Noys, and Dominic Fox.

Wolves' Nature

A tension is immediately evident between the malignancy of black metal writ large and the ecological concerns of Wolves in the Throne Room. The band members are aware of this as they have stated in interviews they wish to steer away from the purported eco-political limpidness that they associate with the blackness of black metal. In opposition to most 'nihilistic black metal' Wolves marry radical Eco-Anarchism (or Deep Environmentalism) with a form of New Age Paganism. Simply put, any psycho-philosophical motivation in the vicinity of the philosophical constellation of nihilism or the otherwise misanthropic, is disregarded in their approach to both black metal and environmentalism. While Wolves are critical of the dead-endness of melancholic ecology, the question becomes whether the figure of the human, in their case a pagan one reunited with nature (or at least a human with such potentiality), need be, or should be, maintained, for the sake for the future of ecological work and ecological thought. Wolves in the Throne Room keep open the possibility of both an apocalyptic nihilism (through ecological catastrophe leaving the now verdant surface of the planet to be reclaimed by the few) as well as a hopeful positivity (through a pre-modern utilization of a pagan nature).

My wager is that the inhumanness of black metal's blackening is in fact more ecologically useful than reliance on either the image of humans reunited with nature or with an original home earth, a tranquil Edenic earth as originary ark, or any other paganesque purification of the planet that Wolves in the Throne Room have sonically engineered, narrated, and continue to support. The blackness or blackening that Wolves in the Throne Room deride is a caricature of both negativity and blackness as an aesthetic prosthetic of that negativity. While surely not all black metal artists embody forms of negativity beyond a more self directed or selfishly (or ego-centered) nihilism, this does not corrode the theoretical and political efficacy of negativity and negation (blackness as the related ethico-political trajectory) to the point of uselessness.

In too quickly dismissing this form of aesthetic negation (as well as its underlying theoretical roots) Wolves in the Throne Room relies on an uncritical positivity of nature, a form of positivity similar to those discussed and critiqued by Benjamin Noys in his text *The Persistence of the Negative* (which I will discuss more in depth below). This positivity in Wolves in the Throne Room's lyrical imagery relies on a kind of reversibility of the environmental damage done to the planet.

The hope for ecological reversal that is found in Wolves in the Throne Room's music, a longing for a return to a non-existent harmony, suggests an ecological model that is alien to dynamics, to energetic modes of existence, as well as to the complexities of feedback loops as they relate to ecological systems. That is, in relying on ancient and pseudo-Pagan aesthetic models of nature, Wolves in the Throne Room set up nature as a set of entities which are being damaged or defiled – processes which will be ceased only by the destruction (or at least massive reduction) of the human race.

The thrust of the rest of this chapter is to argue that Wolves' model, and other ecological black metal bands such as Botanist (to say nothing of other Cascadian Black Metal they have been called) over emphasize the thingness (or material stability) of nature, thereby implying that the earth is an infinitely regenerative Gaia-like-entity and/or that the possibility exists for an unrestricted reversibility of the damage that has already been done to the earth (as the privileged representation of nature-for-humans).

In both 'Vastness and Sorrow" and 'Cleansing' from their album *Two Hunters* (2007), through predominantly medieval imagery, Wolves in the Throne Room obliterate the image of enslaved (or manufacture fueling) nature leaving either sun blasted desolation or enchanted wood in its place for future heathens to enjoy in Dionysian celebration. The last song of the album promises a rebirth of a sun God and the eventual rebirth of all of the earth. Yet the descriptions of surface cleansing suggest not a renewal of all of nature but a reset of the ways of human living with nature; that even the invoked threat of apocalyptic cleansing is one that is caused by nature yet limited to those living in free capitalist societies. As an anonymous member put it in an interview:

> I am inspired by the anger and hatred I feel towards foolish and greedy humans. It is terrible to watch beautiful forests and farms scraped away to make room for hideous death-boxes. I am equally inspired by deep gratitude and love for nature and a desire to find a traditional and life-affirming way of living.[1]

The side effect here is that the target of Wolves in the Throne Room's lyrical critique is that of capitalistic humanity, an entity which seems to interfere with an Orphic relation-to-nature, that is the greed of humans is what covers over our peaceful and deep relationship to nature thereby negating views of nature which complicate not only its violent status but also our heavily mediated relation to it. That a spiritual communion with nature exists uncritically and that this form of thinking is completely alien to the thinking that produces the tools of capitalist existence is too quick a judgment.

Malevolent Grain (2009) continues the logic of the debasement of nature but puts it in ostensibly more anti-capitalist terms. Instead of the existence of man in nature it instead challenges the fruitlessly desiring nature of human beings aesthetically immobilizing them in a frozen waste of indecision. The prescribed escape is always one of a backwards temporality – suggesting both that it is possible for all of humanity to go (culturally and technologically) backwards and that in a pre-industrial state humans are in a perfectly harmonious relationship with nature and that the forms of that nature are something that one can go back to.

In their most recent release *Celestial Lineage* (2011) Wolves in the Throne Room shift to more mythic territory – frequently invoking nature spirits and gods of various realms. References such as 'Deities of frost crave an offering to storms' and 'Sky-lords towering above' give the entire album the feel of diagonally ecological concerns being coupled with an odd form of becoming a self-fashioned god. In this most recent album, Wolves in the Throne Room seem at their least ecological and their least critical.

Two of the striking points of the album are the instrumental songs 'Rainbow Illness' and 'Permanent Changes in Consciousness.' They are interesting in that the titles both convey very critical tones but, since they are devoid of lyrical content, it is hard to grasp what exactly it is they are meant to critique (if anything).

Botanist's Nature

What sonically sets Botanist apart from its Black Metal contemporaries is that amidst the familiar barrage of blast beats and guttural screams there is a stark and crystalline sound of the dulcimer, which introduces a sharpness of a different register. The pseudo-anonymous front-man of Botanist has constructed a fairy tale-like world on which his lyrics rely and pull imagery from. This world seems to be like the 'actual' world as still nature and yet also a more fantasmatic operation. He describes himself in his online biography in the following way:

> The songs of Botanist are told from the perspective of The Botanist, a crazed man of science who lives in self-imposed exile, as far away from Humanity and its crimes against Nature as possible. In his sanctuary of fantasy and wonder, which he calls the Verdant Realm, he surrounds himself with plants and flowers, finding solace in the company of the Natural world, and envisioning the destruction of man. There, seated upon his throne of Veltheimia, The Botanist awaits the

> day when humans will either die or kill each other off, which will allow plants to make the Earth green once again.[2]

This is clearly evident in the lore that Botanist uses, as listed on their website. These terms are used to ground the ecological (or more accurately neo-pagan) world that Botanist's music and lyrics operate within and on which he names as the Verdant Realm. The Chlorophllyic continuum for instance is 'The great collective that unites all floral essences throughout. A sort of astral plane of plants' or 'The Budding Dawn: At the end of the world, at the apocalypse of man, when people either kill themselves or each other off, The Budding Dawn will come to pass.'[3]

In this sense Botanist's world, the Verdant Realm, seems as constructed (though at least admittedly so) as that in which/on which Wolves in the Throne Room operates. Botanist also utilizes negativity far more openly than Wolves. Another term from Botanist's lexicon is 'Azalea: Whether a demon of the plantae underworld, the vengeful spirit of Nature, or merely an embodiment of schizophrenia, Azalea is the voice in The Botanist's head, instructing him on how to bring about the fall of Humanity.'[4]

Botanist seems to be more self-conscious of the limits of constructing an untouched nature outside of the reach of human damage. Furthermore, the lyrical themes of his songs are reinforced by the (mostly) scientific names of plants that make up the song titles. The lyrics themselves shift between fairly straightforward descriptions of various kinds of plants with a touch of vegetative vengeance added which involves an anthropomorphisation or injecting of a bestiality into plants in order to give nature a human-like anger. In this sense, Wolves in the Throne Room combine pre-humanity with humanity whereas Botanist constantly invokes a post-human plant nature as possibly overrunning the human.[5]

There are also images in Botanist's lyrics which invoke a similar separatist aesthetic-politics as that found in Wolves in the Throne Room. The final lines of the song 'Invoke the Throne of Veltheimia' are:

> Seated there in solitary, sylvan authority
> The world from afar I watch
> From my post of entropy
> Thronged by floral alliance
> I await the fall of time
> And the Armageddon of mankind[6]

The problem becomes that of separating separatist negativity (or negation) from a utilization or practice of negativity (whether ethical, political, environmental) that continuously (if not always directly) negates in a logic of better than both. When theorists of ecology such as Paul Wapner rally against the doom and gloom of environmentalism,[7] they overlook the fact that uncritical positivity is perfectly compatible with capitalist accumulation at the cost of ecological sustainability. Against the imagistic worlds of nature constructed by both Wolves in the Throne Room and Botanist, what is required is an aesthetics of nature which is always open to an incalculable outside that constantly and consistently eats away at any stable ground beneath it.

Ecology versus Nature or the Negativity of the Outside

The familiarity, or more literally safe-closeness of an aesthetic formulation of nature as an idyllic set of things and not a changeable system, maintains a human-nature relation which privileges both terms as separate and static. Such thinking is a symptom of the long standing problem of discussing nature, as Timothy Morton has put it, as something always 'over there'. As Morton argues in the first chapter of *Ecology without Nature* (2010), this is the problem of ecomimesis, that form of writing which attempts to get beyond language.[8] In its strong form it is an inside-out situatedness[9] whereas in the weak form it merely invokes the place of where is writing both of which invoke a poetics of ambience.[10]

In contrast to the distant yet close form of nature taken up in Wolves' and Botanist's aesthetic, Morton suggests that since lifeforms are made of other lifeforms and since everything is interconnected, then all background and all foreground disappears.[11] Morton's critique, which appears in different forms in both *Ecology without Nature* and *The Ecological Thought*, argues that the concept of nature itself needs to be left behind in order for ecology to move forward in its thinking: 'Ecological thinking should not stop forging ahead, thinking unthinkable things and demanding the impossible. It must hold open the possibility of a future radically different from the reality we appear to be stuck in'.[12] The problem is that nature is construed as a solid entity that we wish to be reunited with. But the problem is not a lack of connection with nature but the fact that we, as human beings, are always too much a part of nature, the problem being that we have functioned as-if nature is separate from human being and, perhaps more importantly, separate from human thought. Ecology is not the study of a place or even necessarily a set of places, but the interacting generative mechanisms which produce what we know as the environment. But ecology requires some philosophical blackening as well.

Ecology as both a science and a sub-group of the humanities is fractured by conflicting approaches but none of which would argue for total reversibility. The two dominant strands of ecology are the harmonious organic trend rooted in the work of Frederic Clements to be later opposed by the second strand heralded by Henry Gleason which takes a more individualistic look at ecological systems. These two strands can be reduced to Gaia for the former and chaos for the latter, or long term stability versus only short term meta-stability. But, in both cases, the operational privilege of humans in the course of nature is not engaged.

If nature consistently 'natures' through us, then, following Iain Hamilton Grant, nature thinks just as nature mountains or nature voids, glaciers, or meteors.[13] Given the resulting limit of reflection (as an attempt to reach back to the ground of our existence in nature) melancology in the face of nature is not self-indulgent capitulation (as suicide is for Xasthur's negativity) but is the logical consequence of being thinking beings that cannot think the process of their own thinking or capture their own genesis.

Instead of excising the problem of nature's over-proximity, that its processural havoc perforates the formal ghosts of human and earth like a stubborn fungus, the blackening of ecology would annihilate both as distinct entities but not in such a way to re-idealize nature as God or entity. The decimation of distinctions quickly leads to a panic of philosophical uselessness, where all formations and creations seem to fall together as, to borrow from Bataille, 'water in water' leading to a kind of ontological hopelessness. Here Morton's dark ecology as a 'paradoxical aesthetic' is useful, in that the ugly and horrible becomes the center of an ethics.

But Nature appears horrific as long as we hold too dear our own stability in the face of ontological decomposition marshaled by the reality of time and space. What becomes problematic then is the localizability of the negative (as well as the localizability of the relation of nature in itself and nature for us and us). In general negativity has not received a properly flushed out ecology of its own – often being relegated to a shadowy Double (as in Deleuze) or as a fundamentally limited procedure (Badiou).

The problematic relation to the negative is whether an affirmation of the negative is itself negative or affirmative. As Benjamin Noys shows in his recent examination of thinking the negative, such a move risks irony citing Reza Negarestani's welcoming of epidemic complicity with the negative thereby affirming it. Noys seems to overlook, or at least not discuss, how Negarestani's utilization of negativity is deeply intertwined with his use of openness (as opposed to affordance). Whereas discussions of the open claim to be working in a field of radical openness, they in fact are only a case of affordance according to Negarestani as they are always open to X instead of being in a state of openness in which being open consistently invites disaster.[14]

Whereas Morton's critique of strong ecomimesis always invokes an outside, Negarestani's outside is never a gently swaying of the groves, but an outside that is unthinkable beyond being an outside that is already nested inside, any inside, any sense of stability, is only possible by inviting the voiding process of the outside. In his essay 'Undercover Softness: An Introduction to the Architecture and Politics of Decay' Negarestani writes:

> The ideas of the wholesomeness and decaying (whether in regard to design, function, economy or ideas) of socio-political formations, accordingly, are posited as the latter products of a putrefying system [...] a rotting political formation can germinate other forms which might overlap revolutionary, emancipatory and civilised political formations, but also because Western political formations and civilisations might indeed be the degenerate forms of an already rotten and limitropically decomposed Middle-Eastern or Balkanese socio-political formation.[15]

Some of the numerous ramifications of a so-called politics of decay are that not only does it become impossible to localize decay but politics of decay becomes a politics which builds towards the exterior.[16] The ecological usage of such a politics, (of a kind of negativity disavowed by much of ecological black metal) seems critical – focusing on an entity of nature as a local phenomenon or focusing on a large scale concept of nature immune to outside influences at base, leaves out the vulnerability of nature as we see it, as well as the limits of any aesthetic-political construction whatsoever.

Next I will attempt to express how blackness as negativity is often taken to be a closed or overly simplified form of negation and negativity that appears to be useless for living (whether politically, aesthetically, or otherwise) as such.

Ecology of Negativity

Taking up ecology and Wolves in the Throne Room's use of it, negativity is always-already rooted in the human either in terms of the pathos of finitude (as a self inflicted sadness, or kind of auto-immune melancholy) or in what Nick Land has called Transcendental Miserabilism where the negative is over-enlarged and made to be a massive irreproachable entity – his privileged example being capitalism.

As Land puts it 'For the Transcendental Miserabilist, "Capitalism" is the suffering of desire turned to ruin, the name for everything that might be wanted in time' it is the object of 'resentful denigration'.[17]

In the above cases negativity is nested in a particular form in which the user of that negativity is flawed in their approach to the world – either they cut at themselves or cower at the sight of some fanged system out there. In the aforementioned interview with a member of Wolves in the Throne Room, an unavoidable complicity in the economic system is mentioned, as the anonymous band member notes 'we are all hypocrites'. Given this, it is hard to know exactly how Wolves in the Throne Room view their own agrarian separatism in the larger scheme of the relation of ecology and capitalism. Given capital's operational fondness for the positive, it seems not too unreasonable to appeal to the negative in order to better ascertain the sedimented relation of human and nature and how the economic works as an ideological between the two.

Badiou's use of negation is a particularly pernicious codification of the negative in which it is allied with and not against capital and specifically, capital as a denaturalizing machine. Badiou has connected critical philosophies to negation, as well as narcissism, and, most important for our discussion here, has stated that the negation of capital negates the difference of life and death and we all become ghosts.

In Badiou's course lectures at the European Graduate School in 2009, he focused on the theme of negation; he ascribed to it not only the aforementioned egoism but also a strange temporality thereby jumping between an ontic and a transcendental negation. Instead of the 'useful negation' of classic revolutionary politics, Badiou names a contemporary nihilism (for which he blames Schopenhauer) as the nihilism of youth, a nihilism of immediate life (and not the true life) thus the present becomes only the destruction of the past and the void of the future. Again the negative is merely a pathological circuit tending toward suicide or totally unlocalized and dismissed in the machinations of consumerism. In the *Mathematics of Novelty* Sam Gillespie argues that Badiou incorrectly classifies nihilism as a repudiation of the world both past and future.[18] And yet, it would seem that Badiou's thinking of the rupture of politics would grant more space for the negative. Giants of thought which garner the same or more attention than Badiou however fare far worse in their understanding of the negative and negation.

Following Deleuze negation is merely a form of difference, a difference that points outside the world, or to a non-belonging, a non-belonging which covers over the 'first yes' as Noys critiques the tendency in Derrida; that the automatic and response of reason is that of the yes, of positivity, culminating in a kind of weak affirmationism constructing a non-committal political platform.[19] Somewhat oddly, for both Deleuze and Derrida both negativity and negation seem reduced to the noetical movement caused by the prefix de- (deconstruct, deterritorialize, etc). In the closing chapter, Noys addresses Badiou pointing out his closeness to but ultimate departure from the negative. Badiou claims that the world, as a world of finitude, denies affirmation, that the world tells us not to be too positive, it tells us that the world is destructive. Yet false positivity seems a far larger problem and sweeter succor to the market, as certain forms of media, such as black metal, remain for more resistant to capitalist recuperation than the positive. Furthermore, the negative (darkening and blackening) are taking as always relative to the self, whereas the positive is always social and useful. This usefulness covers over the fact that the negative goes beyond the subject, which is why the negative is often rerouted back to the subject, as an internal problem. As Noys suggests however: 'This negation generates the new of the collective agency of courage in the absence of the event, intervallic resistance that predicates itself on disarticulation and ruptural "violence", by turning back a previously reactionary violence towards liberation. What it excavates are the possibilities that exist if we do not subordinate negativity, if we think it beyond and against the disjunctive synthesis of active and passive nihilism which are nothing more than meagre reflections of the everyday violence of capitalist creative destruction.'[20] Ecological thought desperately needs this kind of negativity as it is quite likely that any ecological event could very well be the manifestation of a positive feedback loop which will spiral towards unceasing disaster.

Given the over-proximity of nature, the scalpel of the negative seems a far more useful device, as it may take violent articulations of nature in order to realize the necessity of serious change and not idyllic backwards-looking. Diagonally utilizing Ray Brassier's discussion of noise and capitalism, black metal, and blackening is an aesthetic process that remains indigestible to capitalism, as something that cannot be recuperated. Yet if blackness is dismissed as 'just noise' then the utility of its negativity becomes re-relativized, as an outside that merely determines the positive.

The same could be said of nature and the natural as it has become defined as that which is not ruined or created by human capitalistic procedures. For ecology to have any useful import it cannot remain relational to particular forms of nature, it cannot be seen as distinct from the intentionality of human actions otherwise nature remains 'over-there' just as the negative remains either 'in here' (the brains of disheveled malcontents) or in some completely externalized abstraction.

The Purported Sadness of Inhumanness

To return to Wolves in the Throne Room, in an interview from *Sounds Under the Surface*, the band writes:

> Black Metal is, fundamentally, about two things: firstly, it is an utter and complete rejection of modernity. The 'common sense' principles of the enlightenment - science, logic, rationality, humanism, reductionism, materialism - are revealed to be a sham. In place of modern, liberal, democratic, capitalist society, Black Metal demands that we return to a pre-modern modality. I suppose we all have our own ideas about what that would look like. Secondly, Black Metal expresses a deep and profound sadness. Modern people have lost so much of what makes us human. Our traditions, languages, stories have been washed away by a globalized monoculture. Humans are at war with all that is good and beautiful in the world. Black Metal is an anguished cry of humanity's failure.[21]

The troubling thought process here is that while the sadness described is one of opening humanity to nature it is then filtered back through myth and fable circling back to the failure of humanity and thus our relation to nature supplants nature itself.

Instead a more tactical or open-ended sadness is required in thinking nature. Dominic Fox's excellent text *Cold World: The Aesthetics of Dejection and the Politics of Militant Dysphoria* addresses the melancholic effect of various forms of music as it relates to politics. He opens the text in the following way: 'Sadness does something to the way we see the world. In the experience of deep sadness, the world itself seems altered in some way: coloured by sadness, or disfigured by it. Rather than living inside us, as our normal passions do, our sadness seems to envelop everything.[22] And later on and in specific regards to black metal he writes: 'The cold world of black metal is a deliberate freezing of the world, fixing it within a terminal image, in order that its frost bitten surface may be shattered by anonymous, inhuman forces rising from the depths of the self'.[23]

Following Fox's logic the blackness of black metal puts the world, at least in its affective percolating, under anesthesia. On the one hand this would seem to put the world at a frozen distance but, if we follow Morton, this distance was only ever illusory to begin with, then it makes what is inhuman in both human beings and nature evident as non-aesthetic, or that which does not lend itself to positivized connectivity. This is to suspend the forced choice of leading to Derrida's first yes. Nature natures through the self, if we walk into the woods thinking that we can go there to 'better commune with nature' we are kidding ourselves – not only does it push nature 'over-there' aesthetically and politically but it also neglects the organic and inorganic processes which are gradually peeling the life off of our bones which are just as much a part of nature. Again, it is easy to see the use of a politics of decay for ecology. If we lose the place of nature, then nature does not disappear, but our sanctuary of unnaturalness, both in our constructions and in our humanness. To quote from the end of Morton's *Ecology without Nature:* 'Ecomimesis offers the illusion of a false immediacy that is belied by the immersed yet laid-back aesthetic distance it demands.

Nature, if it is anything at all, is what is immediately given, which at its simplest is pain. A melancholy emerges [...] In the sadness of its very capacity *not* to present immediacy, the aesthetic dimension gives body to the immediacy that hyper-aesthetic ecomimesis, pretending to be anti-aesthetic, wishes to force down our throats'.[24]

Morton's texts, as well as Negarestani's discussion of decay, force us to realize that if nature itself (or the unthinkable outside) is capable of synthesis then our aesthetics are doubly synthetic yet also natural. They are most damaging when they pretend to be natural in a sense that only serves our own perceptions. If there is theoretical utility in Wolves in the Throne Room's primativism, or green anarchism, and so forth, it is not the salvaging of a lost intimacy, to be reflected back to ourselves, but, again following Fox, to animate the inorganic forces which pass through us but that we have some capacity to change. A horrific nature then is not beyond us, its material vastness is, yet we can reconfigure its effects locally, the question of both naturephilophie and ecology, is what are the limits of this applicability, and how does aesthetic blackening (of black metal, of the critical freezing of melancholy), help clear the field of the applicability?

Blackening helps distinguish aesthetic connectivity from actual connectivity, as well as question the localizability of the negative and nature. The latter becomes a force magnifier of the latter, which, if it circles back to the negative, to the human, it is not to close the circle of humanity from nature, but to show how inhuman thought and human being are in the flow of a dejected nature. We cannot even hold onto place, since all solidity (actual and philosophical) bio-degrades, it becomes blackened by thought – negativity accelerates the degradation of nature making thought the most natural of nature's products.

Notes

1. Kim Kelly, Interview with Wolves in the Throne Room, *Hails and Horns Magazine,* available online at http://ravishinggrimness.blogspot.ca/2007/10/interview-wolves-in-throne-room.html
2. Botantist, Available online at botantist.nu
3. Botanist, Available online at http://botanist.nu/lore.html
4. Ibid.
5. Here I am indebted to Alex Williams.
6. All lyrics are taken from http://www.darklyrics.com/w/wolvesinthethroneroom.html.
7. Paul Wapner, *Living through the End of Nature: The Future of American Environmentalism* (MIT Press, 2010), p 180-183.
8. Timothy Morton, *Ecology Without Nature.* Harvard University Press, 2010: 31.
9. Ibid. 32.
10. Ibid. 33.
11. Timothy Morton, 'Thinking Ecology: The Mesh, The Strange Stranger, and the Beautiful Soul' in *Collapse: Philosophical Research and Development,* vol. VI, Falmouth: Urbanomic, 2010: 198.
12. Timothy Morton, 'Ecology After Capitalism', in *Polygraph: An International Journal of Culture and Politics,* n22. Duke University Press, 2010: 58.
13. See Ian Hamilton Grant's contribution to the inaugural Speculative Realism Conference in Ray Brassier, Iain Hamilton Grant, Graham Harman and Quentin Meillassoux, 'Speculative Realism', in *Collapse: Philosophical Research and Development,* vol. III, Falmouth: Urbanomic, 2007.
14. See Benjamin Noys, *The Persistence of the Negative: A Critique of Contemporary Continental Theory,* Edinburgh University Press, 2010.
15. Reza Negarestani, "Undercover Softness: An Introduction to the Architecture and Politics of Decay," in Collapse:

Philosophical Research and Development, vol. VI (Falmouth: Urbanomic, 2010), p 383-384.

16. Ibid.
17. Nick Land, ed. Ray Brassier and Robin Mackay 'Transcendental Miserabilism' in *Fanged Noumena: Collected Writings 1987-2007,* Urbanomic, 2011: 624.
18. Sam Gillespie, *The Mathematics of Novelty,* 144.
19. Noys, *The Persistence of the Negative,* 42-43.
20. Noys, 157.
21. Available online at http://www.metallian.com/wolvesinthethroneroom.php
22. Dominic Fox, *Cold World: The Aesthetics of Dejection and the Politics of Militant Dysphoria,* Zer0 Books, 2009: 1.
23. Ibid. p 56
24. Timothy Morton, *Ecology without Nature,* p 182.

Musca amusica

Scott Wilson

Halo of Flies Over My Head
I am decaying Satan's Wrath
The one to walk planet earth alone
Spreading disease, death and war ... Impaled Nazarene,
'Halo of Flies' *All That You Fear* (2004)

Attractive to the flies ...
I am their mephitic trough ...
a buzzing which engulfs all ...
Through compound eyes
I envision eternity
Lugubrum, 'Attractive to Flies', *De Vette Cueken* (2004)

The fly ought to be used as the symbol of impertinence and audacity; for whilst all other animals shun man more than anything else, and run away even before he comes near them, the fly lights upon his very nose.
Arthur Schopenhauer, *Studies in Pessimism* (137).

'True kvltists like their black metal to sound like bees in a tin'.
Terrorizer 188 (Sep. 2009)

1. The buzzing of life without being

Flies are a frequent trope in both black and death metal. For the latter, buzzing flies pullulating over a rotting corpse lyrically figures death metal's pulverizing a-subjective affections of the body; for the former, flies are related to a metaphysical problem bound up with how, in relation to the principle of the One, univocal being or the One God, evil poses the question of duality or the multiple. Of course this is a conventional problem, but flies take it in many interesting directions. Index of the fallen world of filth, disease and suffering, the ubiquity of *musca domestica* have led them to become a wonderful figure for the precariousness of life in an economy of violence and virulence.

But if flies are indicative of life, theirs is a life, in a philosophical or ontological sense, without being. That is to say a life below the threshold of being measured on a human scale, insects being regarded generally as simple organic mechanisms that could be straightforwardly engineered. They are not regarded as subjects or selves, perhaps only in a general theory of panpsychism would they be presumed to have consciousness; they do not have *Geist* or Spirit; for them there is no *Dasein* even as their annoying 'being-thereness' is perpetually part of the environment for much of the human being-in-the-world.

No doubt since the migration of homo sapiens from Africa, *musca domestica* have been the constant companions and noisy neighbours of human beings, lodging in the margins of human civilization, incubating and pupating in its shit and garbage, feeding on wounds and rotting flesh, defecating and vomiting waste matter teeming in deadly bacteria and viruses: typhoid, cholera, dysentery, tuberculosis. They constantly test the ingenuity of knowledge concerning the limits of the human condition and the human organism's adaptation and agreement with its environment. This perceived annoyance and threat is often taken as a metaphor, such that being 'a fly in the ointment' is the desire of anyone hoping to subvert a repressive system and so on, that is disturb and reconfigure the environment. At the same time, not 'hurting a fly' is the acme of Christian pity and Buddhist piety; deep ecologist Arne Naess famously asserted that human beings have no more 'right to life than a mosquito', drawing an equivalence that, while it apparently raises the fly to the level of the human and its self-proclaimed 'rights' (thereby rendering them meaningless) actually does the opposite,[1] thereby finding its correlate in the familiar cultural reversal that imagines human beings reduced, in horror, to the level of the fly. As Eugene Thacker notes, it is in the horror film genre especially that the non-being of life is imagined:[2] *The Creature, The Entity, It's Alive! The Stuff, Them!* (a film about bees), to which could be added of course Kurt Neumann's *The Fly* (1958) remade in 1986 by David Cronenberg. These latter movies are different in that they envisage a human-fly hybrid for which both horror and fascination derives from the incommensurable difference between the two creatures whose perceptions and experiences relate to two entirely different worlds that reside on the same earth and locality. What would it be like to experience the earth as a fly, to inhabit its world? It would be an utterly nonhuman world even in the midst of humanity and its mess. Could this nonhuman world of the fly possibly be thought, speculated upon, and if so, what might be the implications for the environment that both creatures (do not) share?

The house fly then, is in many ways a perfect object of ecological desire. The 'eco'- of ecology which connects it etymologically with economy is related to the Greek term *oikonomikós*, the law of household management. *Musca domestica* (after the latin, *domus*, for house) disturbs the very heart of the *oikos* or *domus* after which it is named. Recognised therein as a companion species, the fly is a co-dweller in our house and environment, living off the waste products that define and embroil every culture: the fly accompanies human beings everywhere, wherever they live, a neighbour with whom they share their home, but who does not treat it like one; indeed the fly is a creature for whom my home is an entirely other place, an entirely non-anthropomorphic world. While it may be impossible to experience fly-world, the very existence of this absolutely alien world (and innumerable others) nevertheless relativizes human thought and the *oikos*, ecology or human life-world that supports it. Thinking the fly would mean detaching thought from anthropomorphism, thereby offering new possibilities for thinking environment generally. Perhaps, the most effective way of doing this would be scientifically, as long as science can free itself from its all-too-human assumptions concerning the consistency and efficiency of systems that essentially reproduce even as they overwrite the quasi-theological desire for meaning and purpose. It would also require the certainty that the mathematical formulae that ground and express the scientific understanding of microphysical and other states beyond the human scale can be said to be truly autonomous relative to that scale. While that question is beyond the purview of this chapter, music, that force that is often supposed to embody mathematics in sonic form, will be taken to be something that provides tangible evidence of another, unintelligible world of nonknowledge that may open up new forms or new possibilities for cognition. For music to be taken in this way, however, requires both a broader and more specific understanding of music than is conventionally the case. The philosopher Arthur Schopenhauer, I will argue, offers a way into this broader and more specific understanding of the potential of nonknowledge in relation to black metal and the music of flies. Black metal in contradistinction to other eco-cultural examples discussed here engages in an aneconomic relation between humans and flies that discloses the anthropogenic limits of ecological thought.

2. Schopenhauer

> Music is as *direct* an objectification and copy of the whole *will* as the world itself ... Music is thus by no means like the other arts, the copy of the Ideas, but the *copy of the will itself*, whose objectivity these Ideas are. This is why the effect of music is much more powerful and penetrating than that of the other arts, for they speak only of shadows, but it speaks of the thing itself. Arthur Schopenhauer.[3]

It is the same will which objectifies itself both in the Ideas

> and in music, though in quite different ways.[4]
>
> According to all this we may regard the phenomenal world, or nature, and music as two different expressions of the same thing — Music never expresses the phenomenon, but only the inner nature, the in-itself of all phenomena, the will itself.[5]
>
> We might just as well call the world embodied music as embodied will.[6]

Neither will nor Idea, music is located in a strange position in Schopenhauer's philosophical system as a force that is both interior and exterior to the world. For Schopenhauer, will is that mythical, noumenal impulse or power that is the in-itself of all things from physical forces like electricity and gravity to human desires and affects all of which are imperfect copies of Platonic Ideas. The latter are objectifications of the will, but they are not the will itself; the will is essentially in-different to Ideas just as it is indifferent to both humans and nature, that is to say both different from and indifferent to these things even as the will is objectified in them. The will as such is the exterior yet also in-human force of human striving, human will: 'the nature of man consists in this, that his will strives, is satisfied and strives anew, and so on forever' in an interminable process that condemns human beings to continual dissatisfaction, suffering and ultimately death – the will wills its own death in human form in its own way. The will becomes a force in humanity and nature through becoming objectified (that is, objectifying itself) in *Vorstellung*: chains of ideas, concepts, presentations and representations, of which the human is one among others. However, the human has no special or privileged place or vantage point with regard to will. As Eugene Thacker writes, 'unlike his Romantic contemporaries ... Schopenhauer views this abstract *Wille* as impersonal, blind, and indifferent to our wants and desires. There is no nature-for-us, much less any being-on-the-side of nature. Furthermore, the *wille* is, in itself, 'nothing', a gulf at the heart of the world as *Vorstellung*.'[7]

Music, meanwhile, is heterogeneous to all of this, even as it repeats it, with a difference. Music is not *Vorstellung*; it is not an Idea, a concept or representation. It is, however, some form of objectification of the will, a copy of the will, but a copy that is so close it is able to express not phenomena or nature, but 'only the inner nature, the in-itself of all phenomena, the will itself.[8] Since this is exactly what the will does vis-à-vis phenomena, music is an exact copy of the will. It is the double of the will. As Schopenhauer also shows, music acts on the human subject in the same way as the will, exerting powerful effects directly 'on the inmost nature of man' in a way inaccessible to the other arts, reason and even mathematics which are bound up in the *Vorstellung* of ideas and concepts.[9] Music bears on, indeed articulates an unconscious knowledge of the 'inner nature of the world' which is beyond rational comprehension and verbal expression but may be expressed in musical composition: 'the composer reveals the inner nature of the world and expresses the deepest wisdom in a language which his reason does not understand; as a person under the influence of mesmerism tells of things which he has no conception when he wakes'.[10] Notwithstanding all these 'figures of speech', language has no place here: knowledge of the inner nature of the world consists in wordless articulations of sound beyond even mathematical formulation – and Schopenhauer is adamant about this, music is not merely *exercitium arithmeticae occultum nescientis se numerare animi* [an exercise in arithmetic in which the mind does not know it is counting]. Music is thus not an aesthetic object whose formal consistency is guaranteed by mathematics, although Schopenhauer elsewhere hesitates about this, since it would be if music were to be regarded as a closed system. As a closed numerical system, music would not be able to 'free itself from numbers without entirely ceasing to be music'.[11] This seems to be why Schopenhauer must regard music as an open system continuous with all the music of the world, all its buzzing and twittering, its sound and fury, from the birds and the bees to thunder and lightning: 'we might just as well call the world embodied music as embodied will'.[12]

Music therefore for Schopenhauer offers a different relation to the world, to the 'inner nature of the world', than to the world as *Vorstellung*. This is because music is always double; it is both mimetic and anti-mimetic at the same time. On the one hand, since it is a copy of nothing but the will it is heterogeneous to all *Vorstellung*; it lies beyond all chains of signification, beyond aesthetic and mathematical systems, and therefore beyond any possible discursive knowledge or experience of the world. On the other, as a copying of the will in articulated sound, music sublimates and negates the will thereby producing and presenting the void – or the unfathomable dark matter – within itself, the structural *ex-nihilo* out of which sprang the will in the first place, into which the will dissolves in its self-negation. It therefore establishes a position for itself outside of the will. How is this position exterior to both will and *Vorstelling* 'known' or experienced? Unconscious knowledge of this position is signalled by the experience of *a*musia relative to the world as 'embodied music'.[13] The 'void' is signalled for Schopenhauer when the world as embodied music is experienced as a violent dissonance in a way that can be understood as a form of amusia.

The neurological condition of amusia is a form of agnosia, which is the disappearance, pathology or deviation of a highly selective aspect of one's phenomenal model of reality. Amusia never concerns simply a case of tone deafness or indifference to music; it does not describe a world of silence so much as the perception of often agonizing noise where there is music. It is not the nonperception of music, but the perception of music as noise. The notion of amusia also therefore presupposes that music can disclose a fissure in the brain's model of external reality that frames phenomenal experience, hinting at a reality outside that model: the unknown impulse that generates painful 'amusic'. The 'malfunction' of the system of perception, the disjunction between the brain and its reality, is betrayed by the musical repetition of noise. In the same way that Jacques Lacan appropriated the condition of aphasia as a basis for his quasi-linguistic model of the unconscious, so amusia can be taken as evidence of a specifically audio unconscious. That is to say in a way not restricted to biological models where music is a particulate system and external force analogous but distinct from language that produces unconscious effects, traces of a world outside of human consciousness and knowledge. While science finds its consistency in repetition, a notion of *a*musia as a power of the unconscious concerns the irreducible specificity of this 'malfunction', of how music is experienced as a profound dissonance *for some one* that nevertheless discloses the limited nature of the (imaginary/symbolic) system that gives the phenomenal experience of music a semblance of meaning in so far as it is pleasurable.

Appropriately, Schopenhauer does not discuss this in any other way than through recourse to his own experience. Helen Zimmern writing in 1876, 16 years after his death, comments on Schopenhauer's acute sensitivity to the music of the world and its propensity to produce a degree of discordant agony that cuts him off from all ideas, all *Vorstellung*. Describing his thought processes in terms of a hunt for ideas, Schopenhauer says,

> Those ideas which I capture after many fruitless chases are generally the best. But if I am interrupted in one of these pursuits, especially if it be by the cry of an animal, which pierces between my thoughts, severing head from body, as by a headsman's axe, then I experience one of those pains to which we made ourselves liable when we descended into the same world as dogs, donkeys, and ducks.[14]

The cry of an animal – Schopenhauer evokes, in the barking of dogs, the braying of donkeys and the quacking of ducks, the bucolic music of the countryside – literally severs his head from his body, placing him at the very limit of being in acephalic agony at complete variance with the world even as he 'descends' into an animal world beyond human thought. This radical 'headless' disconnection, then, is at the same time for Schopenhauer also a profound if agonizing connection with the exterior world of the animal in the inner experience of dissonant *a*musia.

The pain is an effect of the amusical dis/connection with the world (or worlds, we might add) of other creatures, the pain of 'descent' that is not necessarily the result of the pain inherent to those worlds as such. Pain is a faculty of the human brain and consciousness, as is evident in phenomena such as the phantom limb and anaesthesia generally. Indeed for contemporary science the reality or existence of consciousness and pain – the firing of neuronal C-fibers – outside of human brains and brains like them is highly questionable.[15] This is a view that is anticipated by Schopenhauer in a famous comment from *The World as Will and Idea* on the higher capacity of suffering in complex beings relative to apparently simpler life forms. Every time a man swats a fly, Schopenhauer suggests, he implicitly 'acknowledges that the fly suffers less from being killed than he suffers from being annoyed by it'.[16] Here we see that for the man, the relation between himself and an animal is organized by an economy of suffering and enjoyment, articulated by the locus of sound, in which the fly's annoying presence implies an enjoyment gained at the expense of the philosopher's suffering that even the killing of the fly fails to compensate. The relief sought in the killing of the fly is another way in which man's suffering and enjoyment is located in the earth and violently extracted from it in a struggle over goods and satisfactions. This economy is also of course ecology. While ecology may or may not condemn killing flies, it is itself nothing other than a promise to redistribute the world's goods based on knowledge of the world as *Vorstellung* of good and bad goods, an allocation of resources in human terms that are ultimately related to the law or *nomos* of household management. But what is the good that is represented by the fly whose buzzing amusical presence hovers at the limit of human tolerance and experience?

In *Studies in Pessimism*, Schopenhauer writes, 'The fly ought to be used as the symbol of impertinence and audacity; for whilst all other animals shun man more than anything else, and run away even before he comes near them, the fly lights upon his very nose'.[17] For Schopenhauer, the presence of the fly upon the philosopher's nose represents a kind of sovereignty that by contrast suggests the human world is condemned to conformity and cowardice. While Schopenhauer anthropomorphizes the fly's apparent 'impertinence and audacity', we must assume that this appearance is merely an effect of the fly's indifference, its failure to recognise anything of humanity or the human world. To begin to think from the perspective of the fly, the philosopher would need to regard his own nose as an entirely unfamiliar even alien terrain. Pitching on the philosopher's nose, the fly transforms it into another world in which it ceases to remain human, turning his own nose into a landscape that is completely inaccessible to him.

Swatting the fly – and in the process bringing his nose back to himself in the self-inflicted blow – comically illustrates the economic point about man suffering more from the fly's annoying presence. But the fly is absolutely exterior to this economy. The yawning gap opened up between man and fly is traversed only, perhaps, by the music of the fly, the sound of its 'audacious' freedom and 'impertinent' autonomy relative to human knowledge. In Schopenhauer's *a*musia, his horror and agony at the sound of animals that decapitates his organ of thought, there is an unconscious apprehension of this profound dissonance, resonating long after the death of the fly, that reverberates from a place heterogeneous to any possible economy or ecology of suffering. There is no possible compensation.

But perhaps there is compensation – not through swatting the fly in pain and hatred, but through loving it. Is compensation to be found in loving one's neighbourly fly as oneself? This is the suggestion made by Timothy Morton in his seminal book *Ecology Without Nature* (2007), a proposal which I will consider next.

3. Timothy Morton, ecological love and the jouissance of the fly

> Man is ... a funny sort of animal, is he not? Where in the animal kingdom is the discourse of the master? Where in the animal kingdom is there a master? ... if there were no language there would be no master ... because language exists you obey. Jacques Lacan[18]

> 'Jouissance of the Other ... of the body of the Other who symbolizes the Other, is not a sign of love'. Jacques Lacan [19]

In *Ecology without Nature* (2007) Timothy Morton mounts an attack on the 'eco-mimesis' that characterizes much environmental art and criticism. In the wake of Romanticism, 'eco-mimesis' constructs a fantasy of immersion in the natural world that is at the same time interdependent with and sometimes indistinguishable from the contemplative state of the 'beautiful soul' whose pleasure precludes acknowledgement of participation in the environment and consequently ethical responsibility. In contrast, Morton wants to abolish the dream of nature and replace it with an ecology that recognises the creatures of the world as independent subjects with whom we should interact as such. Morton concludes his book by suggesting that the 'best way to have ecological awareness is to love the world as a person'.[20] Furthermore, he writes, 'the best way to love a person is to love what is most intimate to them, the "thing" embedded in their make up'.[21] His specific example is provided by William Blake's poem 'The Fly': 'Am not I / A fly like thee? / And art not thou / A man like me?'

What Morton means by 'thing' seems to be not so much related to Heidegger (where it is broached only to be rejected) but to Lacan and to the centrality of the Thing or '*das ding*' to Lacan's *Seminar VII* on the ethics of psychoanalysis.[22] What, then, is the fly's thing, or the thing of the fly? It is a strange question because for Lacan, *das ding* is an effect of language; only speaking beings relate to a Thing around which the (death) drive, articulated by the *Vorstellung* of the subject, its means of self-representation, circulates. For Lacan, human beings are pre-eminently speaking beings; language is necessary for someone or something to be loved – or hated – as a person. I am not sure that flies speak (although certainly they buzz which is another question), so they could not, in Lacanian terms, be said to have a 'thing' 'embedded in their make-up', as Morton suggests. However, certainly flies and indeed their buzzing might be said to represent some 'thing' of jouissance for speaking beings.

For Lacan, the very structure of the signifying chain that produces speaking beings implies some thing outside it upon which the chain uncertainly grounds and articulates itself.[23] The immersive world of immanence imagined for the world of nature is sometimes associated with the jouissance that has to be sacrificed in the name of human civilization, language, technology, rational and moral thought, taboo and so on. For psychoanalysis, it is towards this (for humans, impossible) jouissance that the drive aims, thereby becoming a death drive because it is located beyond the pleasure principle that marks the limit of civilized comforts that are always of course more or less comfortable for some. Projected in the void, the 'thing' is identified as both the absolute good beyond the symbolic order and the absolute evil of suffering implied through its deprivation by the Other. This Other, moreover, is usually represented by another person, or anthropomorphized object, one's neighbour, whom Christ commands that one love as oneself. Lacan notes that Freud 'stops in horror' at the Christian commandment to 'love thy neighbour as thyself' since it summons the unfathomable hostility that inhabits the neighbour that one recognises on the basis of one's own hostility. 'And what is closer to myself than that kernel of jouissance in myself to which I dare not approach?'[24] At the interior limit of the thing (on the basis of which Morton suggests we must love another creature as a person), equivalence is established between jouissance and suffering: 'he' always enjoys at my expense and vice versa. Animals are located squarely in this economy when Jeremy Bentham makes what is probably *the* founding ecological statement relative to 'man' and his animal neighbours: 'The question is not can they reason, can they talk, but can they suffer?'[25] If they can suffer, they can also enjoy, and it is certain that man sees that everywhere he looks. It is on this essentially economic and imaginary basis (calculating the jouissance of the other) that ecology seeks to intervene in the world. Some kind of economic relation based in enjoyment – play and happiness – also appears to be central to Blake's poem that is quoted by Morton.

> Little fly,
> Thy summer's play
> My thoughtless hand
> Has brushed away.
> Am not I
> A fly like thee?
> Or art not thou
> A man like me?
> For I dance
> And drink and sing,
> Till some blind hand
> Shall brush my wing.

If thought is life
And strength and breath,
And the want
Of thought is death,
Then am I
A happy fly,
If I live,
Or if I die.
William Blake (1757-1827)

Morton reads the poem as a 'Cartesian meditation' that has the structure of a 'Möbius strip' that characterises eco-criticism in which thought and immersion (or the thought of immersion) are the underside of each other. Since the Cartesian cogito posits the identity of thought and being ('if thought is life', asks the poem, echoing Descartes's 'I think therefore I am'), then the absence of thought signifies death or at least unreality since its existence can be doubted away. 'The Cartesian view', writes Morton, 'condemns us to be no better than flies, since our physical form does not determine our "thought."' That is to say that the Cartesian view condemns us to be no better than flies at the level of the perishable body and its jouissance, though not its thought which lives on, heterogeneous to the body. But at the same time, this enables an identification with the fly, Morton suggests, 'beyond the usual sentimental identification through distance ... the human becomes a fly ... instead of bemoaning the fate of living beings ... the poem identifies with the "evil" (the "thoughtless," "blind" mechanical operation) and with the insect'.[26] Here is another illustration of Morton's 'dark ecology' that rejects the 'hippy aesthetic of life over death', or the 'Bambification of sentient beings' in the full acknowledgement of death and suffering the compensation for which is the ephemeral 'play' of Blake's fly and the 'happiness' found in its aesthetic enjoyment as an end rather than a means by the poet. In this passage, Morton's dark ecology is a kind of Lacano-Cartesian hybrid that encourages speaking beings to love flies as people on the basis of their 'thing', their jouissance that is continuous with the 'evil' that is blind mechanism or, to be psychoanalytical, the death drive. 'Then am I / A happy fly, / If I live, / Or if I die'. At this point the Lacano-Cartesian side of dark ecology flips over to disclose a Bethamite utilitarian underside. Indifferent to life or death, the undead death drive is discovered as the sole locus of happiness that necessarily requires the regulative thought of 'social mediation' in order 'to aid the creature', on the basis of what society thinks about the creature's jouissance, with which it identifies as its thoughtless bodily condition, and the effects of this thoughtlessness on other creatures and the environment.[27] For Morton, then, the poem has the doubleness of a Cartesian-Utilitarianism in which the life of thought provides the rationale for an ecological management of jouissance that is understood as a locus of (un)happiness and death in which humans and animals (even flies) are equivalent.

Where the primary function of ecological thought becomes the production-preservation and regulation of the jouissance of the drives (and of animal instincts understood in terms equivalent to the drives), Morton's dark ecology takes on the same structure as contemporary capitalism where, in Lacan's analysis, the master signifier is concerned with accounting for the right to jouissance. In his Milan Discourse (1972), Lacan provides an algorithm for capitalist discourse by adjusting slightly the Discourse of the Master. Capitalist Discourse is produced when the subject ($) displaces the signifier of the master from the position of agent to that of (repressed) truth below the bar.

In ecological terms, we could say that Man-the-master (Man who masters the environment precisely as an effect of naming it) is displaced by the animal-subject ($) who is liberated through its right to jouissance/happiness (*a*) which bears on it from the position of production. The signifier that marks the difference between 'man' and the 'animal' is displaced and they enjoy an imaginary equivalence in which an animal can be loved as a person even as humans are understood purely in terms of their perishable bodily drives and interests, calculated statistically, and frequently understood in 'bio-economic' terms of 'swarm' behaviour, 'hive minds' that 'buzz' in the network biosphere. It is of course this system of 'bio-economic' capitalism (S2) that must 'socially mediate' and produce the conditions that enable the animal-subjects ($) to enjoy and be happy. (S1) represents the laws of governance that command and regulate capitalism (S2) and its institutions to produce the surplus jouissance (*a*) that enables the animal-subjects to enjoy more or less equally in bovine contentment. Following the arrows, it can be seen that the discourse works in a continuous loop like a machine. In his Milan address, Lacan commented that 'it is the cleverest discourse that we have made. It is no less headed for a blowout. This is because it is untenable ... it suffices so that it goes on casters (*ça marche comme sur des roulettes*), indeed that cannot go better, but that goes too fast, that consumes itself, that consumes itself so that it is consumed (*ça se consomme, ça se consomme si bien que ça se consume*)'.[28] The animal-subjects consume themselves in the all-consuming machine, but they do it more or less painlessly; jouissance is regulated, distributed through the excess commanded by the 'blind hand' of the bio-economic machinery of joy – or at least until the blow out – where the flies are 'happy' whether they live or they die.

4. Damien Hirst and A Thousand Years of even darker ecology

Timothy Morton begins *Ecology Without Nature* (2007) by suggesting that the environment must be an end (like an artwork) not a means, but concludes the book by saying that 'ecological criticism must politicize the aesthetic', thus introducing a certain circularity into his argument.[29] Politics is nothing if not a discourse of means, precisely the means towards the good society and the good life however and for whomever that is defined. A certain impasse is reached here given that the door to an aestheticized politics that would not be a means to an end but an end in itself is already marked, as Morton notes, by 'fascism, the cult of death'.[30] At the same time, subjecting all art to a regime of political utility is to return it to a different kind of totalitarianism. But Morton's Cartesian-utilitarian dualism, as exemplified by his analysis of William Blake's poem 'The Fly' perhaps offers an alternative rationale for a sustainable ecological system that might be seen, notwithstanding its 'darkness' to be utopian. Once again using the metaphor of the fly, Morton writes 'to emerge from the chrysalis of the beautiful soul, we admit that we have a choice. We choose and accept our own death, and the fact of mortality among species and ecosystems'.[31] To realise a system in which the life of thought could provide the rationale for an ecological management of jouissance, the locus of happiness and death in which humans and animals are equivalent, choice must be placed at the centre if it is not to become totalitarian. This system would of course need to be designed, and therefore granted being as an effect of thought, but it must also regulate itself through individual choice – not though political or aesthetic decision. That is to say the system would be equivalent to a work of art, an end in itself because it would generate itself spontaneously within certain minimal rules and conditions, rather than be shaped by an aesthetic system that transcended its own immanent mode of production.

In 1993 Damien Hirst designed a similar kind of system in his artwork *A Thousand Years* (1993). A large steel and glass display case is divided in two by an interior pane with four holes cut into it. Inside, on one side, a rotting cow's head infested with maggots sits beneath an 'insect-o-cutor'; in the other is a white MDF box, a symbolic chrysalis-machine in which maggots pupate into flies. They emerge from the box and are confronted with a choice.

'Moments after their birth', Waldemar Januszczak writes, 'the unluckiest among them fly straight through the hole to the other side, where they are immediately zapped with a short, sharp electronic sizzle. And that's that. There wasn't even enough time to complain that life's a bitch'.[32] Alternatively, luckier ones can head through the holes to the enjoyment of the rotting carcass or dishes of sugar and water. The choice is death or sweetness. The life span of flies is generally limited to around seven days, but for many of course this is is sharply curtailed by the presence of the insect-o-cutor. Others however could certainly live out their lives, mating, reproducing and so on. Certainly more than enough survived to sustain the process of the artwork. And as a kind of generative artwork, *A Thousand Years* has something in common with Brian Eno's installation work such as his multi-screen sound and light installation, *Constellation (77 Million Paintings)* (2007). Here, sound and images are generated by a computer-programme that follows a number of simple bio-digital rules yet manages spontaneously to create 77 million unrepeatable aural and audio experiences. Eno's generative art is another kind of environmental art that is not so much an instance of eco-mimesis as 'economimesis', in the phrase of Jacques Derrida, where art does not imitate nature so much as its mode of production;[33] it is an example of an art, in the tradition of John Cage, that imitates nature in the manner of operation. Hirst's artwork produces just as much variety out of minimal elements as Eno's, and perhaps more drama. Certainly, it invites identification as it offers the art lover the opportunity to view the whole lifespan of a creature from birth to death in a way that, even under confined conditions, owes much to chance and individual choice. As Timothy Morton writes of Blake's poem, The Fly, the work sets up a dual process of identification with 'the "evil" (the "thoughtless", "blind" mechanical operation [of the insect-o-cutor] and with the insect'.[34]

Evil is of course certainly evoked in the title of Hirst's piece,

A Thousand Years, recalling the 'thousand year Reich' promised by the National Socialists in Germany. Given this, it is impossible not also to see in Hirst's piece a reference to Auschwitz. But this is *not* just the extermination machine of a cult of death, this is also a breeding factory and a sustainable environment. Hirst thus brings out the dark continuities between fascism, ecology and capitalism along an aesthetic plane. The piece evokes Auschwitz, but also the ways in which animals are bred in captivity for slaughter; and not just bred, but artificially inseminated, genetically manipulated, over-produced in unprecedented ways and numbers. The correlation between this and Auschwitz invites the contemplation of greater horrors: imagine, 'for example, instead of throwing people into ovens or gas chambers (let's say Nazi) doctors and geneticists had decided to organize the overproduction and overgeneration of Jews, gypsies, and homosexuals by means of artificial insemination, so that, being more numerous and better fed, they could be destined in always increasing numbers for the same hell, that of genetic experimentation or extermination by gas or fire'.[35] This is, perhaps, the darkly satirical element to the work. But precisely as such, ecological desire is provoked and affronted by the way in which the work relies on the equally dark correlation between flies and human beings made, as we have seen for example by deep ecologist Arne Naess when he asserts that 'I will never say I have a higher right to life than a mosquito', mosquitoes of course having been 'responsible' over the years for millions of human deaths, but in so doing help to maintain the balance of life on earth, a balance that is threatened by human over-population. Poised between the solar death of the insect-o-cutor and the nurturing corpse of the earth, the fly-humans live out their brief allegorical lives in a utopian-dystopian sustainable environment as an art work.

While there is no need to speculate about authorial intention, one is tempted to ask, following Schopenhauer, what exquisite sensitivity must Hirst possess to require the audacious buzzing of flies to be compensated by the music of its eternal annihilation, played out in every 'sharp electronic sizzle'? Hirst's fly *a*musia balances his suffering against the extermination of both humans and flies (imagined or real) on the plane of aesthetic enjoyment. What Hirst has nevertheless produced is a machine for both realizing ecological desire and satisfying its death drive. The machine produces happy flies pupating in both an artificial (the pupator) and natural environment (the rotting carcass), feeding on sugar, that are endowed with human 'choice' whether to live or die so that they might be perceived as individuals with a singular destiny. They can fly to safety or they can fly too close to the insect-o-cutor and be zapped. The fact that many do the latter maintains the fantasy of ecological balance. Imagine the congestion without it. Furthermore, perhaps, left to an indefinite future subsequent evolutionary adaptation might result in avoidance of or immunity to insect-o-cutors; we cannot know in advance what evolutionary mutation might follow. Confronting the unknown of future extinctions and evolutionary change is for Morton 'the ultimate rationality'.[36] It is a confrontation that Hirst organizes for the ecological art lover even as he or she is left to contemplate in satisfaction the humane results of intervention in the management of his noisy neighbour's jouissance as rationality's death drive is sustained through the sound of perpetual sizzling annihilation.

5. The rise of Beelzebub

Halo of Flies Over My Head
I am decaying Satan's Wrath
The one to walk planet earth alone
Spreading disease, death and war ...
Impaled Nazarene, 'Halo of Flies' *All That You Fear* (2004)

The most characteristic sound of black metal is the low-res buzzing of the guitars propelled, like a hoard of insects, by the clattering body of percussion. 'True kvltists', according to an assertion from *Terrorizer*, 'like their BM to sound like bees in a tin'.[37] The sound breaks from all previous incarnations of rock and metal to produce a noise, in relation to the latter, that is singularly dissonant, a sound that reverberates around a metalhead like a halo of flies.

A track from Impaled Nazarene's *All That You Fear*, 'Halo of Flies' starts by evoking a world divested of the symbolic form of authority that is erected in the idea of God as the sum of all fears. The fear of God, which is 'an essential expression in a certain line of religious thought ... a tradition that goes back to Solomon', is 'the remedy for a world made up of manifold terrors'. The fear of God, writes Lacan,

> is fear of a being who is only able to exercise his cruelty through the evils that are there, multifariously present in life. To have replaced these innumerable fears by the fear of a unique being who has no other means of manifesting his power than through what is feared behind these innumerable fears, is quite an achievement'.[38]

This metaphorical operation which is for Lacan 'paternal' is also 'the principle of wisdom and the foundation of the love of God' (266). This example of the-fear-of-God as paternal metaphor or 'quilting point' comes from *Seminar III*, otherwise known as *The Psychoses*, where the argument runs that psychosis is indeed the effect of the absence of such a suturing of a particular signifier over a field of multiple signifiance. No doubt because they have read their Lacan, the milieu of Impaled Nazarene's *All That You Fear* is accordingly psychotic, where the subject is 'schizobound' in a world that, since it consists of nothing but multiple fears, is indistinguishable from hell:

> Welcome to your Hell

Where all fears are reality
Paranoia strikes hard
Harder, beyond your wildest dreams
Halo of Flies Over my Head
I am decaying Satan's Wrath
There to walk planet earth alone
Spreading disease, death and war

As with much of contemporary black metal, this track locates itself in the space between humanity and its lack of agreement with its environment, in the space of disease, both mental and physical, death and war, a world denuded of all physical and metaphysical comforts even as it extends the locus of discomfort to the very heavens of the cosmos. Given the name of the band, one can only assume that Impaled Nazarene take as their point of inspiration the moment of Christ's despair on the cross. The moment where Christ's attempt to embody, through sacrifice, the summation of all fear and provide the foundation for the love of God fails as Christ's agony opens itself to a God whose cosmic indifference exposes Him as so complicit in evil that he dissolves back into the multiple terrors of terrestrial life from whence he came. In Impaled Nazarene's 'Halo of Flies', planet earth has been divested of God and therefore become Hell, but this hell is equally divested of Satan whose decaying wrath and rotting corpse give way to the halo of flies that take flight from his maggot-ridden carcass as a new figure of transcendent multiplicity.

While there are numerous references to flies in the various genres of metal (perhaps since Iron Maiden) the ultimate reference is to Satan or Beelzebub as 'Lord of the Flies', or as Malkuth put it, 'Great Black Goat God (Lord of the Flies)' (1994). One version of the origin of the name Beelzebub is a Hebrew insult at the followers of the God Baal. When pronounced 'ba'al', the word signifies a pile of dung. The followers that surround

Baal are thus likened to flies, 'zebub'. Dung flies. From such heterogeneous origins, Beelzebub emerges in the Christian tradition, sometimes as another name for Satan himself, but more often as his own First Lieutenant in the hierarchy of rebel angels. In the Demonic hierarchy of Johann Weyer, sixteenth-century Dutch physician and demonologist, Beelzebub actually takes the principle position after having staged his own successful infernal rebellion, displacing Satan to second position just above Euronymous. So Beelzebub, Lord of the Flies is also a figure for the overthrow or overcoming of Satan and the ascension of some other order, the order of dung flies.

While the reference to Satan and Beelzebub is no doubt primary in the iconography of black metal, the use of the phrase 'lord of the flies' cannot fail, especially given its own kind of ubiquity, to recall William Golding's famous novel of the same name. In the novel, the cult of the Beast (another name for Satan, of course) is exposed, a key example of the delusion of primitivism and savagery, as at first the rotting corpse of an airman and then as a decapitated, pullulating pigs head swarming with flies; the sacrificial offering to the Beast misperceived as the Beast itself. 'They were black and iridescent green and without number; and in front of Simon, the Lord of the flies hung on his stick and grinned'.[39]

It is in this form that the beast *becomes* the Beast in a different way through the hideous teeming acephalic noise of the flies that swarm about its decapitated head. As the Beast begins to talk, in Golding's novel, the process of self-identification and self-transcendence that holds the God-Satan-Man triad together is maintained and sustained in another Christlike sacrifice as Simon unwittingly takes on the Beast's mantle and is hunted down and killed by the other deluded children-become-savages. In some of the more interesting treatments of the fly motif in black metal, this process is arrested and transformed through parasitic consumption. It is the flies, not the corpse or the animal's head or the boy or all the other substitutes in the chain of sacrifice that makes the Beast: a Beast that while black, iridescent green and without number melts the flesh into 'a mephitic trough', a 'Styx of digestive liquid' (Lugubrum) in which 'Transformed man [is] dethroned', Nominon, 'Hordes of Flies' (2005). For Nominon, the process of complete post-parasitical transformation – 'Innate insects part of me /Parasite inside eating me / Host of flies born inside – sees the Satanic multiple resurrected from the swarming darkness of base matter where death has no dominion: 'Absence of life I am the lord of flies'.[40]

'The pile of guts was a black blob of flies that buzzed like a saw' writes Golding, in his novel, as the dead airman is transformed into his surrounding environment.[41] If knowledge – both human and animal – 'is the agreement of the organism and the environment from which it emerges',[42] the black metal buzzsaw resonates as a halo of flies around a central point of nonknowledge encapsulated in a pile of stinking guts, evidence of life without such an agreement, in an *a*musical sound that exults in and exacerbates this lack of agreement. 'Without [this] knowledge', writes Bataille, 'without the identity of the organism, and without this agreement, life could not be imagined', even as he tries to imagine it in the form of 'the unconsidered flight of a possible into the heart of the impossible that surrounds it'.[43]

In black metal's buzzing, its *musca amusica,* sound takes flight, the noise of Ba'al Zebûb's divinely inexistent ascension, into the heart of the impossible. The sound resonates along a vector of *a*musical ex-sistence towards an altogether other, nonanthropomorphic environment. Collective and multiple, 'through compound eyes / I envision eternity'.[44]

Notes

1. The full quote is 'I may kill a mosquito if it is on the face of my baby but I will never say I have a higher right to life

than a mosquito', quoted in Arne Naess, Obituary, *The Guardian*. 15.01.09. This equivalence actually implies that any creature may kill any another if it senses that it is a potential threat, thereby evoking the animal world as such quite devoid of any 'rights' other than the right to kill, perhaps.

2. Eugene Thacker, *In the Dust of this Planet*. Winchester: Zero Books, 2011.
3. Arthur Schopenhauer, *The World as Will and Idea* trans. Haldane & Kemp, 1964. I, III: 333.
4. Ibid.
5. Ibid: 338.
6. Ibid: 340.
7. Eugene Thacker, 'Three Questions on Demonology' in Nicola Masciandaro (ed) *Hideous Gnosis: Black Metal Theory Symposium I*. CreateSpace, 2010: 188.
8. Schopenhauer, Ibid: 338.
9. Ibid: 329, 336.
10. Ibid: 336.
11. Ibid: 331.
12. Ibid: 340.
13. Ibid: 340. For a fuller account of *a*musia see Scott Wilson, '*a*musia, noise and the drive: towards a theory of the audio unconscious' in Michael Goddard, Benjamin Halligan and Paul Hegarty (eds), *Reverberations*, London: Continuum, 2012.
14. Helen Zimmern, *Arthur Schopenhauer, his life and his philosophy*. London: Longmans, Green & Co., 1876: 49.
15. See V.S. Ramachandran and Sandra Blakeslee, *Phantoms in the Brain*. London: Harper Perenniel, 1998. See also Rey, G. (1983). "A Reason for Doubting the Existence of Consciousness", in R. Davidson, G. Schwartz and D. Shapiro (eds), *Consciousness and Self-Regulation Vol 3*. New York, Plenum: 1-39. Churchland, PM and Churchland, P.S., (1998)

On the Contrary: Critical Essays 1987-1997. Cambridge, Massachusetts: The MIT Press.

16. See Anders, *Evolution of Evil* : 195.
17. Arthur Schopenhauer, *Studies in Pessimism*. NY: Cosimo Classics, 2007: 137.
18. Jacques Lacan, 'Discourse of Jacques Lacan at the University of Milan on May 12, 1972', trans. Jack W. Stone. *Lacan in Italia*, 1953-1978. En Italie Lacan, *Milan, La Salmandra*, 1978: 32-55: 32.
19. Jacques Lacan, *Encore*: Seminar XX, trans. Bruce Fink. New York: Norton, 1999.
20. Timothy Morton, *Ecology Without Nature: Rethinking Environmental Aesthetics*. Harvard UP, 2007: 201
21. Ibid., 201.
22. See Morton, ibid.: 198, 202-3. See also Jacques Lacan *The Ethics of Psychoanalysis:* Seminar VII, trans. Dennis Porter. London: Routledge, 1992.
23. Lacan, Seminar VII, 252.
24. Ibid, 219.
25. Jeremy Betham, *Introduction to the Principles of Morals and Legislation,* second edition, 1823, chapter 17,
26. Ibid, 202
27. Ibid.
28. Lacan, 'Milan Discourse', 11.
29. Morton, *Ecology Without Nature,* 205.
30. Ibid.
31. Morton, *Ecology without Nature,* 205.
32. Waldemar Januszczak, 'Laughing in the Jaws of His Critics' *The Sunday Times,* 08.04.12 'Culture': 6-7, 6.
33. See Jacques Derrida, 'Economimesis' in Julian Wolfreys (ed) *The Derrida Reader*. Edinburgh: University of Edinburgh Press, 1998.
34. Morton, ibid., 202.
35. Jacques Derrida, 'The Animal that therefore I am'

36. Morton, *Ecology*, 205.
37. *Terrorizer* 188. Sep. 2009.
38. Jacques Lacan, *Seminar* III: *The Psychoses*. London: Routledge, 1993, 267.
39. William Golding, *Lord of the Flies*. London: Faber & Faber, 1997, 152.
40. Nominon, 'Horde of Flies' from *Recremation*, 2005.
41. Golding, 152.
42. Georges Bataille, *The Unfinished System of Nonknowledge*, ed. Stuart Kendall. Minneapolis: University of Minnesota Press, 2001, 221.
43. Ibid, 221-2.
44. Lugubrum, 'Attractive to Flies', *De Vette Cueken*, 2004.

Black Metal Theory

Dominik Irtenkauf and Nicola Masciandaro

Dominik Irtenkauf (DI). *First of all, black metal theory could be understood as some special kind of metal studies. Yet I can find some traces of philosophy in it as well.*

Nicola Masciandaro (NM). The impulse from the beginning has been for something that goes beyond, without necessarily precluding, diagnostic or analytical discourse about black metal. No one merely listens *to* music, without participating *in* it. It is an object that infects and possesses the subject. So philosophy stands for the *practice* of thought, for thought as participation, as more than just studying or thinking *about* something. On this point black metal theory opposes the perverted secret identity between fan and philosopher in contemporary culture, namely, the situation according to which the fan is an unconscious or sleeping philosopher and the philosopher a mere fan. Black metal theory expresses a need to reopen music to the philosophy of music and philosophy to the music of philosophy in a black way. If philosophy is thought practicing the love of wisdom (*philo-sophia*), black metal theory is thought practicing the love of black metal.

DI. *It seems to be more about speculative interpretations of a musical sub-culture than developing a coherent system of theory. Is that perception correct?*

NM. Yes. And yet there is 'coherence' to black metal. There is a principle according to which we rightly insist and argue that things are and are not black metal. In this respect black metal theory territorializes the potentiality of a non-systematizable coherence, a substance without law. Or we could say that black metal is formally equivalent to Kurt Gödel's incompleteness theorem, that its *topos* or place is the black spaces or unreachable interiors/exteriors that system per se cannot reach. As these spaces are different with respect to different coherent or axiomatic systems, so black metal is not something universally fixed, but a virtually mobile unreachable thing, like an unmineable mineral that weirdly relocates its inaccessibility according to the equipment on the surface.

DI. *If so, can there be a specific methodical approach to black metal theory? Can it be relevant to develop such a method from the subject of research itself, i.e. black metal and its connotations?*

NM. Nothing significant is produced without method, which simply means the *way* of doing something. Arriving anywhere requires a specific way. And it is precisely in relation to the *specificity* of method, to its necessary individuation, that there is no general way. As Nietzsche says, '*"Das — ist nun mein Weg, — wo ist der eure?" so antwortete ich Denen, welche mich 'nach dem Wege' fragten. Den Weg nämlich — den giebt es nicht!*'[1] In other words, if black metal theory is anything significant, it must exist within many specific methodologies, the truth or utility of which is *absolutely indifferent* to whether or not they are followed or implemented.

DI. *What importance does black metal theory attach to the scene's activists such as musicians, journalists and followers of the kvlt?*

NM. This is a strange question to answer because it seems to address 'black metal theory' as if it defined a specific viewpoint or set of values towards persons and vocations. Perhaps the question is analogous to the kind of questions that get posed to black metal artists regarding the importance of the 'fans' or the 'scene' to their music, questions that spark responses of total indifference and sincere fidelity. All I can say is that black metal theory is neither for anyone nor for no one. I do not even want to say that it is for the people who practice it. At a practical material level it does not seem to be. More positively, I think black metal theory attaches importance not to social identities and roles, but to the *act* of penetrating once again into the essence of black metal, an act whose value might be compared to the release of kind of intoxicating atmosphere. Participants in the first two symposia included all the kinds of persons you mention, as well as people not otherwise involved with black metal.

DI. *Can statements by black metal musicians help to start a first interrogation with the music's material?*

NM. Of course. All statements about black metal are always already a form of black metal theory.

DI. *There were books like* Lords of Chaos *which dealt with black metal in a journalistic way.*[2] *There is a new book in Norwegian dealing with Scandinavian black metal's evolution. Mostly, they tell anecdotes and are not very interested in developing theoretical lines. These publications respectively their authors indulge in psychological interpretations of seminal moments in the history of this musical style. Is that a proper way to deal with black metal?*

NM. That is one way, though it is not necessarily 'proper', in the sense of belonging to black metal. I can appreciate the generic utility of intelligent factual accounts of black metal events. But I am much more interested in 'accounts' of black metal that are somehow also black metal events in their own right.

DI. *In* Hideous Gnosis,[3] *there were some philosophers mentioned in the context of understanding black metal. Is there a certain tradition in the history of ideas that could be easily linked to this kind of music?*

There are many traditions that are relevant, as well as several modern thinkers with natural affinities to the genre. Too many to list here. More importantly, black metal perpetuates itself via a satanic logic that corrodes and occludes its own resources *while allowing them to remain apparent*. You could say that black metal practices what Walter Benjamin called the art of citing without quotation marks. Rebelling against the logic or order whereby the citation produces authority, black metal weaponizes citation against its own authorizing aura. For black metal, repetition IS the original.

DI. *Some contributors did also publish in the experimental journal*

Collapse *from the UK. Is there a story behind this connection? The journal's editors seem to follow an approach to phenomena that helps to minimize the distance to black metal music.*

NM. The intersection seems due to some overlap in tastes, and more specifically, to the obvious intimacies between noise and speculation. Reza Negarestani's involvement with the volume of *Glossator* on black metal, which was planned before the first symposium, has also been instrumental.[4]

DI. *Considering metal music's striving for direct speech, this might affect black metal theory. How much value are you willing to attach to this aspect?*

NM. Black metal theory will develop according to its own logic and the diverse desires of the persons who practice it. I am not concerned with how it may be affected by the principle of 'direct speech', which is deeply ambivalent anyway. More interesting to me are the significant parallels between metal vocal styles and theoretical discourse, especially with regard to questions of immanence and the aesthetics of impenetrability. Most of the discussion around BMT has focused on one sense of the term, i.e. black metal theory as the theory of black metal. The significance of the other equally important sense, though more or less evident in the contributions, is less acknowledged: black metal theory as the black metal of theory.

DI. *In the end, there is the question: why intellectualism anyway? Cannot this music better do without questioning the core of its material?*

NM. Why not? Especially if black metal theory does improve the music, i.e. the black metal in my head. I think an essential function of black metal theory to expose and explore the non-difference between thought and metal.

DI. *Seemingly, black metal theory appeals to a certain circle of people. Is there a long-time prospect for this movement? I find it quite stimulating in matters of creative renewal in the field of writing. Plus there are vivid connections to occultural studies as well.*

NM. What is the 'circle' to which black metal theory appeals? The 'collision' between black metal and theory certainly offers many possibilities for development and will appeal to different people for different reasons, perhaps especially because of its newness and because of black metal's esoteric and anti-modern dimensions.

DI. *So far, most texts of black metal theory that I know of show strong links to the genre of essay. Let me outline this style more thoroughly in order to find out the tricks behind "how to talk about a music that refuses to be talked about" like Eugene Thacker puts it in Mute magazine. Essay bears the attempt to try something new and hence unknown in it. Talking about a beast that refuses to be tamed might bring a certain degree of aggression into theorizing. You cannot get a grip on this topic other than using some rhetorical violence. Can this be an option for theory?*

NM. Absolutely. Nothing ventured, nothing won. As Gawain says in Chrétien de Troyes's *Knight with the Lion*, "Now is not the time to dream your life away but to frequent tournaments, engage in combat, and joust vigorously, whatever it might cost you."

DI. *Do you know of any ambitions for augmenting the single texts into one big melting pot of theory? Is there a need for finding a systematic approach to black metal theory or is it better to stay in the flow?*

NM. No, I do not know of any such ambitions. Though it is likely that the encyclopedism of metal culture, evident in projects like Encyclopedia Metallum, A.N.U.S, Black Metal Revolution, Transcix's Metal Archive, will eventually move in the direction of metal theory/studies. But systematic synthesis is another matter. I do not expect a Thomas Aquinas of black metal theory to arrive anytime soon.

DI. *Seemingly, some writers in this field take quite a poetic stance. Can black metal theory still be understood as critical then? Or does it turn into some sort of arts that is to be perceived in a different way?*

NM. I am very much in favour of black metal theory work that does violence to the separative distinctions between poetry and philosophy, art and theory, and so forth. Agamben is correct that modernity is conditioned by a 'scission of the word,' a kind of fatal gap within language that holds the spheres of knowledge and pleasure apart.[5] This is the condition for the birth of criticism, as a distinctly modern way of knowing that 'neither represents nor knows, but knows the representation.'[6] The problem, then, is precisely one of going beyond and creatively destroying criticism, to explode from within its suspension of the infinite immanence of the present.

DI. *Curiously enough, some musicians can relate to this philosophy and they have started their own research some time ago. I think of bands like Ulver and Emperor that seem to be some spearheads of an intellectual movement in black metal. Yet there is a huge scene evolving under the tag 'avantgarde black metal' in Scandinavia and elsewhere. Will they maybe co-work with you in future?*

NM. Anything is possible. I welcome the chance for such collaboration.

DI. *Will black metal theory lead to novels instead of booklets, to acoustic experimentation instead of raw primitive sounds and finally to music's overlapping by books and lectures by the musicians themselves?*

NM. Surely such work is already taking place in various forms. I suppose the question is about whether black metal theory is really a site for the real mutation or migration of black metal into other media, into forms that participate in and are not only about black metal. Right now it seems that black metal can withstand the addition of any adjective placed before it (*this* black metal, *that* black metal), where the difference is registered as one of variety within the genre. Black metal theory engages this process from the *other* side.

Notes

1. 'This is my way – where is yours? As for the right way, the correct way, and the only way, it does not exist!', Friedrich Nietzsche, *Thus Spoke Zarathustra*. III: 10.
2. Michael Moynihan and Didrik Søderlind, *Lords of Chaos: The Bloody Rise of the Satanic Metal Underground*. Feral House, 2003.
3. Nicola Masciandaro, *Hideous Gnosis: Black Metal Theory Symposium 1*: Charleston: CreateSpace, 2010.
4. Nicola Masciandaro and Reza Negarestani (eds) 'Black Metal' *Glossator: The Theory and Practice of the Commentary* 6 (2012).
5. Giorgio Agamben, *Stanzas: Word and Phantasm in Western Culture*, trans. Roland L. Martinez. Minneapolis: University of Minnesota Press, 1993, xvii.
6. Ibid.

Discography

Abgott (2000) *Abgott*, Whiplash Productions.

Abgott (2003) *Fizala*, Helvete and Hate Recordings.

Absurd (1996) *Facta Loquuntur*, No Colours Records.

Agalloch (1999) *Pale Folklore*. The End Records.

Alttari (2007) 'Black Angel Wings.' *Demo* 2. Grievantee Productions.

Antaeus (2004) *Rot*, Battlesk'rs Productions.

Arcanum Inferi (2010) *V.I.T.R.I.O.L.*, Independent, 2010.

Astel Oscora (2009) *Wormshire*, MSR Productions.

Bathory (2002) *Nordland I*. Black Mark Production.

Beherit (1991) *Oath of Black Blood*, Turbo.

Behexen (2008) *My Soul for His Glory*. Hammer of Hate.

Bergthron (2010) *Expedition Autarktis*. Self released.

Black Sabbath (1971) *Master of Reality*, Vertigo.

Blood of the Black Owl (2010), *A Banishing Ritual*, Bindrune Recordings.

Branca (1981) *Ascension*. Acute Records.

Burzum (1992) *Aske*. Misanthropy Records.

Burzum *Svarte Dauen* (1993). Bootleg.

ColdWorld (2008) *Melancholie 2*, Cold Dimensions.

Dark Funeral (1996) *The Secrets of the Black Arts*. No Fashion Records.

Darkthrone (1996) *Total Death*. Moonfog Productions.

Darkthrone (2008) *Frostland Tapes*. Peaceville Records.

Darkspace (2005) *Darkspace II*, Haunter of the Dark.

De Vermis Mysteriis (2003), *Je suis d'Ailleurs*. Self released.

Deathspell Omega (2005), *Inquisitors of Satan*, Northern Heritage.

Dissection (2006) *Reinkaos*. Black Horizon.

Drudkh (2006) *Songs of Grief and Solitude*, Supernal Music.

Endstille (2007) *Endstilles Reich*, Regain Records.

Ezurate (2000) *Infernal Dominatio*. Forever Underground Records.

Fauna (2007) *The Hunt*. Self released.

Funeral Mist (2003) *Salvation*. Norma Evangelium Diaboli.
Keiji Haino (1973) *Milky Way*, Mom and dad Records.
Imago Mortis (2006) *Una Foresta Dimenticata*. Drakkar Productions.
Immanifest (2010) *Qliphotic*. Independent.
Immortal (1995) *Battles In The North*. Osmose Productions.
Immortal (2009) *All shall Fall*. Nuclear Blast Records.
Immortal (2010) *At the Heart of Winter*. Osmose Productions.
Impaled Nazarene (2004) *All That You Fear*, Osmose Productions.
Ithdabquth Qliphoth (2002) *Demonic Crown of Anticreation*, Misanthropic Propaganda.
Thomas Köner (1993) *Permafrost*, Barooni Records.
Liturgy (2011) *Aesthethica*. Thrill jockey.
Lugubrum (2004) *De Vette Cuecken*. Blood Fire Death.
Lustmord (2000) *Purifying Fire*, Soleilmoon.
Marduk (1994) *Opus Nocturne*, Osmose Productions.
Mayhem (1994) *De Mysteriis Dom Sathanas*. Deathlike Silence.
Mayhem (2000) *Grand Declaration of War*. Season of Mist.
Mayhem (2004) *Chimera*, Season of Mist.
Merzbow (2005) *Merzbuddha*, Important Records.
Metallica (1988) *And Justice for all*, Elektra/vertigo.
Mgła (2006) *Presence*, Northern Heritage Records.
The Moaning (1997) *Blood from Stone*. No Fashion Records.
Mütilation (1994) *Black Imperial Blood*, Auto-Production.
Mütilation (1995) *Vampires of Black Imperial Blood*, Drakkar Productions / End all Life Productions.
Mütilation (2003), *Majestas Leprosus*, Ordealis Records.
Nabaath (2006) *Back of Beyond*. Soulflesh Collector Record.
Nominon (2005) *Recremation*, Konqueror Records.
Nurse With Wound (1988) *Soliloquy for Lilith*, Idle Hole Records.
Pest (1998) *Hail the Black Imperial Hornsign*. Demonion Productions.
Pest (2003) *Desecration*. No Colours Records.
Raison d'Être (2007) *Metamorphyses*, Cold Meat Industry.

Sarcofago (1987) *I.N.R.I.*, Cogumelo.
Sargeist (2005) *Disciples of the Heinous Path*. Moribund Records.
Satan's Host (2008) *The Great American Scapegoat 666*. Moribund Records.
Satan's Host (2012). *Power~Purity~Perfection...999*. Moribund Records.
Satyricon (1996) *Nemesis Divina*, Moonfog/Century Media.
Satyricon (2002) *Volcano*, Moonfog/Capitol.
Satyricon (2006) *Now, Diabolical*, Roadrunner/Century Media.
Skagos (2010) *Skagos/Panopticon* split, Flenser.
Skagos (2010) *Ast*, Eternal Warfare.
Striborg (2004) *Spiritual Catharsis*, Finsternis Productions
Striborg (2008) *Autumnal Melancholy*. Southern Lord.
Sunn O))) (1988) *Grimm Robe Demos*, Hydra Head Records.
Ulver (2003) *A Quick Fix of Melancholy*, Jester Records.
Watain (2001/2008) *Rabid Death's Curse*, Season of Mist recordings
Winterkälte (1997) *Structures of Destruction*, Grooveshark.
Wold (2007) *Screech Owl*, Profound Lore Records.
Wolves in the Throne Room (2007)*Two Hunters*, Southern Lord.
Wolves in the Throne Room (2009) *Black Cascade*, Southern Lord.
Wolves in the Throne Room (2009) *Malevolent Grain*, Southern Lord.
Wolves in the Throne Room (2011) *Celestial Lineage*, Southern Lord.
Wormlust (2006) *Wormlust*, Volkgeist.
Xasthur (2002) *Xasthur*, Moribund Records.
Zyklon (2011) *World Ov Worms*, Candlelight Records.

Contemporary culture has eliminated both the concept of the public and the figure of the intellectual. Former public spaces – both physical and cultural – are now either derelict or colonized by advertising. A cretinous anti-intellectualism presides, cheerled by expensively educated hacks in the pay of multinational corporations who reassure their bored readers that there is no need to rouse themselves from their interpassive stupor. The informal censorship internalized and propagated by the cultural workers of late capitalism generates a banal conformity that the propaganda chiefs of Stalinism could only ever have dreamt of imposing. Zer0 Books knows that another kind of discourse – intellectual without being academic, popular without being populist – is not only possible: it is already flourishing, in the regions beyond the striplit malls of so-called mass media and the neurotically bureaucratic halls of the academy. Zer0 is committed to the idea of publishing as a making public of the intellectual. It is convinced that in the unthinking, blandly consensual culture in which we live, critical and engaged theoretical reflection is more important than ever before.